CARIBBEAN AMERICAN NARRATIVES OF BELONGING

CARIBBEAN AMERICAN NARRATIVES OF BELONGING

Vivian Nun Halloran

THE OHIO STATE UNIVERSITY PRESS
COLUMBUS

Copyright © 2023 by The Ohio State University.
All rights reserved.

Library of Congress Cataloging-in-Publication data available online at https://catalog.loc.gov
LCCN: 2022051154
Identifiers: ISBN 978-0-8142-1511-1 (cloth); ISBN 978-0-8142-5869-9 (paper); ISBN 978-0-8142-8285-4 (ebook)

Cover design by Susan Zucker
Text composition by Stuart Rodriguez
Type set in Minion Pro

∞ The paper used in this publication meets the minimum requirements of the American National Standard for Information Sciences—Permanence of Paper for Printed Library Materials. ANSI Z39.48-1992.

CONTENTS

Acknowledgments		vii
INTRODUCTION	Performing Caribbean Americanness	1
PART 1 • SHAPING A MORE PERFECT UNION		
CHAPTER 1	A Vision of Belonging in Political Campaign Books and Civic Memoirs	21
CHAPTER 2	"Big Citizens" and Public Advocacy	48
PART 2 • COMING OF AGE		
CHAPTER 3	Picturing Caribbean American Childhoods	67
CHAPTER 4	Education, Love, and Belonging in Young Adult Fiction	82
CHAPTER 5	Miles Morales as Multimodal Caribbean American Superhero	106
PART 3 • SEEING OURSELVES REFLECTED BACK		
CHAPTER 6	Visualizing Belonging	123
CHAPTER 7	Staging Caribbean American Lives in the Shadow of *West Side Story*	145
CONCLUSION	Aspirational Whiteness and the Limits of Belonging	168
Works Cited		181
Index		197

ACKNOWLEDGMENTS

This book would not have been possible without the help and support of the Department of English at Indiana University, especially Michael Adams in his role as Chair. Naz Pantaloni III, head Associate Librarian of IU Libraries' Copyright Program graciously helped me check my references and find suitable images for the cover. I also want to thank the many scholarly audiences who listened to versions of this project.

I extend a sincere thank you to the manuscript reviewers whose thoughtful responses and critiques helped me beef up the theoretical underpinning of the argument I make in this book and encouraged me to focus on contemporary texts. I thank them for their encouragement.

I thank Billy Halloran for sharing his expertise on videogames and the MCU universe with me. Likewise, this manuscript has benefitted from Thalia Halloran's help with word choice and her willingness to discuss the recent scandals concerning aspirational Caribbean identity. As always, David Halloran is my ideal reader and best editor.

Finally, I acknowledge that the vast selection of popular narratives written and illustrated by and for Caribbean Americans makes this an excellent time to study the impact this group of artists and activists is having on American culture and politics in real time. I hope this study is soon joined by others that investigate more fully the impact of Caribbean American musical artists such as Bad Bunny, who performs his Caribbean Americanness by simultaneously insisting on the particularity of his island-specific cultural capital even as he lives and popularizes his music within the continental United States.

INTRODUCTION

Performing Caribbean Americanness

In the conclusion to *American Like Me: Reflection on Life Between Cultures* (2018), Honduran American actor America Ferrera explains her motivation for assembling the essay collection during the middle of the Trump presidency, characterized by its negative and damaging stereotypes about immigrants. She clarifies that the contributors are her "friends, peers, and heroes" and says that her goal was "to share their stories in this book so that we might build community" (304). The textual polyphony of voices she assembles all grapple with the task of narrating their positionality within the country in which they live and claiming a space within it. Ferrera acts as a conduit when she summarizes the diversity of responses to her request for personal replies to the question that plagued her as a child: "*What do I call an American like me?*" (xxii). Ferrera writes:

> We connect to our roots clumsily, unknowingly, unceasingly. We call ourselves "American" enthusiastically, reluctantly, or not at all. We take fragments of what was broken, severed, or lost in history, and we create whole selves, new families, and better futures. We live as citizens of a country that does not always claim us or even see us, and yet, we continue to build, to create, and to compel it towards its own promise. (304–5)

This statement illustrates the type of identificatory process this book will investigate by focusing on Caribbean American narratives of belonging. Like

Ferrera, my goal is to understand how American politicians, civil servants, novelists, actors, playwrights, and performers with family roots tracing back to the Caribbean claim their place within American society through narrative acts of community-building with one another and with their fellow Americans.

Four of the contributors to *American Like Me* are Caribbean American. Novelist, essayist, and cultural critic Roxane Gay explains the challenges Caribbean Americans face while growing up as bicultural subjects: "There were different rules for each world I moved through, and I had to learn those rules quickly. I knew nothing about boundaries or other such *American* things. My American classmates rarely understood the rules I lived by at home, and my parents were bewildered by the permissiveness of those classmates' parents" ("Roxane Gay" 60). Young Roxane felt unable to reconcile the two clashing world views, but as an adult, Gay now understands that the bureaucratic barriers her parents faced during their immigration journey influenced their suspicion of "boundaries" as artificial obstacles interfering with familial intimacy and love. She interprets their Haitian refusal to comply with dominant culture parenting norms as proof of their "irrepressible, boundless" love for her (62). In turn, her written work deliberately blurs distinctions between the public and private thereby asserting her Caribbean Americanness in the refusal to censor herself according to either American or Haitian sensibilities.

The three other Caribbean American essayists all identify as Puerto Rican, and their prose pieces discuss interactions with strangers. Broadway and film star Lin-Manuel Miranda recalls how the shared celebration of Three Kings Day fostered a sense of kinship with his fellow Latinx classmates in elementary school, bridging the social barriers that normally kept them apart:

> We are the only Latino kids in our grade, and on most days we are friendly but not close, each in our respective corners, unsure of how to share a world and a culture we ordinarily keep at home. But on January 6, we are basically on par with Jesús, because the Three Kings picked the five of us, and all the other Latino kids in the world, and bestowed us with gifts, just like him. (197)

This passage defines "belonging" externally, as the mark of the Three Kings' favor. A shared cultural marker like the observance of epiphany with presents simultaneously marks the Latinx children as distinct from their classmates who belong to the dominant culture and receive presents only on Christmas Eve or Christmas Day, but this recognition of a mutual difference has a very positive dimension in Miranda's formulation: it puts the Latinx children on a par with the Savior as the only recipients of these monarchs' munificence.

Olympic gymnast Laurie Hernandez describes feeling similarly affirmed when her Puerto Rican fans recognize her: "It's like I have a big extended family everywhere I go, and I couldn't be more honored" (231–32). Hernandez's fame and prestige grew from her success in gymnastics competition and her presence in the public sphere become a point of pride for the Puerto Rican community writ large. These encounters with her fans based on their shared ethnicity make the young athlete feel more connected to her late Puerto Rican grandmother even as others celebrate her achievements in the name of the larger context of breaking barriers for Latinx representation. However, not all recognitions of difference are positive or neutral. Sometimes having some Caribbean American background as part of a multiracial identity can also be a source of frustration when one's physical appearance does not match people's perceived assumptions of the phenotypes associated with these various cultures.

Claiming a Caribbean American identity asks the wider society to recognize and affirm hybridity in a way that fundamentally challenges binaristic conceptions of race and nationality. The pressure to conform to normative either/or categories comes from communities on both sides the Caribbean American construct. Singer and actress Auli'i Cravalho, the voice of the title character in Disney's *Moana*, found this out first-hand as a child growing up in Hawai'i. Her essay recalls how she proudly shared her complex heritage with peers during show and tell in school: "'I'm Puerto Rican, Portuguese, Hawaiian, Chinese, and Irish'" (152). However, her classmates' reaction was tantamount to calling her a liar, saying she looks "too white" and thus she does not "look like anything you said you are'" (153). To this day, Cravalho wishes she had thought of a smart retort at the time. Instead, the essay expresses her confidence about looking just like herself and not trying to match anyone else's expectations of what she should look like.

This study analyzes how Caribbean American cultural works and performances of belonging within the United States point to a new direction in diaspora studies. The backward homeward look is no longer the sole paradigm through which Caribbean Americans understand and represent their experiences of living within the United States. To appreciate the impact of this change and its future ramifications, scholars must consider how US-based Americans of Caribbean heritage have developed new networks not only to better reflect their own intersectionality as people who face multiple oppressions at once but also to map out how strategic partnerships with other groups can work to dismantle systemic oppression. For those who trace their heritage to the Caribbean basin, belonging to the United States is not an either/or choice but rather a "yes, and," to borrow a phrase from improv comedy. Being American no longer requires full assimilation to dominant white society or the social pressure to give up one's connection to Caribbean culture and heritage. Binaristic approaches to discussing race and power can be clarifying, but in their refusal to recognize hybridity, they can become barriers to progress that close off potential alliances and exclude whole communities from the wider movement for reform and justice.

As the opening examples demonstrate, there is an undeniable Puerto Rican bias in my selection of primary texts and examples drawn from current events for this project. That is due, in part, to my own background and predilections as a Puerto Rican woman whose family moved to the mainland United States during my teenage years. Given my upbringing and inclinations, I find it natural to be more attuned to (and celebrate) my fellow Boricuas' presence within American culture than to other Caribbean American contributions. As a Caribbean studies scholar, I look beyond my own background and specifically place the Puerto Rican texts I analyze in conversation with those by other Caribbean American interlocutors. As both cultural actors and subject matter for visual, musical, and performative entertainment, Puerto Ricans have been part of American popular culture for over a century. The sheer abundance of material by and about Puerto Ricans explains the overrepresentation of this type of Caribbean American experience in the case studies I examine throughout this volume but this affinity and impulse to celebrate is undoubtedly a contributing factor as well.

Notably absent from my investigation are texts by artists or writers from the US Virgin Islands, the other American territory within the Caribbean purchased from Denmark in 1917. Ten years later in 1927, Virgin Islanders were granted citizenship, which put them on a par with Puerto Ricans in the in-between world of territorial status since the United States seized control of Puerto Rico in 1898 after the Spanish-American War and extended US citizenship to islanders in 1917 through the passage of the Jones-Shafroth Act. Virgin Islanders and Puerto Ricans became colonial subjects when the United States laid claim to both the peoples (US citizens) and their islands (US territories) as its legal possessions. This type of "belonging" involves unidirectional ownership and it is beyond the bounds of what this study will cover. Citizenship and territorial/legislative oversight are legal statuses that govern impersonal processes like taxation or the issuance of identity documents like passports. Questions and issues in these fields call for a different intellectual framework that lies outside the scope of this work. Instead, this study will focus on the personal and lived experience individuals narrate or perform.

In the pages that follow, I consider and analyze written, visual, and performative narratives through which American people of Caribbean heritage describe what it feels like to belong within the United States as part of a broader definition of the American people. I argue that these narratives' celebration of the collective contributions of people from this region to the cultural and political life of the United States challenges the uniform and exclusive identity categories currently in use in public and academic discourse. The term "Caribbean American" emphasizes the geographic specificity of the "Caribbean" basin above racial, ethnic, or linguistic particularities because this region's shared history of colonialism, enslavement, indenture, environmental devastation, and extractive industry exploitation shaped the vibrant mixture of indigenous, African, Asian, Middle Eastern, and European peoples that make up contemporary populations across the region. "Caribbean American" works as a strategic conception of identity that can embrace the particularity of Puerto Rican, Cuban, Haitian, Barbadian, Trinidadian, or Jamaican identity and simultaneously recognize their ties to a wider community.

I use the term "Caribbean American" to describe the people whose heritage can be traced to this region precisely because it signals a different relationship to race and ethnicity, and to belonging and power, from what is traditionally associated with the Black/white color line in the United States. In my quest to avoid duplicating the binaristic logic through which American race relations operate, I claim a space for intellectual inquiry and analysis that investigates intergroup tensions such as colorism, anti-Blackness, linguistic discrimination, and virulent nationalism and also recognizes instances of cross-cultural allyship and cooperation, of people sharing the burden to make oppression more bearable. To this end, I mention people's island-specific national identities whenever it is known, while reserving the adjective "Caribbean American" to describe patterns of behavior, groups including people whose heritage encompasses more than one national origin, or cultural products that portray a given Caribbean experience as emblematic of the region or its diasporic population.

There is simply no one way of being Caribbean so, therefore, Caribbean diasporic communities in the United States exhibit a broad spectrum of ethnic, racial, religious, linguistic, and political behaviors that feed its diversity. Édouard Glissant's theories of Caribbean people's valorization of interdependence offer a critical paradigm for reading across difference and toward a mutual recognition and comprehensive appreciation. Glissant's insights have helped me define how I understand Caribbean American experiences of belonging as affirmations of interconnectedness. In his *Poetics of Relation*, Glissant discusses two main metaphors through which Caribbean immigrants in France think through their own identity within their new homeland: either as the unidirectional assimilationist impulse of the "Root identity" (143) or through the more dynamic and fluid exchange of the "Relation identity" (144). For Glissant, the essential distinction between the two identity categories comes down to a difference in how they imagine the relationship between the self and the inhabited physical space. Those who adopt a "Root identity" have "rooted the thought of self and territory and set in motion the thought of the other and of voyage" (144). An example of this would be Roxane Gay's experience of feeling torn between which national identity to express at any given time—Haitian at home and American outside. Glissant explains that such a dilemma as "one of the most dramatic consequences of interdependence," further explaining: "When identity is determined by a root, the emigrant is condemned (especially in the second generation) to being split and flattened. Usually an outcast in the place he has newly set anchor, he is forced into impossible attempts to reconcile his former and his present belonging" (143). Like Glissant's male emigrant, the young Roxane Gay experienced a Root identity as she felt caught between her parents' cultural identity and that of her peers. As an adult, she has made space for her Relation identity as Haitian American through her various texts exploring this aspect of her belonging within the United States by making community with other feminists and survivors of sexual violence, to name just a few.

As Glissant theorizes it, Root identity is backward looking, and thus more characteristic of diasporic communities that define themselves primarily through their active connections to the country of origin. In contrast, Relation identity is not temporally bound; it "is linked not to a creation of the world but to the conscious and contradictory experience of contact among cultures" (144). This defining interactivity marks the experiences of belonging I analyze in the memoirs, novels, shows, films, and performances. Someone who identifies through "Relation," as Glissant defines it "does not think of a land as a territory from which to project towards other territories but as a place where one gives-on-and-with rather than grasps" (144). Thus, despite its imperial relationship to the Caribbean islands, the United States is important as the place where Caribbean Americans interact with their compatriots and feel accepted and like they belong through this group identity and mutual recognition.

This study explores cultural production and performance on their own terms and, thus, will not delve into the questions regarding who enjoys or is denied the benefits of full or first-class citizenship within the nation state. These questions are fundamentally appropriate and the existing legal and social science scholarship in these areas is strong. The wider cultural developments discussed in this selection of written and visual narratives can be studied fruitfully from a perspective informed by history and the humanities.

The assembled memoirs, young adult novels, picture books, comics, television shows, musicals, and televised performances examined here are narratives of self-identification through which the writers, civil servants, illustrators, performers, and entertainers show what it is like to fit in or be included within the body politic which also allow for analysis of the perception and experience of being excluded. I am persuaded by rhetorician M. Elisabeth Weiser's claim that, "narrative, space, and object promote aesthetic experiences that allow individuals to identify with collectives" (4). For the most part, I chose the written, visual, and performative texts under discussion because of one of two factors: either their relevance to popular culture or their aesthetic value as works of art or life writing that are deeply moving, push genre boundaries, or contain beautiful lyrical passages. Among the best-known cultural creators whose artistic works I discuss are Lin-Manuel Miranda, Edwidge Danticat, Roxane Gay, and Elizabeth Acevedo. Others, like the 2020 Super Bowl halftime show headlined by Shakira and Jennifer Lopez, any of the comic book series featuring Caribbean American superheroes, the musical *On Your Feet* about Gloria and Emilio Estefan, or episodes of the sitcom *One Day at a Time*, are simply lots of fun to watch or read. However, I included two types of texts for their civic virtues in full awareness that their prose is more pedestrian than lofty: political and civic memoirs and reportage about current events. With rare exceptions, such as Sonia Sotomayor's evocative descriptions of her childhood and personal life, the content of their narrative—the *what* of their tale—is much more important than *how* writers impart this information, although the authors' identity and positionality—as state senators or other civil servants, or people with professional or family connections to the current or past White House administration—may be reason enough for fans to buy a copy. Thus far extends the reach of celebrity culture.

Whereas Weiser's analysis takes the museum as the primary site for her rhetorical analysis, I contend that popular and widely available Caribbean American written and visual narratives of belonging likewise promote "individual identification with the national 'we,'" through the promotion of an identity of Relation and interdependence that challenges the ossified nature of national myths in favor of a new story that grows out of such interaction. Weiser explains that "identification with an ambiguous 'we' calls forth a need to present a national myth that is more dialogical, more flexible, and more capable of incorporating fully those ambiguities of the individual subjects making up the 'we'" (11). Because their experience is not solely defined through the lens of race, ethnicity, linguistic background, or religion, Caribbean American cultural producers present us with visions of strategic ambiguity through which to imagine and bring about a more inclusive American "we" in the future. Thus, the operational definition of belonging at the heart of this book encompasses three possible manifestations:

- first, a memoirist's or character's expressed sense of fitting in within a given subset or group of people;

- second, my explicit explanation of how Caribbean ("gives-on-and-with") Relation identity works within the texts and performances under discussion; and
- third, an affirmation or recognition of Caribbean American belonging from an external source, someone or some agency that is situated firmly within dominant American society.

Individuals who write, produce, or star in such narratives of belonging to the United States rely on or activate elements of public memory to make their accounts broadly relatable, if not necessarily universal. In his influential study of public memory and patriotism in the United States, historian John Bodnar defines public memory as "a body of beliefs and ideas about the past that help a public or society understand both its past, present, and by implication, its future. It is fashioned ideally in a public sphere in which various parts of the social structure exchange views" (15). Bodnar differentiates between a country's two main types of cultural expression: official and vernacular. The texts this book discusses fall under the category of "vernacular," because they are written, composed, or performed by people in their private capacity as citizens rather than being formal acts of state performed by government functionaries. Bodnar defines vernacular cultures in contradistinction to official cultures, as "an array of specialized interests that are grounded in parts of the whole. They are diverse and changing and can be reformulated from time to time by the creation of new social units such as soldiers and their friends who share an experience in war or immigrants who settle a particular place. They can even clash with one another" (14). The rise of social media in the decades since the publication of Bodnar's book has blurred the boundaries between official and vernacular cultures significantly. As a category, the vernacular remains valuable as a lens through which to analyze a culture's diversity and flexibility, while at the same time acknowledging a lack of formal cohesion or official endorsement. In the next case study, I will analyze the vernacular cultural elements of the inauguration of Joe Biden as the forty-sixth president of the United States and apply Glissant's notion of Relation identity to understand how journalists and public critics interpreted the cultural implications of this official event's choreography and scripting.

BIDEN INAUGURATION

Joe Biden's inauguration was an official event like no other: a ceremony that took place behind barricades and amidst the scarce crowds that pandemic social distance protocols demanded. There was enough pomp and circumstance to mark the majesty of the occasion. There were also prominent visual reminders that the country was in mourning, such as the *Field of Flags* on the national mall, a tribute meant to represent the more than 400,000 American lives lost by the time of the inauguration. A professionally choreographed affair, the entertainment that took place in between the various stages of the official proceedings included vernacular elements that highlighted the talents of people with Caribbean backgrounds as well as those who acknowledged the influence of Caribbean Americans within contemporary society thereby enacting the first manifestation of belonging discussed previously. Nuyorican singer Jennifer Lopez performed a medley of patriotic songs including "This Land is Your Land" and "America the Beautiful." She then switched languages from English to Spanish to proclaim the last words of the Pledge of Allegiance: "una nación, bajo Dios, indivisible, con libertad y justicia para todos."[1] Ms. Lopez punctuated this patriotic display by singing the title verse from one of her signature songs, "Let's Get Loud," before once again affirming that, "This land was made for you and me." These improvisational gestures were polarizing since they reminded some viewers and listeners of the limits of belonging to the imagined community of the nation: Google searches and social media posts attested to the fact that not everyone understood the phrases in Spanish or appreciated the self-referential addition of Latin pop / hip hop into the otherwise staid occasion. Though some critics thought the inclusion of her own song was done for purely commercial purposes, I read it instead as a conscious nod back to her explicitly political Super Bowl performance one year earlier, which featured children being freed from their cage-like enclosures as the performer and her child sang alternating verses from "Let's Get Loud" and Bruce Springsteen's "Born in the USA." I will discuss that performance in more detail in a later chapter.

Two other moments from the official inaugural celebration illustrate my larger claim that people of Caribbean heritage have taken to the public stage to both articulate and demand a fuller understanding of what it means to belong within America. They both involve Lin-Manuel Miranda, though the first one only does so through allusion. Inaugural poet Amanda Gorman's "The Hill We Climb" includes two references to Lin-Manuel Miranda's blockbuster Broadway musical, *Hamilton*. The next day, one of the morning television shows interviewing Gorman arranged a surprise visit by the Puerto Rican hip hop multi-hyphenate and the two bonded over their shared appreciation of the founding father. This interaction was a spontaneous performance of Relation identity where the United States serves as "a place where one gives-on-and-with," especially in the context of the new president's inauguration. Through

---

1. Translation: "One nation, under God, indivisible, with liberty and justice for all."

politically aware verse that calls out systemic racism and inequity, both wordsmiths celebrate their shared nation while also reminding us that we should make the dream of the inclusive democracy a reality for more Americans.

The second performance was part of the televised inaugural celebration that replaced the usual inaugural balls. Actor Tom Hanks talked about Biden's well-known love of Irish poetry and introduced Lin-Manuel Miranda to read the president's favorite passage from Seamus Heaney's English verse translation of Sophocles's play, *Philoctetes*. From the stage at the United Palace Theatre in Washington Heights, Miranda speaks lines from the play referencing the adversity and calamity that can befall humanity. As he begins reciting the stanza that Biden quotes most often, an image of the president joins him on-screen and together they proclaim the words that provide solace for the new leader of the free world: "once in a lifetime / that justice can rise up, / And hope and history rhyme." The newly sworn-in president of the United States reciting Irish verse alongside the Nuyorican hip hop Broadway impresario best known for playing a "Caribbean" founding father present a vision of multicultural America that seeks to "build back better"[2] from the oppressive nationalism of the Trump era, during which the self-satisfied celebration of empty populism and an "America First" policy rolled back earlier efforts to dismantle existing structures of oppression.

As celebrities, Miranda, Lopez, and even Gorman participated in this official ceremony to inspire patriotism in the viewing audience. In contrast, White House correspondent Yamiche Alcindor's tweet about Kamala Harris's swearing-in ceremony as the new vice president of the United States constitutes a vernacular performance of cultural belonging:

> What a moment for our country and for women of color in particular.
>
> The first Latina Supreme Court Justice, Sonia Sotomayor, administers the oath of office to the Vice President, Kamala Harris, the first black, South Asian, and woman to hold this office. (@Yamiche)

As a cultural text posted from her work Twitter account, Alcindor's tweet is at once an "official" act of news reporting and also a personal expression of her reaction to the official ceremony from her positionality as a "woman of color." The tweet is also a performance of Caribbean American belonging and an expression of patriotic pride because it shows a Haitian American journalist (Alcindor) celebrating a Puerto Rican jurist (Sotomayor) swearing in

---

2. The White House explains President Biden's "Build Back Better Plan" to rebuild America on its website: https://www.whitehouse.gov/build-back-better/.

a woman of Jamaican and Indian descent (Harris) into the nation's second-highest office. This tweet enacts Glissant's Relation identity because it situates the women's Americanness within the framework of interdependent validation: by tweeting about the "particular" sense of pride she feels when watching the swearing-in ceremony, Alcindor displays a dynamic and collective self-understanding ("gives-on-and-with") by symbolically including both Sotomayor and Harris within her personal sense of belonging within "our country." This is the second manifestation of Caribbean American belonging I mentioned earlier.

Alcindor's vernacular public utterance of belonging is an example of the politics of Relation identity. Whereas Alcindor's tweet is the vehicle through which she extends her sense of belonging to include others, media critic Erik Wemple of the *Washington Post* performs the third manifestation of belonging by affirming Alcindor's exemplary Americanness. He celebrates Alcindor's performance as a White House correspondent during the early days of the COVID-19 crisis under the Trump administration as emblematic of the highest standards of professionalism: "As Alcindor stands and rams through her questions, she is becoming the symbol of American journalism: strong, unflappable and polite." Wemple's approving assessment of his Haitian American colleague suggests that he not only includes her within his own definition of Americanness but, also, that he has changed his own views of what "American journalism" could be based on Alcindor's admirable conduct while interviewing a rather treasonous elected official. Wemple's description of her work is proof that he not only accepts but also celebrates Alcindor's sense of belonging to the nation as well as their shared profession.

I conclude this section of inauguration-related public performances of belonging by returning once more to a discussion of how President Biden incorporates the vernacular even as he performs the official function of marking the start of National Caribbean American Heritage Month in his capacity as the chief executive.[3] June 2021 marked the first time a Caribbean American person, Kamala Harris, has served as the nation's vice president. Thus, President Biden acknowledged her and the other Caribbean American members

---

3. Elsewhere, I have traced the history of the presidential proclamation of June as "Caribbean American Heritage Month" as the result of a Black woman's dedication to honor her Caribbean American political mentor (Halloran). The bill's sponsor was Representative Barbara Lee (D-CA) and the woman whose achievements the proclamation is meant to honor was Barbadian American US Congresswoman Shirley Chisholm (D-NY). Inclusion in the official governmental calendar that celebrates the achievements and contributions of various segments of the polity is one metric through which to measure or quantify belonging to the nation. Thanks to Congresswoman Lee, Caribbean American people have been recognized in this way without interruption since the end of the George W. Bush administration.

of his cabinet whose heritage is Cuban American, Puerto Rican, and Jamaican American, respectively, in that year's proclamation:

> Caribbean Americans have made our country more innovative and more prosperous; they have enriched our Nation's arts and culture, our public institutions, and our economy. I am honored to celebrate this National Caribbean-American Heritage Month alongside Caribbean-American barrier-breaking public servants in my Administration—including Vice President Kamala Harris, Secretary of Homeland Security Alejandro Mayorkas, Secretary of Education Miguel Cardona, and Domestic Policy Advisor Susan Rice—all of whom continue to be sources of pride and inspiration for Caribbean Americans across the country. (White House)

This paragraph highlights that people whose heritage traces back to the Caribbean region are now quite literally in the "room where it happens," to quote a verse from the musical *Hamilton*, advising the president and helping shape policy to make the United States a "more perfect union." Perhaps more important than the shout-out the president gives to members of his administration is his explicit acknowledgement that systemic racism and inequities in health outcomes are problems that affect Caribbean Americans and others, and ones that he plans to address as part of his governance strategy.

THE DARK SIDE OF BELONGING

Throughout the book, I apply the term "Caribbean American" to texts or performances about Caribbean American people or characters even when the authors or co-creators of such texts claim no Caribbean heritage themselves. My rationale for doing this is to focus on the work the texts do, rather than privileging an author's or artistic collaborator's personal biography as the only determining factor for inclusion in this context. I advocate for the more widespread use of the term "Caribbean American" while fully recognizing its invented nature following the example of novelist Viet Thanh Nguyen. In a recent op-ed, Nguyen defended the need to continue using another invented term, "Asian American," because the political value of such an identity category gets to an important point about belonging: "No claim to American belonging will end the vulnerability of Asian Americans to racism and cyclical convulsions of violence. And what does it even mean to claim belonging in the United States? If we belong to this country, then this country belongs to us, every part of it, including its systemic anti-Black racism and its colonization of Indigenous peoples and land." Nguyen's capacious understanding of the complexity of belonging underscores the fact that this state of being is a dynamic process, rather than a one-way ticket into acceptance by the majority. To belong to the United States as either an Asian American or a Caribbean American means to own up to the histories of inclusion and exclusion, the racism as well as the opportunity, the problem as well as the solution. The multi-modal narratives I analyze in this book present Caribbean American versions of actual or imagined lives within the United States as much as they reflect deeply personal visions of what the idea of "America" means to the narrators and/or protagonists.

I draw a distinction between the dynamic and collective self-understanding of Relation identity ("gives-on-and-with") that Americans of Caribbean heritage share with their compatriots through their respective narrative texts and the fixed and unchanging Root identity of the national self-mythologizing they question, critique, and explicitly seek to reframe. Even when the Caribbean American writers or public figures I examine hold xenophobic or anti-Black views, their overall goal is to persuade others to their way of thinking and, thus, broaden the circles in which they navigate to arrive at a big-tent version of whatever dogma they espouse. Consider, for instance, that Caribbean American people also make headlines for the wrong reasons. One such negative interaction that captured nationwide headlines was the altercation between the so-called "SoHo Karen" and a Black teenager whom she falsely accused of stealing her phone. During a televised interview with Gayle King, the wrongful accuser, Miya Ponsetto, denied her actions were racially motivated because as a Puerto Rican woman and "a woman of color" she was incapable of being racist, a claim Ms. King quickly refuted. The incident itself and the subsequent interview both highlight how discourses surrounding race, ethnicity, and *latinidad* often obscure or deflect charges of anti-Blackness within Hispanophone Caribbean cultures.[4] In an article for *Refinery 29*, Jasely Molina asks us to go beyond appearances to fully appreciate the ironic complexity of this interaction when she explains that the teenager Ponsetto accused and physically tackled in the hotel is also of Puerto Rican heritage:

> Let it be known that Harrold Jr. is also of Puerto Rican descent. At the base, white Latinas like Miya Ponsetto benefit from white privilege, yet they'll use this privilege to choose when they can or cannot demonize Black people in the white spaces that accept them as one of their own. Then, they'll use this

---

4. For a more in-depth discussion of Latinx anti-Blackness, see Tanya Katerí Hernández's *Racial Innocence: Unmasking Latino Anti-Black Bias and the Struggle for Equality*, (Beacon Press, 2022).

same Latinx identity and exploit the oppression of other Latinx people to defend their racist actions. But if an officer arrived at the scene at the time of the incident, they wouldn't see two Puerto Ricans: they'd see one white woman accusing one Black young man—and historically, we know how that story goes.

Interpreting this situation through a Caribbean American lens, rather than defaulting to reading such interactions through the American framework of the Black/white color line or even racially tinged intra-Latinx tensions, highlights the anti-Black prejudice inherent within US Caribbean diasporic populations. This leads to a strident critique of the attitude of Caribbean exceptionalism that has consistently stymied successful collaboration and allyship between Caribbean diasporic populations in the United States and the Black community.

The flipside of narratives of belonging are narratives uncovering fraudulent claims of belonging that have been debunked. While I said earlier that establishing the relative success of people's claim of belonging was beyond the purview of this project, I will discuss two high-profile identity appropriation scandals by former faculty members at the George Washington University to frame my discussion of the increased visibility people with heritage ties to the Caribbean have achieved in contemporary American social, political, and cultural discourse. The first is the recent confessional post by a white and Jewish associate professor of history, Jessica Krug, admitting she built her whole professional and publishing career on the lie that she was an Afro-Caribbean woman. She writes, "People have fought together with me and have fought for me, and my continued appropriation of a Black Caribbean identity is not only, in the starkest terms, wrong—unethical, immoral, anti-Black, colonial—but it means that every step I've taken has gaslighted those whom I love." This statement enumerates the negative impact of Krug's actions without apologizing for it. The scholarly response on social media was swift and unforgiving. In a Twitter thread, Professor Yomaira Figueroa, who is Puerto Rican, quickly pointed out that the timing of this admission was not coincidental: "The only reason Jessica Krug finally admitted to this lie is bec on Aug 26th one very brave very BLACK Latina junior scholar approached two senior Black Latina scholars & trusted them enough to do the research & back her up." Figueroa's comments help us understand that even when framed as a mea culpa, Krug's statement deliberately stole the spotlight from, and effectively silenced, the Black Latina scholar who could prove her self-representation was nothing but racial masquerading.

A second highly publicized instance of someone falsely claiming a Caribbean American identity that did not correspond with his own biography came to light in May 2020. The story unfolded in the obituary pages of the *Washington Post* after the deceased, novelist and former assistant professor of English, H. G. Carrillo, had succumbed to COVID-19. When Mr. Carrillo's birth family reached out to the newspaper with information that the author's public account of his life was his own fabrication, the *Washington Post* corrected the obituary, included an editor's note to explain the situation, and added the following explanation about how the dead man's husband found out: "And this weekend, in his grief, he suddenly learned that his husband (true name Herman Glenn Carroll, it turns out) was not the childhood Cuban immigrant he claimed to be—that Hache's personal origin story, which he shared publicly and with those close to him throughout his adult life, was an extension of his fiction, a product of imagination" (Duggan). The updated obituary also mentioned the novelist's mother's reaction, saying she had taken offense that he had obfuscated his own background. Two fabricated identities: Krug's crossing racial lines and Carrillo's claiming an immigrant experience he had not undertaken. Both performances of passing are examples of aspirational Caribbeanness based on deeply felt anti-Blackness. These two examples serve as cautionary tales that also support my claim that Caribbean American identities are now so established within American society as to be considered worth stealing for the sake of their perceived cultural capital.

BELONGING

In assembling the primary sources to analyze in this project, I was mindful that "belonging" is neither a lasting condition nor a panacea for all instances of cultural oppression. Instead, in laying claim to the identity of being "American," Caribbean American writers, artists, and performers do not get to pick which aspects of that national character they identify with or reject, as Nguyen so keenly observes: "If we belong to this country, then this country belongs to us, every part of it, including its systemic anti-Black racism and its colonization of Indigenous peoples and land." The three examples just discussed, two of aspirational Caribbeanness and one of aspirational whiteness, both converge around the impulse to put Black people down to prop themselves up. Black Americans have noticed this and are fighting back to promote greater awareness of Black ethnicities within the United States. In his book *Because of Our Success*, legal scholar Kevin Brown, for example, makes the case for excluding what he calls "Black Multiracials," or mixed-race people with one Black parent, and global "Black Immigrants" and their children from qualifying for race-based programs in the United States meant for groups he terms "Ascendant Blacks," whose American ties go back further than three generations. Although I do not share Professor Brown's views on affirmative action or other limits on belonging, my discussions of race and ethnicity within American society grow out of my understanding of the complexity and overlapping of these large, diverse demographic categories.

ARCHIVE AND METHODOLOGY

This book brings together an eclectic assortment of cultural products that explicitly address the Caribbean American process of finding a way to belong within American society. While most of the primary texts under discussion in this study are the work of artists and public figures who have attained some measure of public recognition, my aim was to present a broad sense of the many aspects of American cultural and political life to which people of Caribbean American heritage are contributing. We have reached a critical mass of people with family ties to the Caribbean as influential interlocutors in the public dialogue surrounding the current state and future direction of American cultural and political life.

Part 1 examines texts that blur the line between official and vernacular. Sometimes these texts are idealistic and forward-looking, such as the campaign books and civic memoirs that are the focus of chapter 1. Though neither Marco Rubio, Ted Cruz, nor Kamala Harris won the presidency of the United States, their individual visions of a more diverse and prosperous America make for interesting reading as a canon of possibility. In contrast, Sonia Sotomayor and Karine Jean-Pierre discuss both the fulfillment they get from serving their country but also give frank insights into the hard work that goes into making government function the way it is supposed to. The second chapter examines two extremes of Caribbean American activism: on the one hand are public icons like Ricky Martin, Roxane Gay, and Karamo Brown, who have weighed in to one of this era's most public reckonings with the problem of sexual violence through their memoirs and anthologies, sharing their respective accounts of surviving rape, perpetrating intimate partner violence, fighting human trafficking, and enduring unrelenting pressure to disclose their sexual orientation before they were ready, in the service of critiquing rape culture and toxic masculinity. Activists use narratives to persuade others to their way of thinking.

Part 2 features fictional narratives that shine a light on intergenerational struggles that teenagers and young adults face as they negotiate just how much of their Caribbean heritage to claim while making their way through the education system in pursuit of the promise of the American Dream. Chapter 3 focuses on children's picture books because they represent intergenerational textual and visual performances meant to be shared and experienced together across a variety of registers. Children and their adult readers see different but interrelated narratives unfolding depending on their respective literacies and interests and together can construct complex understandings of what Caribbean American children's lives are or can be as depicted in texts by Edwidge Danticat and Junot Díaz, among others. Chapter 4 discusses young adult novels by Elizabeth Acevedo, Jennine Capó Crucet, Nicola Yoon, and Ibi Zoboi that feature protagonists who negotiate a variety of obstacles, from undocumented status to teenage pregnancy and everything in between during their transition from Caribbean children to American adults. Chapter 5 analyzes how the *Miles Morales* comic / film / novelization / video game franchise negotiates the hero's "Blatino" bicultural identity differently depending on which modality he appears in. This examination of how Caribbean American young people perform both their cultural heritages differently in the twenty-first century than people of their parents' generation did in the twentieth follows a theme introduced in one of the novels discussed in chapter 4 but complicates it by adding the supernatural dimension to the usual high school drama.

Cultural texts work on different registers than the merely textual as part 3's focus on televisual and comic book works explores. The visual performance of Caribbean American lives shapes how audiences—readers and viewers alike—see themselves represented as part of current and alternative futures in shows like *One Day at a Time* and *Red Table Talk: The Estefans* in chapter 6. This chapter opens with my reading of the 2020 Super Bowl show co-headlined by Jennifer Lopez and Shakira. Arguably the most fashionable way of presenting Caribbean American belonging in the second and third decades of the new millennium has been through musical theater with catchy beats and astounding feats of lyrical dexterity. Chapter 7 traces how Broadway musicals and their film adaptations like *Hamilton, In the Heights,* and *On Your Feet!* explicitly connect Caribbean Americanness and the immigrant experience to protest the last administration's racist weaponization of immigration policies to incarcerate those who look to the United States for refuge and to separate families who brave great perils to reach our borders.

The book concludes by considering how a Trinidadian American memoirist compares her life in the United States to various dysfunctional romantic relationships she has overcome throughout her adult life. While writing from a self-imposed exile in her birthplace, Tiffanie Drayton expresses her frustration with having her Americanness seen only through the monolithic lens of race—as Black—which flattens out her ethnicity as a Trinidadian. While Drayton's experience is the opposite of Miles Morales, for example, whose biculturality forms the basis of his popularity, her discomfort with being relegated to a "caste" system where she is considered "only" Black, coupled with the memoir's absolute lack of any reference to Drayton's new Caribbean life add up to an unfiltered performance of American anti-Black screed even as she explicitly decries the systemic and personal racism she personally endured as a child and young woman. Because *Black American Refugee* talks about the damaging effect of aspirational whiteness on Drayton's psyche, I discuss it alongside Kimberly Guilfoyle and Enrique Tarrio, both of whom have positions of power within American white supremacist political organizations (the Trump campaign and the Proud Boys, respectively) intent on policing and limiting just who can participate fully within the nation. These three narratives are part of a larger manifestation of the valorization of whiteness as a cultural rather than racial designation, what some have described as "multiracial whiteness."

As a group, Caribbean Americans have arrived even if there is currently no consensus surrounding who exactly is included under this descriptor or any substantive grassroots movement to adopt the moniker "Caribbean American" as an umbrella term around which to organize across difference. As a cultural critic, however, I make the case that the considerable power of this group of citizens is hard to appreciate unless we have a common language to discuss their achievements. This book provides one way to take stock of their impact.

PART 1

SHAPING A MORE PERFECT UNION

CHAPTER 1

A Vision of Belonging in Political Campaign Books and Civic Memoirs

On January 6, 2021, an insurrectionist mob stormed the US Capitol to disrupt democratic processes and overturn a free and fair election. In their reporting about the day's events, newspaper accounts, talking heads, and social media posts emphasized that among the legislators under attack were Vice President Mike Pence and Vice President-Elect Kamala Harris in her capacity as senator from California. As with so many of these barrier crossing moments, instances that highlight the increasing diversity of the United States, most American citizens hailed Harris's election to the second highest office in the land as a mark of progress. To the smaller number of party loyalists radicalized by Donald Trump and activated by social media, the prospect of Harris's assumption of the powers and obligations of the vice presidency was both illegitimate and yet another outrage.

I reference the January 6th insurrection to call attention to a little-noted convergence of three political careers that illustrate some of the historical and cultural forces contributing to the nation's current identity crisis and political polarization. Harris was not the only Caribbean American senator with presidential ambitions present in the Capitol that day. Ted Cruz, the junior senator from Texas, disgraced himself by leading a rogue Republican assembly of senators and members of Congress to protest the certification of the election results. It was another in a series of cynical political stunts that followed the 2020 election, but this time its impact on a disgruntled and disoriented group of Trump voters had fatal consequences. While Harris was under siege and Cruz was whipping up the winds of revolt, Marco Rubio, senator from Florida and the third Caribbean American former presidential contender, disappeared from the wall-to-wall coverage of the unprecedented events.

The fact that three politicians of Caribbean American descent were swept up in these events is no fluke. The turmoil surrounding the 2020 election and the resistance to its outcome has its roots in some white Americans' growing xenophobia, a sense that the nation is being swamped by immigrants and stolen from them right in front of their eyes, an ideology called the Great Replacement theory (Guerrero). Increasingly, members of various immigrant communities and people from all races, gender identities, sexual orientations, or ability status are running for office; their increased visibility, along with and the nation-wide movement to increase diversity and inclusion across all areas of society make Trump's followers afraid and resentful. Harris, Cruz, and Rubio were not the first people of Caribbean American heritage to run for office; that honor belongs to Shirley Chisholm, the daughter of Guyanese and Barbadian immigrants.

The Congresswoman from New York was a trailblazer who took her presidential campaign all the way into the Democratic Convention in 1972. Harris found Chisholm's example to be so inspiring as a fellow Caribbean American that she advocated for the erection of a statue in the Congresswoman's honor in the US Capitol in 2018, a full year before inaugurating her own presidential campaign (Toure). Ten days after the assault on the Capitol, Harris tweeted a shout-out to her hero, acknowledging the debt she owes her elder: "Shirley Chisholm created a path for me and for so many others. Today, I'm thinking about her inspirational words: 'I am, and always will be, a catalyst for change'" (@KamalaHarris). The vice president's admiration for Chisholm is a part of a larger movement to celebrate this pioneering politician's unabashedly inclusive platform and her staunch refusal to compromise her vision to raise funds. Chisholm's campaign slogan, "Unbought and Unbossed," was a trending hashtag on Twitter in the lead-up to the 2020 election. In April of that same year, Chisholm was a featured character in the TV miniseries, *Mrs. America*, in which Uzo Aduba played her. Meanwhile, there are also two filmic biopics about her under development: *Shirley* set to star actor/director Regina King and *The Fighting Shirley Chisholm*, produced by Amazon Studios and starring Oscar-winning actor Viola Davis. Fifteen years after her death, Representative Shirley Chisholm is having a moment.

I discuss the campaign books written by Chisholm's successors (a Democrat and Republicans, respectively)—Kamala Harris's *The Truths We Hold* (2019), Ted Cruz's *A Time for Truth* (2015), and Marco Rubio's *American Dreams: Restoring Economic Opportunity for Everyone* (2015)—as an archive of possibility rather than a set of failed visions. Read together, these texts constitute a compendium of competing visions for an unrealized American future in which the values gleaned from their shared Caribbean upbringing serve as guides for how best to move the American project forward. They also help to identify how embracing a Caribbean American identity offers an effective response to Donald Trump's endorsement of the nativism and racism that motivated many of the insurrectionists.

In a 2008 article for the *New Yorker*, historian Jill Lepore explains that "campaign biographies" are a distinctly American literary genre and have been the hallmark of presidential campaigns dating back to the nineteenth century.[1] She credits James Parton with first describing "campaign literature" as uniquely American "trash." Campaign books' lack of pretentiousness, their publishers' widespread distribution networks, and the multimodal platforms through which such accounts may be consumed (hardcover, paperback, e-book, audiobook) ensure that Harris's, Cruz's, and Rubio's depictions of their Caribbean families and upbringings reach a variety of reading publics of different abilities, interests, and ideological world views. The authors of *The Truths We Hold, American Dreams,* and *A Time for Truth* use their Caribbean American identities to write themselves into the well-established political trope of the worthy immigrant. In their narratives, these politicians leverage their own experiences as children of immigrants to portray their respective parents' journeys to the United States as exemplars of the overarching national myth of origin that casts immigration as a positive force in America.

These three texts make the same general argument: the candidates' Caribbean heritage made them into better Americans, and the lessons they learned at home taught by their immigrant parents fueled in each of them a desire to serve their compatriots as their elected chief executive. Even as they leverage their respective exoticism as a distinctive qualification, Harris, Cruz, and Rubio are also at pains to convey just how patriotic and all-American they are. This chapter analyzes these twin constructions of national belonging—to the ancestral homeland through affective ties and to their American homeland by virtue of their US citizenship and political aspirations—to suggest that Harris, Cruz, and Rubio articulate something new in their combination: a Caribbean American Relation identity that is forward-looking and envisions a new collaborative future that Americans can build together, in contradistinction to the backward-facing, nostalgic tone more characteristic of Root-identity

---

1. In an article for the *New York Times* in 2007, Julie Bosman suggests the title "candidate lit" to describe the books published by public figures seeking their party's presidential nomination. Since the term did not catch on, though the publishing trend continues, I chose to use the more pedestrian terms "campaign book" or "campaign memoir" throughout this chapter.

diaspora discourse that affirms affective ties with the people still living in the islands they left behind.

I read each candidate's accounts of shared themes—their parents' immigrant journey, their ties to the familial homeland, and their professed work ethic—as distinct rhetorical performances of their aptitude for civic service as well as of their strident patriotism. I am also interested in the moments when Harris, Cruz, and Rubio position themselves vis-a-vis their constituents as fellow Americans, but with a Caribbean difference. These carefully balanced autobiographical performances of their Caribbean American civic belonging highlight their campaign books' utilitarian function of introducing a potential candidate to the national stage. In this endeavor, I follow in the footsteps of literary critics Stephanie Li and Gordon Hutner, who argue for the validity of such critical analysis of the genre in the introduction to their edited volume of *American Literary History*:

> While political texts that often read as little more than self-indulgent propaganda may seem an unlikely focus of academic study, especially as objects of literary analysis rather than examples of cultural comment, writings by and about presidents and presidential candidates are crucial to understanding the increasingly blurry boundaries between truth and fiction, private and public, politics and entertainment. (421)

I am less interested in fact-checking each candidate's claims about their family's immigration journey than I am in examining the affective and evocative work these stories do to establish the candidate's fitness to lead the United States. I focus my literary analysis of these texts on how each depicts the story of the candidate's Caribbean roots to connect with voters and share their respective visions for a possible American future they can all share.

Li and Hutner consider how this popular mass-media genre shapes political discourse and influences citizens' likelihood to exercise their civic duty at the ballot box:

> What does it mean for a president or presidential candidate to craft a story and an image that is already compromised by the most obvious of political agendas? How does the rhetoric of the presidency impinge upon stories that must be both intimate and persuasive? And what role do journalists and political commentators have in influencing not just readers, but voters? (419–20)

This vernacular genre promotes the idea that the narrative presents an intimate portrait of the person running for office, as much because it contains "relatable" episodes from their private, family life, as it is because readers incorporate it into the rhythm of their personal routine by reading it at home or listening to the audio version during one's commute to work. Campaign books hold up a candidate's life as a civic exemplar: these are people who feel so moved by the plight of their fellow citizens that they articulate a compelling vision of how to change the status quo and rally supporters to their cause. To convey the illusion of intimacy, campaign books mete out just enough information about the individual's family background and domestic life to strike the right tone with multiple segments of the American electorate simultaneously. The goal is to create enough reader interest and public support to sustain their campaigns through to the primaries and the presidential debates.

In contrast, book sales rather than polling results are the metrics through which to determine the success of a related autobiographical genre, the civic memoir. Puerto Rican Associate Supreme Court Justice Sonia Sotomayor's *My Beloved World* (2013) and Haitian American White House press secretary Karine Jean-Pierre's *Moving Forward* (2019) combine personal accounts of growing up stateside as the children of Caribbean parents with a behind the scenes glimpse of government in action. As government "insiders," Sotomayor and Jean-Pierre shed light on the how their respective government agency works, whether it is the legal deliberations of the federal judiciary or the high-stakes decision making in the White House. Conveying these scenes of drama and intrigue in the context of their memoirs allows these DC power players to explore the individual and personal dimension involved in doing the Republic's work. Throughout their texts, these Caribbean American professionals exhort their readers to become more active citizens.

Where the campaign books written by Harris, Cruz, and Rubio plead their case to the electorate writ-large, Sotomayor and Jean-Pierre share their personal experiences of overcoming various forms of oppression and use their memoirs to increase the visibility of women of color in government service. Campaign books are written in the subjunctive, outlining what the politicians *would do* if elected. Civic memoirs, in contrast, are written in the present perfect, from the vantage point of those who *have been* making government work for the people. They point to what they have accomplished to show what members of the Caribbean American community can do when given a chance.

My Beloved World and *Moving Forward* address themselves to an audience of readers who are not inherently familiar with how federal government agencies function: recent immigrants, people from low socioeconomic backgrounds, who identify as minorities, who grew up in a single-parent household, who suffer from chronic illness, naturalized citizens, members of the LGBTQ+ community, and first-generation college students. These readers are not their only, or even their primary audiences, however. It is a testament to their skills as effective cultural translators that Sotomayor's and Jean-Pierre's memoirs simultaneously instruct their white readers about the distinctive family and community dynamics of their respective Caribbean American backgrounds. In the introduction to *Moving Forward,* Jean-Pierre illustrates this pressure to succeed for one's ethnic or national group when she explains the significance of an old photograph she carries in her wallet as a memento of her family's first trip to Washington, DC:

> There we were, seated on the base of the railing in front of the South Lawn of the White House, with the Truman Balcony in the far background. Jeannot gave me the photo to remind me of the pride my family takes in my success, of all of the people in the Haitian American community I carry on my shoulders. (13)

This anecdote reinforces her family's shared sense of ownership over her professional achievements: Jean-Pierre's success is not only hers, but it validates the generational and community expectations that are unavoidable aspect of public service for first- and second-generation immigrants.

In contrast, Sotomayor feels a personal obligation to share her story. She acknowledges the responsibility she feels to act as a role model for others whose circumstances make them identify with her in the preface to *My Beloved World:*

> The challenges I have faced—among them material poverty, chronic illness, and being raised by a single mother—are not uncommon, but neither have they kept me from uncommon achievements. For many it is a source of hope to see someone realize her dreams while bearing such burdens. Having caught people's attention in this way, I've thought long and hard about what lessons my life might hold for others, young people especially. How is it that adversity has spurred me on instead of knocking me down? What are the sources of my own hope and optimism? Most essentially, my purpose in writing is to make my hopeful example accessible.

Though Sotomayor feels duty-bound toward those who look to her as an inspiration, the fact that she has to say this explicitly to justify her decision to "write more intimately about my personal life than is customary for a member of the Supreme Court" means that she, too, speaks to two complimentary readerships at once: the children of adversity who share her experiences and a white middle class group of readers who are trying to figure out their subject positions as consumers of this narrative (n.p.). This passage is one of the rare moments where Sotomayor does not identify herself or her situation through a reference to her Puerto Rican heritage.

My Beloved World and *Moving Forward* function as personal testimonies demonstrating what exercising one's civic duties and responsibilities looks like. Sotomayor and Jean-Pierre share an expansive vision of when citizenship begins and what skills are necessary to fully live out one's responsibility as an active member of the nation state: it goes beyond the ballot box and starts as early as one can check out books at the local public library. For these authors, a citizen is someone who is curious, informed, and committed to making a difference that improves the lives of those around them.

Elected public officials (Harris, Cruz, and Rubio) and civil servants (Sotomayor and Jean-Pierre) are charged with enacting their citizenship more often than members of the public. I find Robert Asen's assertion in "A Discourse Theory of Citizenship," useful in understanding both how individuals go about activating or ignoring their civic duty as citizens, as well as how politicians running for office frame their calls for action when addressing this very audience:

> Multiplicity makes citizenship possible by situating it as something one can take up, rather than as a condition that is always or never present. People do not—and should not—enact citizenship all the time. Full-time citizenship imposes a false simplicity on people's complicated lives and frames citizenship as a burden rather than a process of active, willful uptake. (196)

By voting for our senators and representatives, we agree to outsource the duties of citizenship to those individuals whose ambition it is to carry out these functions professionally and act on our collective behalf. The assembled group of campaign and civic memoirs not only serve as proof of their authors' patriotism, but they also invite readers to become more acquainted with candidates and their platforms. In so doing, *The Truths We Hold, A Time for Truth, American Dreams, My Beloved World,* and *Moving Forward* engage in what Robert Terrill calls the "*inventional* capacity of rhetoric," through which political communities are conjured into existence:

> To recognize citizenship as a mode of rhetorical speech is to recognize it also as constituted in and through rhetorical speech. Citizenship, in this mode, is the role into which a discourse invites its audience, signified by the par-

ticular discursive resources through which the invitation is offered and the stylistic tokens that the discourse provides as ways through which to enact this role. (14–15)

By reading a politician's campaign book or a government employee's civic memoir, people engage in acts of citizenship as a discursive practice in which they entertain the writer's vision for how the nation would ideally function under his or her governing philosophy or thanks to their hard work. Where Terrill's critical project analyzes Barack Obama's presidential rhetoric to find and signal how these texts provide points of entry for Americans to enact their civic roles, the literary pretensions of the texts that make up this case study are considerably more modest, and thus I have tailored my theoretical intervention to scale. Terrill deploys an innovative methodology, "inventional critique," which "aims to make a contribution to the rhetorical education of democratic citizens" (11). In contrast, my approach combines close readings and performance analysis to evaluate the degree to which these memoirs imagine an inclusive view of an American civic landscape in which the government: responds to the needs of Americans of all stripes by increasing personal freedoms (*A Time for Truth* and *American Dreams*); taxes large corporations to help fix the economy (*The Truths We Hold*); treats everyone fairly under the law (*My Beloved World*); and allows everyone who wants to do so to cast a vote (*Moving Forward*). The performative dimensions campaign books and civic memoirs come into play when they leverage references to their authors' biographical Caribbeanness to engage with their ideal readers as fellow citizens and potential voters.

AUTOTOPOGRAPHY AS A CRITICAL LENS

My analysis of campaign books' performative dimensions as works of political theatre rather than meditations on citizenship grows out of my appreciation of Deirdre Heddon's theoretical framework in *Autobiography and Performance*. Heddon examines the theatrical dimensions of autobiographical narratives performed before live audiences and explains:

> The task of autobiographical performances that engage with explicitly political remits is threefold: (i) to use personal experience in order to render visible oppression and inequality; (ii) to render simultaneously such experiences historically contingent (and therefore possible to change); (iii) to deny any simple referentiality between a life and its representation while acknowledging that representation is itself a discursive technology. (31)

Though Heddon's inquiry focuses on the artistic and political dimensions of theatre pieces based on autobiographical elements, I apply her concepts to analyze the performative elements of politicians' and government workers' autobiographical self-representations to their intended audiences of likely voters and fellow Americans. For one thing, both performance artists and politicians frequently recount versions of their life stories on stage. For another, the book and the stage provide platforms through which autobiographical performances can take place in a concentrated and uninterrupted manner and can demand the audiences' full attention. Heddon calls this process "autotopography" and argues that this style of writing

> intends to foreground the subjectivity involved in plotting place; autotopography is writing place through self (and simultaneously writing self through place). Autotopography, like autobiography, is a creative act of seeing, interpretation and invention, all of which depend on where you are standing, when and for what purpose. (90–91)

Campaign books and civic memoirs inherently engage in verbal or rhetorical mapping since they superimpose the particularity of their featured candidate or government worker onto the expansiveness of the national stage. Harris, Cruz, Rubio, Sotomayor, and Jean-Pierre write themselves into place in three distinct and overlapping ways in both genres:

Campaign Books

1. mapping the candidates' physical relationship to their ancestral Caribbean homelands
2. tracing the candidates' educational journeys in higher education
3. collapsing the physical distance separating their offices in Washington, DC, from those in their respective districts

Civic Memoirs

1. recounting personal visits to their parents' home island
2. tracing their higher education journey
3. narrating the arc of their professional careers

My close readings of key passages of autotopography from these works will illustrate how they make strategic use of the candidates' Caribbean or American heritage to better connect with their intended audience of likely voters and proclaim their sense of belonging within the United States.

MAPPING CONNECTIONS TO THE CARIBBEAN

On December 3, 2019, Senator Kamala Harris gave up her bid to oust President Trump in the 2020 national elections. Up until then, her campaign had generated some early buzz. The biographical video, "America's Promise," available both on YouTube and her official campaign website, introduced Harris nationally by emphasizing the candidate's preferred self-presentation as "an American." As family photos appear on-screen, Harris proudly recalls her Oakland roots by briefly discussing her parents, Donald Harris and Shyamala Gopalan, who "met as students at the University of California." The voiceover narration entirely omits any reference to their shared status as immigrants to the United States; Harris's and Gopalan's respective birthplaces, India and Jamaica, remain unnamed. Instead, the narration stresses her parents' activism "in the civil rights movement." In her first appearance on screen, Harris claims activism as her birthright: "I was taught that I had a responsibility to be a part of the fight for justice." While her own commitment to social justice aligns Harris's campaign rhetoric with that of previous African American leaders, most notably former president Barack Obama, her relative silence regarding her status as the child of immigrants stands in marked difference to the former president's portrayal of his Kenyan American father as an elusive but interesting figure in his first memoir / campaign book, *Dreams from My Father: A Story of Race and Inheritance* (1995). Both the elder Mr. Obama and Mr. Harris were gone from their children's lives early on due to divorce, but where Barack Obama rounds out his story by discussing a visit to his father's homeland as a young man, Kamala Harris waxes poetic in her campaign memoir about her late Indian mother's enormous strength, personal drive, and unwavering support for her daughters. She hardly mentions her father. Instead, the story of Harris's trips to visit his ancestral homeland unfolds visually within *The Truths We Hold* through a selection of photographs that show young Kamala posing with relatives in Jamaica. I contend that the strategic written and visual references she makes to visiting Jamaica as a child in the memoir constitute a useful instance of autotopography because they attest to her kinship ties to the island.[2]

---

2. The one place about which Harris remains almost silent in this memoir is Canada, where she spent her teenage years.

To campaign in the Trump era, Harris decided she needed to distinguish her own political discussions of identity from Barack Obama's celebratory rhetoric and from the vitriol of Trump and his minions. She also refused to engage directly with political operatives trying to reactivate the Swift Boat / Birther playbook to disqualify her candidacy through innuendo and gross inaccuracies and lies. A feature article on Kamala Harris published by the *Washington Post* illustrates this tension in its very title, "'I Am Who I Am': Kamala Harris, Daughter of Indian and Jamaican Immigrants, Defines Herself Simply as 'American.'" Journalist Kevin Sullivan repeatedly discusses her parents' immigrant statuses, even though he acknowledges the candidate's refusal to incorporate this information into her public self-definition:

> Harris's background in many ways embodies the culturally fluid, racially blended society that is second-nature in California's Bay Area and is increasingly common across the United States.
>
> She calls herself simply "an American," and said she has been fully comfortable with her identity from an early age. (Sullivan)

Harris's refusal to engage in identity politics prompts those telling her story by proxy, such as Sullivan, to fill in the gaps for an audience they perceive wants to know the specifics of the politician's family background. In insisting on her American identity, she asks her would-be voters to recognize that Caribbean Americans, Jamaican Americans, and Indian Americans are already part of the nation. Harris's strategic refusal to leverage her Caribbean family history to seem more "relatable" to potential voters in her campaign book marks a turn away from the political playbook that previous presidential contenders of Caribbean heritage had used before. She is well-aware that her Indian name and Black skin announce a hybridity that distinguishes her from most other candidates. Rather than explain how she navigates difference and cultural tension, Harris insists on her presence in the moment in all her complexity. By describing herself as "an American," Harris reclaims the label away from the former president's platform of toxic nationalism; she redefines American identity as a more benign and inclusive brand of nationalism that can encompass the totality of both her Jamaican and Indian heritages, as well as anyone else's.

Neither Ted Cruz nor Marco Rubio challenged Donald Trump as he made a failed reelection bid in 2020. Four years earlier, the two had gone head-to-head in the long march to the 2016 Republican national convention. As self-identified sons of Cuban exiles, each man's retelling of his family's departure from that island became a central feature in their campaign's presentation of the candidate to the American electorate. Later, each of these narratives came under media scrutiny. Jason Horowitz from the *New York Times* traveled to Rafael Cruz's hometown of Matanzas, Cuba, and interviewed his contemporaries to fact-check his son's version of his freedom-fighting exploits. In response, the Cruz campaign doubled down on their official version of events and blamed any discrepancies on political rivals' efforts to discredit the Senator and his family.

Marco Rubio handled questions about the accuracy of his family's immigration story more honorably. On October 20, 2011, the *Washington Post* published an article fact-checking Rubio's account of his family's departure from Cuba against their actual naturalization records (Roig-Franzia). The reporter's investigation unearthed a chronological discrepancy: the elder Mr. and Mrs. Rubio had left Cuba more than two years before Castro came to power. Other news outlets, like *NPR* and *The Atlantic* picked up the story and Rubio issued a public acknowledgement explaining that the account he had given of his parents' departure from Cuba was based on family lore, and that he had never personally verified the timing of their journey. *NPR* conducted its own archival research and unearthed an interview Rubio had given to Robert Siegel of *All Things Considered,* which also contained other erroneous statements regarding the timing of his mother's 1961 return to Cuba and how long it took her to rejoin her family in the United States (Welna). Subsequent editions of Rubio's first memoir, *An American Son,* contain "a new epilogue" that explicitly addresses the issue of Rubio's chronological faux pas. His subsequent presidential campaign book, *American Dreams* briefly invokes the senator's ties to Cuba through a poignant description of Rubio's grandfather's death in an ambulance accompanied by his grandson and translator, young Marco. The dramatic opening sets the stage for later discussions of healthcare, insurance, Medicare, and debt, but it also establishes Rubio's authenticity as a bilingual Cuban American. Structurally, the passing of the immigrant patriarch makes way for their American-born children to rise and claim America, the land of opportunity, as their own.

A Time for Truth and *American Dreams* meet the first of Heddon's criteria in their portrayal of the candidates as people of Caribbean heritage, a rhetorical strategy that positions the two senators (via their parents) as hereditary victims of oppression and inequality. Cruz's concept of "opportunity conservatism" aims to "empower" the "least fortunate among us in a way that regulations and bureaucrats never have and never will" (169). In *American Dreams,* Rubio identifies himself primarily through social class, "the son of a bartender and a maid" (x), a distinct shift in tone from his original self-portrayal where he claims a more politically significant lineage, "the son of Cuban exiles" (*An American Son,* 292). These campaign books triangulate their authors' inherited sense of oppression to signal a different, better future. Cruz's *A Time for Truth* and Rubio's *American Dreams* both invoke the notion of divine "blessings" as the reason why they never had to experience the abject poverty that afflicted their Cuban forbears.

Cruz's and Rubio's Cuban heritage lend these candidates' childhood stories an air of uniqueness made them legible to a broad spectrum of immigrant communities as having similar life experiences to those of their families. The absence of intimate ties to Cuba establishes Cruz's and Rubio's satisfactory performances of being members of the Cuban exile/diaspora community in the United States. The Cuba that both Cruz and Rubio invoke is entirely imaginary—it is the product of their parents' nostalgic recollections. Within the larger architecture of Rubio's two-volume campaign oeuvre, the first book, *An American Son,* establishes his autotopography in vivid and descriptive detail. Central to Rubio's autobiographical sense of self are the immigration journeys undertaken by his parents, grandparents, aunts, uncles, and even his older siblings who were born in Cuba. The Rubio nuclear family's subsequent relocation from Florida to Nevada, Marco's circuitous academic journey from being a transfer student as an undergraduate and then living at home with his parents while attending law school, together with the various stops in Rubio's religious pilgrimage from Catholicism to Mormonism, to Protestantism, and back to the Catholic Church, are the backbone of his evolving perception of himself and the role he could play as an advocate for others.

The second book, *American Dreams,* then builds on that thick autotopographic tapestry in two specific ways that at once signal back to Rubio's *cubanidad* and move beyond the need to establish his bona fides because they are a fundamental part of how he lives his life. The first was his service as a translator for his dying grandfather. This reminds readers of his bilingualism. The second is through a throwaway reference to a staple of Cuban cuisine, *ropa vieja,* in the larger context his proposed plan for making higher education more affordable:

> For example, an aspiring cook may have mastered his or her craft from books and free online tutorials, or perhaps from the training of a parent who is a certified chef—or who simply cooks up a mean *ropa vieja* after years of preparing it for the family. These people should have the opportunity to prove their abilities and gain the certification necessary for employment without spending tens of thousands of dollars at a formal culinary school. (*American Dreams,* 105)

The logic of this argument is spurious—the cooking industry is one in which it is not only possible, but perfectly acceptable, for professionals to rise through the ranks from dishwasher to head chef without acquiring formal or costly culinary instruction. However, this passage's innovation is how effortlessly and comfortably it centers a Cuban way of knowing as the norm for a hypothetical citizen seeking to make a livelihood unencumbered by external and unnecessary debt. Rubio does not pause to explain that *ropa vieja* means "old clothes" or that it is a traditional Cuban stew made up of shredded beef and vegetables in a tomato-based sauce. Instead, he treats *ropa vieja* as a synecdoche for every American family's traditional recipe, passed down by their immigrant ancestors. Then, the text adds more layers that correspond specifically to the people whose lives he is trying to improve through the legislative process.

Cruz, for his part, rejects such gestures of hospitality and presents the table as an ideal place to sow discord. From its opening gambit, in which Cruz boasts of disrupting the weekly lunch of the Senate Republicans, *A Time for Truth* consistently depicts its subject as a man apart, an outsider to his colleagues, his party, his ethnicity, and most surprisingly, his constituents. He claims few friendships, the most significant of which is with a fellow Caribbean American from Jamaica, David Panton, who became his roommate and debate partner at Princeton and then his classmate once more at Harvard Law. Throughout the text, Cruz uses autotopography to signal his Americanness when he describes himself and his conservative friend in terms of race and ethnicity rather than emphasizing their shared Caribbean heritage: they are "a Hispanic man and a black man" whose presence at the Ivy Leagues helps the debate team in which they participate appear more diverse (61). Panton "wanted to go into business in Jamaica," while Cruz went on to a clerkship for Chief Justice William Rehnquist (78).[3] Cruz later reverses course when it seems politically expedient to diverge from the attitude adopted by other Republican politicians who surround him when he portrays his grandstanding behavior at Nelson Mandela's funeral as a principled stance he took as a Cuban American:

> In 2013, I was proud to attend the funeral of Nelson Mandela—the only senator to attend, and one of only two Republicans. I admired Mandela because he was a freedom fighter, he stood up to racial injustice and transformed his nation and the world. But, when his odious supporter Raul Castro spoke at the funeral, I walked out of the stadium. (328)

---

3. And it is precisely there, in the Supreme Court judges' chambers, that Cruz's account comes most alive. *A Time for Truth* makes a compelling case for why Ted Cruz would like to be appointed to the nation's highest court someday. The very lack of pretense of any concern with his constituents' welfare of their livelihood betrays that his desire for the presidency is mostly the result of vanity.

This empty gesture, so unnoticed by the world at large that he had to report it within his campaign book so he could claim to be a "truth teller," is emblematic of Cruz's understanding of physical space. What matters to him is where he was standing and whether he could bear to occupy the same public space as the communist leader of his ancestral homeland. At no point does he mention either Cuba or South Africa, relying on readers' willingness to supply such details for themselves and therefore complete the picture.

Cruz's Cuban roots are half as deep as Marco Rubio's since only his father was born on the island.[4] Cruz traces his paternal family's heritage all the way back to the Canary Islands in Spain, thereby clearly establishing his genetic ties to Europe rather than to Cuba's history of racial intermixing. Interestingly, the only uncontroversial story of immigration he tells recounts his great grandparents' arrival to Cuba: "It was to this fledgling nation that my great-grandparents arrived in 1902 from the Canary Islands. Agustin and Maria Cruz boarded a ship with their infant son, Rafael, bound for the New World" (7). This account does not quite show Cruz writing himself into place because the book does not specify whether Cruz has visited either the Canary Islands or his mother's ancestral Irish and Italian lands. The one thing the reference to his grandparents does it highlight Cruz's European ancestry, a not-so-subtle instance of anti-Blackness because it forfends the possibility that any of his Cuban forbears are Afro-Latinx.[5]

Sotomayor's and Jean-Pierre's explanation of their families' respective journeys to arrive in the mainland United States strike a different tone that those of Harris, Cruz, or Rubio because as public servants, neither woman bears the responsibility of making her story emblematic of the larger plight of all immigrants. *My Beloved World* and *Moving Forward* engage in two types of autotopography that reinforce one another. Because the books are personal accounts of public lives with no further aim than to make their subjects legible to their American compatriots, Sonia Sotomayor and Karine Jean-Pierre write themselves into place both as part of the families that brought them up as well as individual adult women who decide what aspect of their Caribbean heritage to claim and for what purpose. Sotomayor was born in the United States,

---

4. His mother is a woman from Delaware.

5. As Cruz's narration of his great-grandparents' sea voyage makes clear, the name "Rafael" gets passed down from grandfather (the baby) to Cruz's father, and it is also the Senator's given appellation, one which he rejects in favor of his mother's more Anglicized version of his middle name as "Ted." While this change helped young Cruz avoid bullying, his father receives it as an insult: "'Ted' immediately felt like me. But my father was furious with the decision. He viewed it as a rejection of him and his heritage, which was not my intention" (35). Cruz also avoids discussing his dual citizenship by virtue of being born in Calgary, Canada, or whether he has ever returned there as an adult.

whereas Jean-Pierre immigrated with her parents as a young child and became a naturalized US citizen as an adult. They share the common experience of visiting their parents' birthplaces, but their travels are markedly different, in part, because of their age gap and also due to the fact that Puerto Rico is a territory of the United States and thus travel to it involves only domestic flights. Trips to Haiti are international flights that require travelers to clear customs. Moreover, Haiti's history of repressive governments and political instability further complicates travel to and from the island.

Jean-Pierre recounts her only visit to Haiti, which she undertook as part of a graduate seminar capstone project offered by Columbia University's School of International and Public Affairs. This trip had significant professional and personal implications, not the least of which was that while Jean-Pierre grew up in a Haitian American household, she was born in Martinique where her parents had immigrated to find employment and she does not speak Haitian Creole. Jean-Pierre's presence in her parents' homeland was mediated through her studies as a graduate student from Columbia. In contrast, Sonia Sotomayor spent her summers visiting relatives in Puerto Rico throughout her childhood. She spoke Spanish at home to communicate with her family, thereby cementing an affective connection that only changed after her father's death and the subsequent strain on the family's finances. These anecdotes affirm their writers' Americanness in contradistinction to the island cultures they encounter but the vivid details Sotomayor and Jean-Pierre employ when describing their visits to their parents' homelands showcase how each woman writes herself into both Caribbean and American spaces through their connection to family.

Sotomayor's childhood visits to Puerto Rico parallel Harris's youthful visits to her extended family in Jamaica. In *My Beloved World,* Sotomayor recalls: "On my earliest trips to Puerto Rico, when I was small including my first as a toddler—it was just Abuelita and I. My mother was determined that she would never, ever go back to the island, but then she changed her mind" (41). The judge suggests that her mother's negative attitude about Puerto Rico was due to frustration over having had such limited opportunities for advancement on the island as a rural woman. Sotomayor writes that her mother, Celina, was:

> recruited into one of the first Puerto Rican units of the Women's Army Corps. Over twenty thousand Puerto Rican men had already served in the U.S. armed forces before the women were included. And although the first units were segregated because of their limited English, it was for many of these women, as for so many of the men who served, how they came to see themselves as rightfully American. (73)

Thus, although English language fluency was not something Mrs. Sotomayor passed on to her offspring, civic duty, patriotism, and a tradition of serving others were values the family cherished. This is the foundation of Sotomayor's sense of civic responsibility—rather than being torn between her heritage and her patriotism, both are part of a continuous experience of Americanness. Sotomayor's account also mentions visits to local beaches, museums, architectural landmarks, and some of her relatives' businesses. For young Sonia, these trips to Puerto Rico shaped her expectations of how far her hard work could take her:

> It was clear to me even then that the people I knew on the island had better jobs than the Puerto Ricans I knew in New York. When we walked down the street in Mayagüez, it gave me a proud thrill to read the little signs above the doors, of the doctors, the lawyers, and the other professionals who were Puerto Rican. It was not something I had often seen in New York. (44)

Sonia's sense of the island's urban areas as places where professional success was both possible and common differed from her mother's own experience growing up poor in a more rural area. However, in noticing the differences between the island and her New York home, Sotomayor's account performs an interesting retrospective autotopography by implying that the seed of her professional ambition was planted during the childhood sojourns in her parents' birthplace. Her impression of those times conveys a sense of orderly life somewhat more slow-paced than New York, but still recognizable. In this regard, Sotomayor's experiences of Puerto Rico affirm a sense of continuity with her regular life.

Karine Jean-Pierre's first visit to her parents' homeland took place when she was an adult. Even then, she felt so conflicted about the prospect of traveling to Haiti and fearful of how the idea would be received by her family that she only told her mother of her plans the day before her flight was scheduled to take off. The opportunity to travel there came about through her friendship with a graduate student who encouraged her to enroll in the course co-sponsored by a collaboration between Columbia University and the Ministry of Haitians Living Abroad (94). This episode gives rise to a complicated discussion of the internalized prejudice Jean-Pierre felt toward Haiti as a young woman growing up in the United States along with her anticlimactic discovery that the Haitians with whom Jean-Pierre interacts regard her as an outsider. In *Moving Forward*, the first self-disclosure comes during her reflection on the cost of not trying to cultivate linguistic skills as a heritage speaker of Haitian Creole:

> We ate a lot of Haitian food like *Pwason Boukannen* (grilled fish), *Dri Kole* (rice and beans), and *Bannnann* (plantains) but I never considered learning the language of Haiti, Creole. If I were honest, I would admit growing up I was, well, ashamed of being Haitian. Part of me had absorbed both a sense of stigma that the AIDS epidemic had created around Haiti and my mother's bitterness towards her birthplace. I had spent so much of my life trying to fit into American life. (95)

Her fellow student's pride in his ethnicity and his enthusiasm for all things Haitian prompts Jean-Pierre to reach this introspective confession. Once she arrives in Haiti after braving her mother's disapproval, Jean-Pierre briefly feels as if the trip is a homecoming of sorts. However, the optimism is short-lived when she overhears locals describing her to one another as "*blan*" or "white," a perplexing interaction she perceives as a racial misidentification:

> I later learned during our trip that *moun blan* or *blan* is a phrase used to describe foreigners. I heard the phrase a few times that week. It was a hard reality for me to reconcile with. Back home in America, I was seen by most people as "exotic," a foreigner with my dark skin, broad nose, full lips, and big eyes. I never felt like I fit in. If it wasn't my Haitian culture, then it was my looks. It didn't matter how hard I tried; I was an "outsider," the "other." My whole life, I have felt a sense of "You are not one of us." How could it be that I finally made it to Haiti and I was still seen as a foreigner, an "other"? I felt rejected by Haiti. (103)

These two passages convey the complex and sometimes contradictory web of stereotypes about both race and culture that determine how national insiders interact with those perceived to be outsiders or marginal to the dominant class. These stereotypes are damaging whether they are internally or externally imposed but, in both instances, they constitute ways of asserting autotopography or the writing of the self in place. They also reveal the strains that a purely binaristic concept of race places on the individual and how it resonates with a Root identity. While this trip confirmed for Jean-Pierre that she did "not feel a deep connection with Haiti," she admits that there was nothing in her background that would have fomented such a positive affective connection. Her mother's bitterness toward Haiti parallels Celina Sotomayor's ambivalence toward the prospect of returning to Puerto Rico. Neither woman can write themselves into place in the Caribbean after having made their way in the United States.

The rest of *Moving Forward* focuses on Jean-Pierre's discussion of how she resolved her sense of being peripheral to American culture through two external actions: the first was regularizing her immigration status by becoming a naturalized citizen and the second was pursuing a career in politics that has spanned from the local to the national level. Because neither Jean-Pierre nor Cruz learned their Caribbean parents' first language (Haitian Creole or Spanish, respectively), their main exposure to Caribbean cultures is through the American experience of either exile (Cuban) or diaspora (Haiti). Regardless, what all five public servants have in common is that they all hold graduate degrees: as lawyers, Harris, Cruz, Rubio, and Sotomayor earned JDs, while Jean-Pierre holds a Master of Public Affairs from Columbia University.

EDUCATION

All five of the memoirs under discussion portray their authors' experiences of higher education as a formative stage in their personal and political development of a sense of belonging within the United States. Their respective accounts of college life and establishing their careers cast their adult lives as all-American, a necessary precondition to identifying with their constituents and volunteering to work on their behalf in Washington. Though successful within the pages of each book, these tales of the hybrid immigrant child / American adult were meant to also resonate as compelling talking-points on the campaign trail for Harris, Cruz and Rubio, whereas they only serve as illustrations of Sotomayor's and Jean-Pierre's career trajectories. These intellectual coming of age narratives illustrate how each of the Caribbean American political figures construct their textual selves in space.

In *The Truths We Hold*, Kamala Harris states that as the child of two doctorate-holding parents, she had always planned to go to college. She recalls choosing Howard University, a historically Black college or university (HBCU), because she wanted to become a lawyer and this was the school one of her Civil Rights idols had attended: "what better place to do that, I thought, than at Thurgood Marshall's alma mater?" (21). The one thing her parents still had in common many years after their divorce was their commitment to Civil Rights, so this choice was sure to please them both. In her description of the Howard University campus, Harris engages in autotopography by writing herself into a place where she clearly belongs:

> I'll always remember walking into Cramton Auditorium for my freshman orientation. The room was packed. I stood in the back, looked around, and thought, "This is heaven!" There were hundreds of people, and everyone looked like me. Some were children of Howard alumni; others were the first in their families to go to college. Some had been in predominantly black

schools their whole lives; others had long been one of only a few people of color in their classroom or their neighborhood. Some came from cities, some from rural communities, and some from African countries, the Caribbean, and throughout the African diaspora. (22)

This is the only real passage that outlines the rich diversity of students' experiences and backgrounds that characterizes a freshman class, for example. Here, Harris acknowledges that her individual experience is in no way emblematic of how other students experience this historically Black university. This perspective enacts her Relation identity at work as Harris conveys the validation she felt as a mixed-race woman who did not stand out for her difference from others.

Harris mentions some of the social and professional opportunities that Howard offered her during her years there before then briefly explaining that during her time at UC Hastings College of the Law in San Francisco she was elected president of the Black Law Students Association. That is the extent of her discussion of academics. We know less about Harris's intellectual training as part of her legal education than we know about the other memoirists', an ironic consideration given that she made her political career on the strength of her success as an elected district attorney. This brief digression into her college and law school years shows how Harris writes herself back into place first to mark her return to the United States from Canada, and then from Washington, DC, to San Francisco, California, the state where she was born and raised for a time and which she would eventually represent as its first elected Black woman senator.

One recurring theme across the remaining campaign books and civic memoirs is the immigrant parents' insistence that their children take advantage of the opportunities a good education would afford them. Marco Rubio played football in high school and college but proved to be an otherwise indifferent student, though he did graduate from law school. Like Harris, he studied law in the state he now represents as senator. Rubio took out loans to finance his legal studies and admits, "when I raised my right hand and was sworn in as a United States Senator in January 2011, I still owed over $100,000. It wasn't until the publication of my first book, *An American Son*, in 2012, that I was able to repay my loans" (*American Dreams*, 94). To his credit, Rubio's frank discussion of the financial hardships he endured to pursue a professional degree helps him empathize with the plights of his constituents, to whom he describes himself explicitly as, "a cautionary tale for young Americans" (*American Dreams*, 94). Sadly, the solution he proposes to fix this broken system in the book is to downplay the significance of traditional academic or professional credentials in favor of an ad hoc system that rewards skills acquisition through informal work experiences.

Rubio's path into politics involved him navigating the tense political waters of Florida's expatriate Cuban patronage system. Although he could not work as a lawyer until he had both earned a JD and passed the bar exam, the vocational path he advocates for people with work experience or natural talent, like the *ropa vieja* cook in his example, devalues the importance of the very academic credentials he holds. Cruz's *A Time for Truth*, in contrast, shows how far the connections one makes in elite Ivy League universities open doors for people with political ambitions. His book does not paint a particularly vivid picture of how Cruz succeeded in breaking into Texas politics.

Cruz distinguished himself academically, earning acceptance to the nation's most elite private universities. Even though his father only left Cuba because he was accepted at the University of Texas as an international student, Cruz takes a haughty tone when describing his own experience of the college admission process, striving to both establish his hard-partying credentials while also making it seem as if gaining admission to Princeton was a walk in the park. Like Harris, both of Cruz's parents earned doctorates and expected their child to apply himself academically. In the Ivy League, Cruz found mentors like Alan Dershowitz, who channeled his youthful conservatism and exposed him to the rigorous study of economics and political theory. Only when recounting his law school education does Cruz sound like he legitimately fell in love with his studies; in fact, he explicitly acknowledges how much his choice of law school was an effort to validate his father's expectations for him: "It was hard to imagine anything that might mean more to my immigrant father than for his son to attend Harvard Law School" (67). However, practicing law in his home state was not something Cruz planned on doing long term, thereby deviating from the pattern that characterizes both Rubio's and Harris's careers.

Like Rubio, Cruz also acknowledges that his professional education came at an economic cost. In *A Time for Truth*, Cruz discusses his student loans in a footnote to his account of working on the George W. Bush 2000 campaign a few years after finishing law school. Rather than a "cautionary tale," however, Cruz's account of how he managed his finances ends up being more of a humble brag: "My fixed bills, including my student loans, dramatically exceeded my monthly income on the campaign. Fortunately, in my two years at Cooper & Carvin, I had saved nearly half of my salary, so I was able to live off savings during the campaign" (104). With this statement, candidate Cruz lays bare the economic dimension of his electoral platform—rather than commiserating with those who face more disadvantages than he did, Cruz extols the virtues of thrift and strategic connections to improve one's lot in life.

Whereas the Caribbean American campaign books sought to bridge the physical distance separating politicians' offices from their constituents' home spaces, Sotomayor's book builds on the commonalities she already shares with her audience, such as her love of reading, the help and mentoring she received from others who wanted her to succeed, and her desire to serve her country though the fruits of her labor. In *My Beloved World,* Sotomayor recalls growing up poor in New York City as the child of hard-working migrants from Puerto Rico and taking advantage of every opportunity to indulge her love of learning and leverage her outstanding academic performance into ever-more impactful career choices. Sotomayor's dedication to community service as a college student, as well as the legal acumen she developed through her time in the district attorney's office and in private practice, led to a position as a federal judge and a nomination to the nation's highest court. Her educational journey to the Ivy League parallels that of former first lady Michelle Obama: both were first-generation minority college students at Princeton, and they each use their respective public platforms to encourage young people of color to aim high and reap the rewards and opportunities a college education makes possible.

The *New York Times* emphasized the importance of the judge's elite academic pedigree to her professional success when reporting President Obama's nomination of Sotomayor to the United States Supreme Court in 2009: "In making his first pick for the court, Mr. Obama emphasized Judge Sotomayor's 'extraordinary journey' from modest beginnings to the Ivy League and now the pinnacle of the judicial system. Casting her as the embodiment of the American dream, he touched off a confirmation battle that he hopes to wage over biography more than ideology" (Baker and Zeleny). Thus, from her first entry onto the national stage as a high-profile nominee to serve a lifetime appointment, Sonia Sotomayor's degrees from Princeton and Yale serve as shorthand to convey her success at being American. Whereas Cruz plays off his similar pedigree as proof of his innate brilliance and lack of effort, Sotomayor downplays the selective nature of her alma mater's admission policies in favor of describing her battle against impostor syndrome when talking to young people with more modest academic aspirations.

My Beloved World also honestly portrays Sotomayor's difficulty adjusting to higher education as a first-generation student away from home. Even reviewers discussing her memoir, like acclaimed literary critic Michiko Kakutani, cast the judge's efforts to master the complexities of the English language as signs of her commitment to assimilating to dominant American culture:

In college she received a C on her first midterm paper and realized she needed to learn how to construct more coherent arguments, and that she also needed to improve her English, which was "riddled with Spanish constructions and usage." Over the next few summers, she says, she devoted each day's lunch hour to grammar exercises and to learning 10 new words. She also tried to catch up on the classics—like "The Adventures of Huckleberry Finn" and "Pride and Prejudice"—that she'd missed out on in her youth, when there was little to read around the house besides *Reader's Digest*.

Kakutani's catalogue of Sotomayor's self-improvement efforts makes her sound a little like a Puerto Rican Jay Gatsby. It is ironic for Kakutani to invoke *Reader's Digest* as shorthand to dismiss of the Sotomayor household as lacking in literary cultural capital because young Sonia had not read canonical Anglophone novels by the time she got to college. Sotomayor herself recounts how much her childhood was steeped in and shaped by her grandmother's public poetry readings in Spanish. The epigraph makes clear that the title of her memoir, *My Beloved World,* comes from a verse of Puerto Rican Romantic poet José Gautier Benítez's poem, "To Puerto Rico (I Return)." As the title of her memoir illustrates, her accomplishment unites rather than separates the Puerto Rican space of her home and neighborhood and the civic space of the courts. Though well intentioned, this passage highlights how invisible to most monolingual American audiences is the rich Hispanophone Caribbean American cultural heritage to which Sotomayor is an heir. By discussing her reading habits, Sotomayor conveys that learning is a dynamic process that can take place beyond the classroom.

As first-generation college students, Sotomayor and Jean-Pierre recall experiencing self-doubt at times. At Princeton, Sotomayor was far from home and thus had to reach out to others for help and guidance in making sense of her professors' expectations and connecting with fellow students to build community. In contrast, Jean-Pierre lived with her family while she pursued her undergraduate studies and thus had the added support system of family that Sotomayor lacked. Jean-Pierre felt so much pressure from her parents to become a doctor that she attempted suicide after not doing well in the MCAT exams. The double failure of her exam results and surviving her attempt to die gave Jean-Pierre the impetus to chart a new course for herself by moving out of her parents' home, pursuing graduate studies at Columbia, and coming to terms with her sexuality as a lesbian.

Jean-Pierre says her family's conservative and Christian Haitian cultural norms translated into high expectations they had for their daughter: "Being the eldest of three in a Caribbean immigrant family, I was expected to set the bar high, to be a perfect child. No trouble at school. No drinking. No drugs. No sex. You must be better than that" (40). Jean-Pierre's account of this internalized surveillance successfully conveys the clashing autotopographical impulses across the generations. The parents and diaspora community promote a Root identity based on an outdated notion of Haitian nationalism, while the American-raised child forges their own Relation identity through interaction with others. In a testament to the ingrained bias against acknowledging mental illness, Jean-Pierre mentions that nobody in the family has discussed the incident since: "Even though failing to achieve my childhood aspiration almost destroyed me, I eventually got past my crushing disappointment. To be honest, I'm not sure that my parents ever have" (50). Jean-Pierre cites her parents' inability to disambiguate their own ambitions from those of their children, homophobia, and distrust of therapy as three negative factors of her Caribbean American upbringing that she does not want to pass along to her own daughter.

PROFESSION

The bulk of *The Truths We Hold* is a prolonged autotopographical account of Kamala Harris's professional relationship to the state of California, where she has represented "the people" in some way, shape, or form as a litigator. In this way, her account very much resembles those of New Yorkers Sotomayor and Jean-Pierre. Harris draws on her experience as prosecutor, district attorney, and eventually attorney general to explain her ideas about what type of legislative change would be good for people in her city, state, and the nation. The last third of the campaign book explains how she has negotiated the needs of her constituents and the nation as a one of a hundred senators. She explains that her governing philosophy grows out of what she has learned through her work rather than from listening to constituents or out of values inculcated in her by her family.

American Dreams situates Rubio in two primary locations: in the halls of the Senate building in Washington, DC, as the author or co-sponsor of specific legislation and in a college classroom: "On Monday mornings I teach a class on political science—Florida politics, to be exact—at Florida International University in Miami" (21). When he asks readers to "forgive the Econ 101 lecture" (41) and tries to anticipate objections to his policy proposals— "Before I start hearing from indignant poli sci majors" (90)—Rubio posits the experience of reading the chapter of his memoir as something akin to participating in a virtual classroom. This only works because Rubio's own academic record is average; his lack of Ivy League credentials makes him seem like an unpretentious everyman rather than an aloof egghead as he discusses his teaching duties.[6]

Rubio's autotopographical work corresponds to the geographical reality of his actual electoral district. In *American Dreams,* Rubio foregrounds real-life dilemmas faced by individual constituents that he personally interviewed to make the case that their problems are commonly shared by other Americans elsewhere, and thus the benefits of his legislative initiatives would be applicable on a much larger scale. In *A Time for Truth,* Cruz's autotopography is entirely abstract—the Canada of Cruz's birth and the Texas of his upbringing are devoid of adjectives, whereas the references to both Princeton and Harvard work exclusively as generic backdrops to the debating triumphs he so fondly recounts. Cruz's anecdotes remain within the realms of political strategy and Constitutional case law, rather than including interactions with human beings who are neither lawyers nor legislators.

In contrast, Sotomayor grounds her professional identity in an epiphany she had after being diagnosed with diabetes as a young child. She received a pamphlet outlining job opportunities that would still be possible for someone suffering from the disease and "lawyer" was among the options listed. Sotomayor's emulation of Nancy Drew, her favorite fictional character, allowed her to imagine a future in which she could be a professional.

Nancy Drew's father is a lawyer. He talks to her about his cases and gives her tips that help her solve crimes. They are like partners, father and daughter. Sotomayor writes:

> The world they live in is a kind of fairy tale, where people own homes on winding, tree-shaded driveways: visit summer homes at the lake; and attend charity balls at the country club. Nancy travels, too. She's even been to Paris. What I wouldn't have given to see the Eiffel Tower one day! But even though Nancy Drew is rich, she isn't a snob. And even though it is fiction, I knew such a world did exist. It wasn't Cinderella and pumpkins turning into carriages. It was real, and I was hungry to learn about it. (101).

As described in this passage, Sotomayor's mental map, the socio-geographical landscapes available to her through both her personal experience and

---

6. Rubio is listed as a fellow of the Steven J. Green School of International and Public Affairs at Florida International University. Both Ted Cruz and Karine Jean-Pierre also mention their own stints as college adjunct instructors in their states of origin, though I am not quite sure what to make of these self-congratulatory proclamations of belonging to the ranks of contingent faculty.

her reading, helped her realize that a compromised immune system did not have to limit her horizons. Together with the professionals whom she saw ply their craft in the urban areas of Puerto Rico during her visits to the island, Sotomayor had internalized hard work, home ownership, and travel as external markers of success, of having made it in American society. Thanks to her imagination, her personal ambition was not diminished.

Whereas Sotomayor wrote her memoir after having achieved the culmination of her professional aspirations, Jean-Pierre wrote *Moving Forward* in the middle of her career arc. In some ways, the most interesting part of her professional life is yet to come as she serves in the Biden White House. Jean-Pierre first met Biden while working on the Obama presidential campaign:

> After the rally, Biden came aboard and sat in the seat right next to me. It was pretty surreal. There I was, this Haitian American kid, a black gay woman whose mother is a home health aide and whose father drives a taxi. He was charming and funny. He talked about his progressive record and his work with women, with African Americans, with the LGBTQ+ community. You could tell he was really proud. I was pleasantly surprised and pleased. (191)

Jean-Pierre's self-description in this passage is more striking than the substance of her conversation with the vice president. She refers to her race and gender with the added dimension of her sexual identity, "a black gay woman," qualities that suggest the intersectional oppression to which she could be subjected. However, these adjectives modify her first self-definition as a "Haitian American kid." The two parts of this description are at odds because the first one ties the idea of youthfulness to geography, whereas the second links together the notion of maturity to cultural constructs and biology. The passage establishes that Jean-Pierre is a professional worthy of the attention of the (then) second most powerful leader in the country. Jean-Pierre is part of the winning team that helped the Obama administration earn a second term.

However, in a move that resonates more with millennials and Gen Z readers, Jean-Pierre explains why she left the White House to work at MoveOn.org and develop a new skillset as a political commentator for news outlets. She exhorts her audience to follow her example and find their own way of getting involved in politics: "If you want to take a more active role in the political process-in addition to voting, of course—you should know that there are thousands of jobs and volunteer positions available to you. And almost none of them involve pulling up your roots, loading the van, and driving to Washington, to your state capital, or even to your county seat" (195). *Moving Forward* literally models how its audience can join the ranks of politically active

Americans through inclusion of spatial references and a chapter entitled, "Resources: Political Basics and the Media Maze."

Outside of a presidential election, identity categories of race, gender, and ethnicity play better in national discussions of diversity and inclusion, even as there is no consensus of how to value the contributions each area makes to the nation's culture and to society. Though none of these candidates' Caribbeanness was personally diminished by their failure to win the presidency, the post-election accounts they give of themselves leverage their more regional-based identities. Rubio's *cubanidad* lends him an air of authenticity and gives him entrée into the exile establishment of Miami but his *latinidad* resonates even more with other constituent communities. For his part, Cruz's own connection to Cuba makes him simultaneously legible within the Latinx/Hispanic context of his district while it also conveys a different set of ideological values, such as anti-Communism, and a fiscally conservative ideology, that are not necessarily shared by the Mexican American or Chicanx community in in his district. Not even Harris's self-proclamation as a simple "American" connected broadly with voters until she was reintroduced on the national stage as Joe Biden's running mate. Most importantly, *The Truths We Hold*, *American Dreams*, and *A Time for Truth* all forcefully make the case that people of Caribbean descent are Americans who not only vote but also can and do run things in this country.

Unlike the politicians, the public servants whose civic memoirs are analyzed here offer themselves up individually as exemplars of what Caribbean American belonging can look like in areas beyond the ballot box. In taking stock of their lives up to the point of their respective books' publication, Sotomayor and Jean-Pierre serve as Caribbean American guides showing their fellow Americans how the branches of government work individually and, more importantly, how they contribute to the maintenance of a working democracy. Sotomayor and Jean-Pierre first perform their Caribbean identities by demonstrating due deference to their elders and by describing their secular pilgrimage to their parents' homelands. In so doing, they perform their dual belonging: to the status quo (that is, the government) and to the diasporic Caribbean community. Only once they satisfy these overlapping obligations may Justice Sotomayor and Secretary Jean-Pierre occupy the role of instructor within their own narratives and profess the benefits of full and active citizenship as a concrete way to experience belonging.

CHAPTER 2

"Big Citizens" and Public Advocacy

Working against the stereotype of Caribbean people as exotic hypersexual creatures, three queer Caribbean American public figures have used their life writing narratives to draw attention to the fight against sexual violence: Cuban and Jamaican American reality TV star Karamo Brown, Puerto Rican singer/actor Ricky Martin, and Haitian American writer and scholar Roxane Gay. As celebrities who are public spokespeople for LGBTQ+ rights in the United States, Brown and Martin wrote their memoirs as a response to their fans' demand to know more about their lives. Both men tell stories about their childhoods to explain how their respective Caribbean heritage shaped their outlook and careers. Brown admits to his personal motivation for raising awareness about the incidence of intimate partner violence within LGBTQ+ relationships in *Karamo: My Story of Embracing Purpose, Healing, and Hope* (2019). Martin shares the backstory for his advocacy against sexual trafficking in his memoir *Me* (2010). Roxane Gay has been at the forefront of public conversations discussing the power and necessity of sharing narratives about rape and sexual assault as well as exploring what constitutes feminism through her fiction, academic scholarship, and public writing in many articles and books including *Bad Feminist* (2014), *Hunger: A Memoir of (My) Body* (2017), and the edited collection, *Not That Bad: Dispatches from Rape Culture* (2018). She discusses her bisexuality in these texts, but her sexual orientation is not as big a part of her overall advocacy as is the fight against sexual violence. These three Caribbean Americans weave their biography into their accounts of their involvement in the broad fight against sexual violence and exploitation to suggest that their heritage shaped their quest for social justice in American society. However, their activism could be dismissed as simply a type of "celanthropy," a portmanteau word that combines "celebrity" and "philanthropy" and popularized by economists Matthew Bishop and Michael Green.[1]

Sociologist Chris Rojek incorporated the context into the field of celebrity studies and extended it beyond the mere fact of celebrities endorsing economic solutions to persistent problems. Rojek explains that "celanthropy reinforces the media presentation of the world as a collection of disjoined episodes, incidents and emergencies. This contributes to a non-holistic understanding of power that underscores the question of the structural issues in the construction of culture" (127). Rojek uses the term "Big Citizens" to convey the inordinate amount of power that celanthropists wield. According to Rojek, "Big Citizens" are

> a politicized enclave among celebrities based in the entertainment sector who act as the unelected (and largely unaccountable), tribunes of the people. They use their fame to build public awareness and raise funds in relation to single issue campaigns (opposing human rights abuse in Darfur or providing relief for Hurricane/Tsunami damage) or general nongovernmental movements against inequality, hunger and injustice. While they may liaise with, and even form partnerships with governments, they present themselves as stateless solutions operating outside the Parliamentary system. (128–29)

Though Martin, Brown, and Gay all have different positionalities as "Big Citizens," their celebrity statuses and name recognition affirm their influence over their fans. In this way, their life writing functions very similarly to the Caribbean American campaign memoirs examined in chapter 1. However, whereas those texts appealed to the "American people" to imagine a better tomorrow they could build alongside their candidate of choice, these texts address large social problems grounded in narratives about their famous authors' Caribbean American home lives. Whereas Gay celebrates her Haitian American parents' love for their children and their dedication to creating a stable and happy home environment, Brown's version of his childhood paints it as a dark and troubled part of his life marked by his Jamaican father's physical abuse. Martin, in contrast, had a happy home life but spent most of his youth and

---

1. Although Bishop and Green use the word "celanthropy" several times within their book *Philanthrocapitalism*, they do not provide a very helpful definition. I much prefer Chris Rojek's explanation of the concept, and I cite his work throughout the chapter.

adolescence on the road and in the public eye as a member of the internationally famous Puerto Rican boy band Menudo. This opportunity made him an iconic island ambassador to Latin America, the United States, and the rest of the world. Martin eventually transitioned from a child star to a working television actor in the United States, and then returned to his first love, music, as a solo performer.

As Big Citizens, each of these Caribbean American celebrities leverage their public platforms to raise attention to the social causes close to their heart. Martin's foundation is part of a larger global effort to end human trafficking, while Gay's activism resonates most clearly with the #MeToo movement. However, though Brown has written and spoken about surviving domestic abuse at home as a child and abusing his partners when he was a young man, he has not partnered with any national organization to promote awareness of this issue. However, his participation in the *Queer Eye* franchise means that he currently has a broad public fan base. The autobiographical works under discussion here explicitly set out to model consent and boundary setting; as first-person narrators, Brown, Martin, and Gay repeatedly emphasize that their writings do not reflect the totality of their lived experience. I analyze how Brown's *Karamo*, Martin's *Me*, and Gay's *Bad Feminist, Hunger,* and *Not That Bad* approach four distinct aspects of sexual violence: intimate partner violence, sex trafficking, the pressure to make closeted LGBTQ+ people come out, and a Caribbean American take on the public outcry against rape culture and sexual harassment of the #MeToo Movement. Brown's, Martin's, and Gay's Caribbean American heritage informs the objection each has to the issue they fight against while also highlighting the overlapping and sometimes contradictory identities to which they lay claim.

The values each supports—safety from being abused by a partner, freedom from being trafficked, and the right to speak out about one's rape but also to not be subjected to unwanted sexual attention or abuse in the first place—are ideals that they wish to share with the nation, if not the world. However, the narrative arc of their individual journeys toward activism varies greatly: both Brown and Gay validate the right of victims of sexual or intimate partner violence to own and tell their stories. However, Brown also speaks from experience as a reformed abuser now warning others against repeating his past mistakes.

Martin's account of his advocacy against sex trafficking in *Me*, though brief, is deeply steeped in Orientalism about India and its mystical/religious traditions. Both in the memoir and on his foundation's web page Martin casts himself as a white savior figure who rescues three girls "who were at risk of falling into child prostitution" (179). Communications scholar Robert Heynen and criminologist Emily van der Meulen discuss Martin's anti-trafficking activism as an example of the "witness-rescuer-expert trajectory" typical of celebrities who advocate against a situation that does not affect them personally but which they have seen, taken action to change, and then studied the history and larger implications of in order to persuade their fans to donate to a given foundation or nongovernmental organization (309). Heynen and van der Meulen critique the account of this rescue in Martin's website, arguing that it constructs a colonial narrative that builds up his brand while effacing the ongoing anti-trafficking efforts of local Indian organizations and downplaying poverty as a root cause of such social breakdowns. This celanthropist narrative structure runs the risk of becoming nothing more than a self-aggrandizing gesture that undermines local anti-trafficking work and exploits the victims' suffering. Ultimately, however, Martin limits the scope of his discussion of his anti-sex trafficking work in favor of a more eloquent discussion about the pressure he felt to disclose his sexual orientation before he was ready to do so.

Finally, Roxane Gay's body of work about feminism and on behalf of people's right to claim positive and negative stories about their embodied experiences sets the larger tone against which to understand two other peculiarly Caribbean American incidents within the #MeToo Movement: Dominican American author Junot Díaz's stunning essay detailing his childhood rape and the subsequent outcry against him by Latina writers accusing him of sexual harassment and misogynistic blacklisting. Gay weighs in on Díaz's use of the space she created to shield himself against the complaints he knew were coming.

Another Caribbean American antagonist of the pioneering work Gay has done to legitimate public discourse about one's #MeToo experiences is Kimberly Guilfoyle, a Fox News personality who often invokes her Puerto Rican mother to justify anything she does as tantamount to being a strong Latina woman. I analyze Guilfoyle's anti-#MeToo campaign to publicly defend disgraced Fox CEO, Roger Ailes by disparaging white colleagues who spoke out against workplace sexual harassment by labeling them "weak." This behavior has resulted in lawsuits charging Guilfoyle herself with sexually harassing her support staff. Unlike Gay, whose work is dedicated to creating safe community spaces for people to speak their truths, Díaz and Guilfoyle promote a sense of shame and stigma toward people who speak out against oppression. Though they stand in the minority, Guilfoyle's contrarian views and Díaz's alleged blacklisting help us see the positive impact of Brown's, Martin's, and Gay's activism against sexual violence.

BOUNDARY-SETTING AND SELF-DISCLOSURE

The three primary writers excel at setting boundaries between their public and private lives within their life-writing texts. They do this more explicitly than others because of the nature of their activist work and their desire to manage how their public persona relates to the larger goal of making an impact in the situations they want to change. Karamo Brown of *Queer Eye* knows that his fans want to get a bit of the "behind the scenes" explanation of how he got cast, so he provides that by describing his preparation for the audition:

> With a Word page open in front of me, I started thinking critically about my life from its beginning and *key things I wanted to share*. I began to write down facts, such that my family is Jamaican-Cuban. I wrote down that I was from the South, had attended an HBCU (historically black college/university), and found out I was a father in my early twenties. (250, emphasis mine)

Through the distancing device of meta-writing, Brown conveys the basics of his process without sharing the private thoughts he wrote for himself. This quote summarizes the preparation that went into selling a version of himself that would get him cast in the role he now occupies. Chief among the things Brown wants to share with his audience is the geographical self-description of himself and his family as both Caribbean American ("Jamaican-Cuban") and Southern. These aspects of his existence are ones about which he had no control, and yet Brown's insistence on leading with them, as opposed to the two that have to do with his actions (what university he attended, unknowingly impregnating an ex-girlfriend), means he places great value on how they relate to his overall identity.

Though he discusses the *Queer Eye* casting process in detail, Brown is more careful about mentioning the topic closest to his heart: advocating against intimate partner violence. In the introduction to chapter 4 of his memoir, "Overcoming the Legacy of Abuse," Brown explains his positionality: "There are many stories I want to share, but my mother and sisters have not dealt with their emotions and the trauma that lingers within them when it comes to the physical and emotional abuse doled out by my father" (75). Even though he describes the violence he observed while growing up, Brown avoids speculating about how the women in his family feel about the abuse they endured. He also does not chastise them for forgiving the family patriarch. In setting these clear boundaries, Brown implicitly asks his readers not to judge this aspect of his Caribbean American family dynamic. He also reminds his audience that his father's reliance on spanking, "was what was culturally acceptable at the time in many communities in the United States" (77) but also explains that his own parenting philosophy is radically different. Brown attributes his decision to study social work to his dysfunctional upbringing.

Whereas Brown waits until almost the end of the book to set up his boundaries with the reader, Martin speaks forcefully about his right to privacy at the outset of *Me*:

> I'll talk about many personal matters that I have never discussed publicly before, that it isn't my intention to share every little thing, either. I believe we're all entitled to a certain degree of privacy; there are certain things I keep to myself because they are mine alone and I want them to stay that way. What I would like to do is explore the different paths and experiences that have led me to be the person I am today. (7)

In this passage, Martin speaks as a public figure willing to open up to his fans but only to an extent. He also couches his support of privacy as a universal right, rather than something particular to himself. He later affirms that his decision to share aspects of his life will not mean that he will violate other people's privacy simply to placate his fans' desire to know more about his famous friends: "Even though there are some people who have formed part of my public life, and who are likely easily recognizable, I won't involve them in this history that is not theirs" (11). This clear boundary-setting with his audience constitutes a kind of contract with Martin's friends as well. It also makes for an interesting situation when Martin does name-drop, like his reference to meeting Sonia Sotomayor or saying Madonna gave him good business advice. At any rate, Martin's declarations about what he is willing to discuss are especially important because he will later recount the enormous pressure he felt to come out of the closet before he was ready.

In contradistinction to the more reticent male memoirists, Roxane Gay has written candidly about her life in various nonfiction and scholarly texts throughout the years. Her frankness is the hallmark of her distinctive writing style and her unmistakable narrative voice led to her prominence as a public intellectual. Like Martin does with his famous friends, Gay strategically shields someone's identity, not a friend but her biggest nemesis: the boy she calls "Christopher," who betrayed her trust and led her to a cabin in the woods to be gang raped when she was twelve. She tells the story of this trauma first in *Bad Feminist*, again in the memoir *Hunger*, and once more in the anthology, *Not That Bad*. Repeating the story does not mean that she has said all there is to say about what happened to her. In chapter 11 of *Hunger*, Gay clearly states how she wants her readers to behave after reading her account: "If I must share my story, I want to do so on my terms, without the attention that inevitably follows. I do not want pity or appreciation or advice" (*Hunger* 39). As a rhetorical gesture, this is a plea for reciprocity from her audience that signals they are interlocutors. It is utterly unenforceable and, yet, by stating the limits she wants to impose on the intimacy of public responses to her words, Gay expresses the things to which she does not consent.

The second part of her meta-critical explanation for why she writes about her attack in *Hunger* more closely resembles what Brown's approach in his memoir than the space Martin tries to claim for himself. Gay explains that rather that narrating what happened to her she actually "write[s] around what happened to me" to protect herself from the damage that revisiting this trauma inevitably causes her (*Hunger* 39). Like Brown, she knows her words will impact her family and it is on their behalf that she primarily pursues this evasive writing tactic:

> I write around what happened because I don't want my family to have these terrible images in their heads. I don't want them to know what I endured and then kept secret for more than twenty-five years. . . . I want to protect the people I love. I want to protect myself. My story is mine, and on most days, I wish I could bury that story, somewhere deep where I may be free of it. But. It has been thirty years and, inexplicably, I am not still free of it. (*Hunger* 39–40)

Through her writing, Gay proclaims her sense of belonging to overlapping communities: her Haitian American family unit and the group of women (and some men) who have suffered sexual violence and lived to tell the tale. The essay anthology *Not That Bad* assembles testimony from other victims and strongly condemns rape culture. However, Gay disapproves of trigger warnings because of their chilling effect on writers' freedom in *Bad Feminist*:

> I do not understand the unspoken rules of trigger warnings. I cannot write the way I want to write and consider using trigger warnings. I would second-guess myself, temper the intensity of what I have to say. I don't want to do that. I don't intend to ever do that.
>
> Writers cannot protect their readers from themselves, nor should they be expected to. (*Bad Feminist* 151)

Once more, Gay explicitly sets out the rules of engagement readers should follow if they read her work. She will write what she needs to in a way that is true to herself and only readers who can handle the experience should bother to try. This type of boundary-setting is crucial for someone whose life has been so defined by her activism against sexual violence. It also demands that potential readers give informed consent—if they pick up her books, they should be able to handle what is in them. Only those who can bear it may be included within the community of belonging Gay has created.

These Caribbean American writers use their texts as spaces within which to articulate their respective views on the topic of sexual violence. While Brown strikes a confessional tone, Martin's outrage works on a more abstract level. Gay's righteous anger is multidirectional: it changes its focus from inward to outward and seeks to shake us all out of our general complacency with, and toleration of, a rape culture that encourages victims to tell themselves what they went through was, in the words of her title, "not that bad." Brown, Martin, and Gay want their readers to recognize the persistence of sexual violence as a constituent part of our shared American society. The three authors trace their activism to their Caribbean American upbringing in some way. For these Big Citizens, sexual violence and family are deeply intertwined and whether they wish to indict cultural norms that supported the performance of toxic masculinity (Brown), indulge in their white savior fantasies of correcting other people's lax parenting (Martin), or separate the trauma of rape from the ideal family life they lived (Gay), the idea of family is at the heart of what sexual violence threatens the most.

INTIMATE PARTNER VIOLENCE

Though he is renowned for his ability to make each episode's "heroes" cry on camera in almost every episode of *Queer Eye*, Karamo Brown spent a large part of his youth being angry. In his self-titled memoir, he discusses the anger he felt at his father's abuse of his mother and his corporal punishment of his sisters, as well as how conflicted he felt about his sexuality and, finally, the negative impact his drug addiction had on his life and choices. These issues all coalesce in Brown's Jamaican-Cuban family around the silence regarding a man's authority over his household. The first type of silence to which Brown objects is his father's near-complete reticence about his own childhood: "My father has never shared with us how the household he grew up in shaped him, but from what I gathered, abuse was prevalent" (75). Unlike his own choice of what story to share, Brown's father's silence is a weapon because it refuses to provide any sort of narrative against which his children and spouse may understand his violent actions. The second type of narrative silence is the deeply embedded sexism of the family's parenting style, which assigned clear consequences (corporal punishment) whenever his sisters broke the house rules but not for Brown as the only son. This inequity bothered him, but no one ever discussed it in the open. Likewise, Brown says the only times he saw the consequences of his father's abuse of his mother were when he caught glimpses of the bruises around her body. The unfairness of this treatment led him to develop what he calls "'savior' behavior" by setting himself up as a "protector of women" later in life (80). Brown now understands that he went about defending women from intimate partner violence the wrong way; he often used these circumstances as an excuse to use violence against male perpetrators, thereby performing his own type of toxic, but feminist-seeming, masculinity.

Having witnessed the effect of his father's physical violence against his mother and sisters, Brown then takes ownership about his own inappropriate use of violence within his personal relationships by openly declaring: "from the age of twenty to twenty-four, I was completely emotionally and physically abusive to the men I dated" (84). Brown's own internalized sexism downplayed the relationship part of this violence, rationalizing it by claiming that physical altercations between men are not as culturally frowned upon as they are between men and women. This shift from telling his family's abuse story to his personal reckoning of his abusive behavior toward men signals Brown's sense of belonging within two distinct groups: the Caribbean American family and the LGBTQ+ community. These perspectives overlap when Brown explains that he inflicted the same strategic pattern of injury on his male partners that his father had perpetrated on his mother: "I would do exactly what my father did: I would never touch my boyfriends' faces. I would only hit them in places that I knew they would have to hide" (84). Brown is honest about how badly he treated the men in his life and recalls that his straight best friend would challenge his behavior as hypocritical since it belied his espoused defense of women in dangerous heterosexual relationships. While he blames the lack of role models for healthy homosexual relationships as one of the causes for his abusive behavior toward his romantic partners, Brown also acknowledges that toxic masculinity and homophobia are intertwined. He ends the chapter by discussing what he learned in anger management classes, in which instructors held him accountable for his actions, and how these experiences prompted Brown to hold himself to the same standard.

Brown ends the chapter with an affirmation to the effect that he will never let his anger get the best of him again, and a plea to his readers: "If you recognize the internal and external conflicts that support an abusive culture and make changes—seek out help, make amends, and forgive yourself—then things will improve" (92). This casts Brown's personal account about the process of "overcoming" intimate partner violence as a possible mirror into which his readers can gaze and see if their experiences parallel his. The book, his speaking engagements, and his work on *Queer Eye* are the extent of his public advocacy against intimate partner violence. Though Brown's celebrity status marks him as a "Big Citizen," the scope of his "celanthropy" is small and has no monetary dimension. It simply depends on his readers' self-recognition as a victim, perpetrator, or would-be savior.

SEX TRAFFICKING / COERCED OUTING OF CLOSETED LGBTQ+ PEOPLE

Perhaps because he first rose to fame as a preteen, singer Ricky Martin has long dedicated himself to the global fight against human trafficking of children. In his memoir, *Me,* Martin casts this activism as the culmination of his journey of spiritual self-awareness that took him to India and saw him interact with friends of his involved in nongovernmental structures to care for orphaned young girls. Martin has an eponymous foundation focused primarily on this fight.[2] As Brown does with intimate partner violence, Martin shares his personal quest to learn more about this topic:

> When I took an interest in this cause, I knew it was not going to be easy. I educated myself on even the smallest details, which is how the People for Children project of the Ricky Martin Foundation came to be; through it, we defend children who are being exploited or who run the risk of exploitation. (192)

There is no explanation of what fans should do once they educate themselves other than to contribute to the "People for Children project" of his foundation. When I click on this part of the foundation's website, it directs me to a "Related Action" that advises me to "Stop Watching Violent Porn" and offers to explain the connection between such material and human trafficking. There is no other recourse listed for those of us who already abstain from this form of media consumption. I pause on this not to cast doubt on the sincerity of Martin's advocacy but, instead, highlight to the limits of his "celanthropy." I fully agree with Heynen and van der Meulen's critique of the colonialist dimensions of Martin's activism on this front. Although both scholars oppose celanthropic

---

2. The Ricky Martin Foundation also manages his philanthropic activities in Puerto Rico in partnerships with the March of Dimes and other arts-based campaigns.

involvement in hot-button issues, I do think that Big Citizen platforms like the Ricky Martin Foundation could engage their audiences more meaningfully by drawing attention to local efforts to combat poverty and trafficking in more culturally sensitive ways.

While Martin calls his fight against child trafficking "my cause" (190), the most eloquent plea he makes in the memoir is against a different type of sexual violence: the public's insistent demand that closeted LGBTQ+ individuals disclose their sexual orientations. In the cover story for *People* magazine's 2021 Pride issue, Ricky Martin recalls a traumatic interview a bit more than two decades ago in which Barbara Walters pressured him to answer rumors regarding his sexuality by stating on national television whether he identified as gay. According to reporter Jason Sheeler: "[Martin] says the moment still haunts him. 'When she dropped the question, I felt violated because I was just not ready to come out. I was very afraid.' Martin's entire body shifts. He clears his throat and takes a deep breath. 'There's a little PTSD with that.'" Martin's word choice here is important; regardless of Walters' intention, Martin felt "violated" by the interaction. Remarkably, Martin found the presence of mind at the time to tell Walters he simply did not feel like answering the question. He chose his own time to speak his truth and that coincided with the publication of *Me*.

Martin says being closeted helped him claim the time and space he needed to process the complexity of his sexual desire. Martin's memoir ends with the coming out letter he published on his website and disseminated more widely on Twitter. The document consciously buries the lede, ending with a bang: "I am proud to say that I am a fortunate homosexual man. I am very blessed to be who I am" (271). Because he knows people are interested, Martin forces them to read through the other issues like his advocacy against human trafficking that contribute to his sense of self as both a human being and as a public figure. This is the kind of context Walters's coercion would have deprived him of and Martin is vindicated by having bided his time.

The other community to Martin claims allegiance, both on his own and his sons' behalf, is the Puerto Rican one but with his own peculiar twist. Whereas most public declarations of one's Puerto Ricanness emphasize the biological and metaphysical connection one feels to either their island birthplace or to the Puerto Rican community wherever they happened to be born, in *Me* Martin extends those constraints further across both space and time. He writes: "I am Puerto Rican and so are my sons. I want them to always be conscious of their roots, but more than anything, I want my children to see themselves as citizens of the world, because this is what is going to give them the global vision to be men in the twenty-first century" (244). I read Martin's desire that his sons consider themselves "citizens of the world" metaphorically, based on the example the singer himself has set in the pages that precede this declaration. This is the vision that undergirds Martin's work with his foundation; namely, that he cares about human trafficking as a global problem, rather than simply something that affects his birthplace. In so doing, Martin performs the American part of his Caribbean Americanness most clearly and acts as a flawed, white-savior-y "Big Citizen" with roots in Puerto Rico.

CARIBBEAN AMERICAN #METOO

Roxane Gay's *Bad Feminist* strongly advocates for victim-centered ethical journalism in "The Careless Language of Sexual Violence." In an opinion piece for the *New York Times*, Gay credits Tarana Burke with coining the term #MeToo in 2007 when she started a nonprofit to advocate for victims of sexual harassment ("Louis C. K."). Her more recent anthology, *Not That Bad: Dispatches from Rape Culture* builds on her earlier work and explicitly functions as a public platform for people who have lived through rape, sexual harassment, or abuse to explore their experience and its implication in writing. Gay tempers her repeated accounts of her rape and its aftermath with frequent references to the warm, safe, and loving home environment her Haitian American parents created for her and her siblings. With *Not That Bad*, Gay challenges the enduring cultural acceptance of rape culture because our society lacks the language through which to analyze its implications:

> I was interested in the discourse around rape culture because the phrase is used often, but rarely do people engage with what it actually means. What is it like to live in a culture where it often seems like it is a question of when, not if, a woman will encounter some kind of sexual violence? What is it like for men to navigate this culture whether they are indifferent to rape culture or working to end it or contributing to it in ways significant or small? (*Not That Bad* xi)

In her role as a de facto gatekeeper, Gay sets the criteria for who can belong to the Caribbean version of the #MeToo movement based on whether they listen to the voices she has assembled and learn from them how to question the language that maintains rape culture. I examine two of the gestures Gay makes in the introduction to this anthology: this first one of unpacking the meaning of "rape culture" as an ongoing process that has not been fully understood within public dialogues against it. The second is in her role as the anthology's editor, which gives Gay as a queer, Haitian American woman, a platform to set the tone of public conversations about rape culture henceforward. The somewhat prophetic tone of the concluding statement in the introduction reveals the full depth of her ambitions in this activism: "This is a moment that will, hopefully, become a movement. These essays will, hopefully, contribute to that movement in a meaningful way. The voices shared here are voices that matter and demand to be heard" (*Not That Bad* xii). Gay's vision for who gets to speak includes men who themselves have been victims of sexual violence and that is an important endorsement because if a cause like this is to resonate broadly, it cannot only apply to half of the population. Men need to acknowledge both their culpability and potential for victimhood if we are to truly challenge rape culture.

This preface was necessary to contextualize why Gay as a fellow Caribbean American, would question the motives of Pulitzer-prize winning Dominican American author, Junot Díaz, when he joined in the public discussions surrounding the #MeToo movement in the personal essay where he outed himself as a victim of childhood rape. Shortly thereafter, he was accused of being a perpetrator of sexual harassment and blacklisting. Díaz's accusers asserted that he not only forcibly kissed them, violated their personal space, and disrespected their boundaries but also used his power as a member of the publishing establishment to professionally harm up-and-coming women writers of color. Writing about Díaz for *The Advocate*, Tracy E. Gilchrist mentions Gay as an arbiter of determining the sincerity of a person's writing about their rape: "Many on Twitter, including *Bad Feminist* and *Hunger* writer Roxane Gay, have said they believe his *New Yorker* piece was his 'preemptive strike' intended to mitigate backlash that was certain to occur when accusations of misconduct and misogyny, which many saw coming based on his reputation, were brought to light" (Gilchrist). By naming Gay as both an authority on American rape culture and an emblematic spokesperson for throngs of anonymous Twitter users, Gilchrist recognizes that Gay belongs to multiple groups at once. A full reading of *Not That Bad* demands the inclusion of Zinzi Clemmons's, Monica Byrne's, and Carmen María Machado's allegations against Díaz for sexual harassment and his attempts to blacklist them even though both institutions with which Díaz has long-standing affiliations, MIT and the Pulitzer Prize committee, have cleared him of wrongdoing. A full hearing of the voices that advocate against rape culture demands the openness to understand that a Caribbean American man can be both a victim and a perpetrator. Only such a full reckoning has any hope of making headway and dismantling the system of passive acquiescence, of telling ourselves that things are simply "not that bad."

ANTI-#METOO MOVEMENT

Any good movement gives rise to its own pushback, and the Caribbean version of the #MeToo movement is no different. Junot Díaz chose a strategy of silence, perhaps the most immutable of all refusals. Kimberly Guilfoyle, the former Fox personality who often mentions her Puerto Rican mother in public speeches, chose a different approach to battle #MeToo and demonstrate women can be agents of sexual violence through their explicit support of rape culture. Though she has not written about her experiences, Guilfoyle was involved in the #MeToo fight at Fox News in two roles: first, as one of the most vocal defenders of Roger Ailes, the Fox executive whom on-air host Gretchen Carlson sued for sexual harassment, and then later as the subject of a sexual harassment claim filed by a female assistant. In her 2015 self-help book, *Making the Case: How to Be Your Own Best Advocate*, Guilfoyle sings Ailes's praises. Among the rules she tells her readers to follow is to "be mindful of your own style," advice she gleaned from reading Ailes's book, *You Are the Message*, while an undergraduate at UC Davis (54). Further undermining her own credibility here, Guilfoyle then admits, "I even brought my dog-eared copy of it with me on my first interview with him so he could sign it" (54). This instance illustrates Guilfoyle's willingness to violate the very principle she advocates to others by subordinating her own style to praise that of her bosses, a pattern that will become more meaningful in the context of the toxic work environment at Fox News.

CNN chief media correspondent Brian Stelter chronicles Guilfoyle's efforts to discredit Fox female employees who supported Carlson's claims or otherwise refused to defend their boss, Roger Ailes, from the abuse allegations against him in his book, *Hoax: Donald Trump, Fox News, and the Dangerous Distortion of Truth*. Calling her, "the head of Team Roger," Stelter suggests that Guilfoyle's support for the disgraced leader may have been due, in part, to her own complicity in the sexually exploitative culture at the network; he goes as far as to quote "unsubstantiated allegations in a lawsuit filed by former Fox cohost Julie Roginsky" to suggest Guilfoyle had no problem complying with male executives' requests for sexual favors (67). I find it ironic that the host of CNN's *Reliable Sources* would violate the premise of his own signature show by repeating "unsubstantiated allegations" in print for the sole purpose of slut-shaming Kimberly Guilfoyle. Joe Hayden, reviewing the book for the *Journalism & Mass Communication Quarterly* agrees, pointing out that "the dirt dished up in this book makes for a lurid romp through the wilds of Cable Crazytown." While reviews of Stelter's book have been largely positive, this one gesture of using rumor to tarnish Guilfoyle's personal reputation perpetuates the very type of misogyny Stelter is ostensibly bringing to light.

Investigative reporter Jane Mayer's two *New Yorker* articles on the allegations of Guilfoyle's wrongdoing at Fox News present a study in contrast with Stelter's sensationalism.[3] In March of 2019, Mayer first reported that "Guilfoyle left the network mid-contract, after a former Fox employee threatened to sue the network for harassment and accused Guilfoyle of sharing lewd images, among other misconduct; Fox and the former employee reached a multimillion-dollar settlement" (2019). In a subsequent article published in October 2020, Mayer shared specific and verified details of her former assistant's draft complaint:

> According to a dozen well-informed sources familiar with her complaints, the assistant alleged that Guilfoyle, her direct supervisor, subjected her frequently to degrading, abusive, and sexually inappropriate behavior; among other things, she said that she was frequently required to work at Guilfoyle's New York apartment while the Fox host displayed herself naked, and was shown photographs of the genitalia of men with whom Guilfoyle had had sexual relations. The draft complaint also alleged that Guilfoyle spoke incessantly and luridly about her sex life, and on one occasion demanded a massage of her bare thighs; other times, she said, Guilfoyle told her to submit to a Fox employee's demands for sexual favors, encouraged her to sleep with wealthy and powerful men, asked her to critique her naked body, demanded that she share a room with her on business trips, required her to sleep over at her apartment, and exposed herself to her, making her feel deeply uncomfortable.

Though these allegations are much more detailed and disturbing than what Stelter repeated in his book, Mayer clearly states that they have been fact-checked. These claims are relevant to the larger discussion within this chapter because Guilfoyle's post-Fox career has included leadership roles within the Trump reelection campaign as the head of fundraising. She has also headlined "Women for Trump" events.

These allegations suggest a disturbing trend of Guilfoyle enabling or tolerating displays of toxic masculinity in the workplace that make it an inhospitable space for other women. Guilfoyle had previously faced a backlash from

---

3. Mayer does cite information from Julie Roginsky's "complaint" against Fox News charging sexual harassment by Roger Ailes. The network settled with Roginsky. The substance of the quote Mayer includes in her article has to do with Guilfoyle's efforts to retaliate against Gretchen Carlson, rather than any innuendo about her personal conduct.

female employees at Fox. Chris Ariens featured Guilfoyle in a 2016 article for *Adweek* where she defended Ailes's character against Carlson's allegations of sexual harassment and suggested the latter's lawsuit may have been motivated by her show's low ratings. In the same piece, Ariens reported that "Guilfoyle also found herself named in another complaint last week filed by three former female Fox News make-up artists," who accused her of not objecting when a male coworker, Bradley Stenson, played a video featuring explicit language about sexual acts while the women worked on both on-air personalities. Fox settled this suit as well. Taken together, the evidence points to Guilfoyle as someone who actively supports patriarchal power structures in the workplace even when these target or disadvantage her female coworkers. Guilfoyle contributed to a sexist workplace culture by actively using her position of influence over employees of lesser standing and suggesting they cooperate with executives' sexual demands or refuse to assist investigators trying to document such abuses of power.

Guilfoyle has not defended herself against these allegations of inappropriate behavior. The only statement she has issued to date was in response to Mayer's request for comment on the *New Yorker* story: "In my 30-year career working for the SF District Attorney's Office, the LA District Attorney's Office, in media and in politics, I have never engaged in any workplace misconduct of any kind. During my career, I have served as a mentor to countless women, with many of whom I remain exceptionally close to this day" (Mayer). While this counts as a categorical denial, it sounds hollow because of its immediate evocation of the anonymous "countless women" whom she has helped. Even if true, this claim is hardly exculpatory and, more importantly, by invoking the notion that she has very intimate or "exceptionally close," relationships with a small subset of the women whom she has helped, Guilfoyle inadvertently suggests that these professional relationships have blurred the boundaries and become personal friendships.

Four years earlier, Guilfoyle admitted in the *Adweek* article to being present when Stenson walked in playing the offensive video described in the harassment suit but would not say anything further because the case was still being litigated. However, in the same article she once again leveraged her own professional experience as a female prosecutor to undermine Carlson's credibility as a victim of workplace sexual harassment: "I am a strong woman. I come from a background as a prosecutor. I've tried everything from homicides to gang cases to sexual assault cases to child abuse cases. If I see, hear, or experience anything that I feel is inappropriate you bet I'm going to speak up" (Ariens). Here Guilfoyle alludes to her career credentials as some sort of indicator of the soundness of her moral character. However, she stands accused of failing to live up to her self-descriptions in two specific ways. The first is by failing to support women who spoke up when there was a clear instance of inappropriate workplace behavior by a male coworker. And the second was by "speaking up" only to either shame other women into silence about the abuse they suffered or else to say inappropriate things about her sex life while in the process of carrying out her work duties. In these instances, Guilfoyle's influence has been the opposite of Roxane Gay's: she has made it more difficult for women to stand up and "make the case" for themselves as people who deserve a work environment free of demeaning or exploitative comments and/or suggestions.

Whether as victims or perpetrators of sexual violence, the one thing Caribbean American public figures do not appear to do is stay quiet. Guilfoyle and Gay address the topic of sexual harassment by staying true to their brand: the former by excusing men accused of harassment and berating the women who experienced the abuse, while the latter validates victims' accounts and calls on the culture at large to stop making excuses for sexual violence. Both agree there is sexual abuse, but Guilfoyle's statements cast it in terms of women's weakness whereas Gay acknowledges that it takes a lot of strength and resilience to recovering from the loss of power and agency. Likewise, when it comes to accountability, Gay holds fellow Caribbean American writer Junot Díaz responsible both for his behavior toward other women *and* for his shameless co-optation of the free space she created for victims to speak their pain. She does not, however, deny the reality of the trauma he underwent. In contrast, Guilfoyle excuses prominent white men's sexual improprieties while also being accused of perpetrating her own, thereby suggesting she would like to be judged by the company she keeps rather than the actions she carries out. In both cases, the community to which both Guilfoyle and Gay belong is defined primarily, though not exclusively, along gender lines.

Brown and Martin, in contrast, include their Caribbean American identity as part of their many overlapping positionalities. They are Big Citizens, fathers, sons, and proud out gay men. Both Brown and Martin are careful to situate their own life stories and struggles in the context of other people's difficulties. The public image they present in their books is interactive, engaged with problems bigger than themselves. In so doing, *Me* and *Karamo* join Gay's *Not That Bad* in building their own communities and marking all three texts as distinctly Caribbean American. They issue an invitation for us to take a serious look at the pitfalls that plague our current society and support one another as we seek solutions.

PART 2

COMING OF AGE

CHAPTER 3

Picturing Caribbean American Childhoods

Islandborn, the first children's picture book by Dominican American novelist Junot Díaz, was published in 2018 to great critical acclaim. Though its Afro-Latinx protagonist, Lola, is ostensibly Dominican American, the book avoids naming this or any other geographic location specifically, referring to her birthplace as "the Island," a choice which universalizes the experience of Caribbean Americanness even as it reduces it to insularity and effectively erases Haiti from the map. In response to a class assignment asking students to draw a picture of their "first home," young Lola confronts her own deterritorialization: because she "had left the Island when she was just a baby so she didn't remember any of it," Lola has to rely on her family's and neighbors' communal memories to fill in the gaps and complete her homework. By crowdsourcing material to serve as inspiration for her class project, Lola learns that the Island culture and its history combine a rich mix of beauty, music, comfort, and danger from both human and inhuman forces. These positive and negative connotations are all part of her heritage as a Caribbean American child living in the United States and trudging to school in the snow. People who purchased this book very likely did so because of Díaz's popularity and literary renown as the Pulitzer prize-winning author of *The Brief Wondrous Life of Oscar Wao*. As positive a depiction of acculturation and place-making as *Islandborn* conjures, the impact of this portrayal of a Caribbean American childhood was soon dampened by the author's searing personal confession of the trauma that plagued his own youth in the United States.

In April of 2018, Díaz published a moving first-person account about having survived childhood sexual assault and exposed the negative psychic toll that keeping this secret into adulthood has taken on him ("The Silence"). A month later, Díaz himself faced allegations that he had sexually harassed and intimidated Black and Latina writers, effectively blacklisting them within the publishing world (Trombetta). His employer, MIT, ultimately cleared him of sexual misconduct charges (Romo). The ensuing public debates and investigations into the misconduct allegations drew attention away from *Islandborn*, condemning the picture book to relative obscurity. While I analyzed Díaz's dual narratives as rape survivor and accused sexual harasser against the backdrop of the #MeToo movement in chapter 2, here I posit a reading of *Islandborn* as emblematic of the types of stories produced for and about Caribbean American young children and their parents in the first two decades of the twenty-first century. In extricating Lola's story from the drama of Díaz's fall from grace, this chapter analyzes how Caribbean American accounts of belonging to the United States as presented in picture books for young readers suggest that no one person's failings or personal losses can mar the larger effort of claiming one's place within the broad canvas of American culture.

Picture books like *Islandborn* portray their child protagonist/narrators as bicultural and, often, bilingual, and indelibly marked by their own or their relatives' immigration journeys. What makes these texts Caribbean American, rather than simply Caribbean, is their collective emphasis on fitting in and adding their own immigrant tale to that of their peers to form a larger narrative of the United States as a nation of immigrants. I will offer close readings of five more picture books categorized into two groups: those by prestige writers like Díaz, who have established publishing platforms and existing fan bases, and those published by independent, professional picture book authors. The first group includes Edwidge Danticat's *Mama's Nightingale* (2015), and Sonia Sotomayor's adaptation of her memoir for young readers, *Turning Pages: My Story* (2018). The second group includes picture books published by smaller presses and depicting Caribbean American child protagonists. LaTisha Redding's *Calling the Water Drum* (2016) is a first-person account of a Haitian American boy's loss and survival during the sea voyage from Haiti to the United States. Sandra L. Richards's *Rice & Rocks* (2016) contextualizes the ubiquity of rice and beans as a staple dish to highlight the culinary ties connecting the Jamaican American protagonist to his Puerto Rican, New Orleanian, and Japanese American school friends. Finally, Monica Gunning's *A Shelter in Our Car* (2004), tells the story of how an unhoused Jamaican

American mother and child end up in transitional housing. Taken together, these picture books depict the complex web of sociocultural experiences that shape young people's journeys to belonging and claiming a space as citizens in the making.

Both the young adult novels analyzed in the next chapter and the picture books under discussion here explore how schools' and universities' credentialing function serves as a vetting mechanism through which children and young adults are socialized into the complex public world of American society. The protagonists of the young adult fiction in chapter 4 successfully negotiate their transition from Caribbean teenagers to Caribbean American adults with independent lives of their own only after graduating from high school and getting accepted to college. *Islandborn* and the other picture books under discussion illustrate how young children learn to navigate the complex realities of their kinship ties as these intersect with school assignments or social networks. This pattern suggests that elementary education asks students to purposefully integrate their familial and academic lives into a larger narrative of national belonging.

GENRE AND METHODOLOGY

As multimodal texts, picture books aim to reach two different reading audiences simultaneously: parents or adults who read the words out loud, and the young children who look at the images as they listen to the story. This combined audience engages in dialogue to make sense of the complementary visual and textual narratives and this meaning making takes place multiple times, since repetition is part of the pleasure of this communal reading. Children's literature scholar Carole Scott remarks upon the status of this debate within the field and provides her own assessment of the dynamic interactions between these texts' intergenerational audiences:

> Whereas many of the works that have drawn the attention of critics fascinated by the dual-audience or cross-audienced phenomenon offer opportunities for intricate analysis of narrative technique, perspective, symbolism, and characterization, I believe that picture books give a unique opportunity for what I consider a collaborative relationship between children and adults, for picturebooks [sic] empower children and adults much more equally. (101)

My discussion of *Islandborn*, *Mama's Nightingale*, *Turning Pages*, *Calling the Water Drum*, *Rice & Rocks*, and *A Shelter in Our Car* focuses on the texts' visual and written narratives, rather than speculating about how families may use these books within their own complex interactions. I analyze their narrative and aesthetic literary value as contributions to the ongoing project of increasing Caribbean American visibility internally, as the books thematize the process of understanding the specificity of a given national heritage and culture as defining aspects of the child protagonist's familial identity and also externally, as the child learns that their Caribbeanness is one of many possible ways of being American and belonging to the nation.

This literary analysis stands in contradistinction to most of the published scholarship on children's picture books as tools to enhance literacy, which takes an instrumental view of these texts influenced by social science approaches. The field of literacy studies considers picture books as objects of study for teachers to incorporate into their larger project of increasing the preschool curriculum's diversity of experience and developing cultural competencies. Jamie Campbell Naidoo articulates this sense of mission when writing about award winning picture books by Latinx authors:

> As educators and librarians, one of our goals is to prepare children from all cultural backgrounds to function in our culturally pluralistic society. Having an awareness of the precise social messages about a particular culture—in this case the Latino culture—that children encounter in their literary transactions will help us to facilitate our children's learning and understanding of the metaphorical 'other' in society. (126)

I acknowledge the pedagogical value of including children's literature in the curriculum and its positive impact on students' development, but this area of inquiry falls outside of my purview. As a literary scholar, I analyze how the visual and textual narratives of children's picture books depict and imagine a capacious nation to which its citizens, present and future, feel connected across multiple affective categories: to the family, to the neighborhood, to the school, and beyond. I rely on close reading of passages and images to arrive at my conclusions, rather than deploying textual content analysis that considers the social valences of key words.

Despite these differences of approach, I nonetheless concur with literacy scholars Maria José Botelho and Masha Kabakow Rudman when they claim that "cultural products such as children's literature play a role in 'narrating the nation' and must be studied against historical and sociopolitical contexts, with an awareness of the social construction of nation and culture. Critical multicultural analysis can peel away at the layers of these constructions" (136). My critical approach in reading picture books that encompass different ethnicities and linguistic backgrounds connected to the Caribbean as part of their depiction of the United States as a multicultural nation aligns with the goals of critical multicultural analysis as Botelho and Rudman conceive of it. Furthermore, the transnational nature of the Caribbean American experience demands a more inclusive set of approaches that recognizes the importance of the immigrant experience that shapes Caribbean diasporic communities in the United States. The work of Linda Leonard Lamme, Danling Fu, and Ruth McKoy Lowery has influenced my thinking about how Caribbean American picture books depict and discuss the immigrant experience. These scholars contend that, "Immigrant stories are an important part of American history because the stories humanize the immigrant experience and provide a pivotal segue through which to delve into U.S. history" (123). However, whereas Lamme, Fu, and Lowery's analysis focuses on how teachers can incorporate these texts into the social studies classroom, I will perform close readings of the written and visual narratives of the small archive of primary texts I have assembled, alongside the author's notes that occasionally accompany them. The value of *Islandborn* and its cohort transcends their potential utility as pedagogical tools for educators to challenge embedded power structures. The critical lens I use privileges these texts' aesthetic contributions through which Caribbean American stories of belonging are shared across generations and with broader audiences than the binary insider/outsider status marker might indicate.

CASE STUDIES

To establish a grounded comparison of how these prestige picture books align with the work of professional picture book writers, I followed in the footsteps of education scholars Zaria T. Malcolm and Ruth McKoy Lowery and used my local public library as a resource to find out what Caribbean American picture books are available to local children in my college town in a landlocked state. There, I found Gunning's *A Shelter in Our Car*, Richards's *Rice & Rocks*, and Redding's *Calling the Water Drum*. Like *Islandborn*, Sotomayor's *Turning Pages*, and Danticat's *Mama's Nightingale*, these depictions of young children's lives tackle hard social realities, like school bullying, poverty, and homelessness (*Shelter in Our Car*), and parents dying during the immigration journey (*Calling the Water Drum*). *Rice & Rocks*, like *Islandborn*, thematizes the creation of a communal identity through commensality since rice and beans is a staple dish for many cultures.

Read together, the visual and textual narratives in these picture books imagine national belonging as a Glissantean Relation identity established through a multi-level process of situating oneself and claiming kinship within both local and imaginary communities. American studies scholar Amy Fish points out, "By portraying migration from young people's perspective, children's books allow us to examine the implications of making children the protagonists and spokespersons of migration" (2). Of the six picture books under discussion, half feature children who were born in the Caribbean and then immigrated to the United States: the Dominican Republic in *Islandborn*, Haiti in *Calling the Water Drum*, and Jamaica in *A Shelter in Our Car*. These texts portray a child as both protagonist and spokesperson for (im)migration, even though Lola, Henri, and Zettie are growing up in the United States. The protagonists of the other three books—Saya in *Mama's Nightingale*, Sonia in *Turning Pages*, and Giovanni in *Rice & Rocks*—are US-born Americans, each with at least one family member who left their island of origin (Haiti, Puerto Rico, and Jamaica, respectively). These books all center difficult interactions between the Caribbean American children and others who do not share their backgrounds. And, while these tales do have happy endings, the conclusions do not in any way minimize or erase the emotional pain and hardships the child protagonists experience during the narrative. Books across both sides of the publishing divide demonstrate a shared respect for the trauma children undergo as they navigate their own or their families' immigration journeys and strive to find their place within American culture.

In their respective picture books, Díaz, Sotomayor, and Danticat call attention to the ways Caribbean American family units navigate the difficulties of speaking multiple languages, decoding the dual cultures of their island of origin and adopted homeland, and the divide between the private world of the family and the public arena where formal education takes place and policy issues such as immigration are debated. Like *Islandborn*, *Turning Pages* and *Mama's Nightingale* also appeal to their authors' established reading audiences or fans who can introduce these texts to their younger relatives. Díaz, Sotomayor, and Danticat are a relatively elite group of authors who have access to the publishing pipeline thanks to the demonstrated success of their adult literary texts. Thus, the content of their picture books is on brand for each writer. Díaz discusses the Trujillato in *Islandborn* like he has done previously in the short story collection *Drown* and the novel *The Brief Wondrous Life of Oscar Wao*. The child protagonists in Sotomayor's and Danticat's tales face dire circumstances that impact them directly. Young Sonia describes both her diabetes diagnosis and her father's death in *Turning Pages*, incidents Sotomayor narrates at length in her original civic memoir and its adaptation for middle grade readers: *The Beloved World of Sonia Sotomayor*. And Danticat's choice to focus on family separation due to a parent's irregular immigration status in *Mama's Nightingale* makes sense in light of the author's poignant personal account of her uncle's troubles with the US immigration system's detention camps in the family memoir, *Brother, I'm Dying*. These topics are representative of each writer's larger concerns in the rest of their oeuvres, and thus it makes sense that their texts for early readers portray children's lives as rich and complex, encompassing both sorrow and joy.

Díaz's sunny text acknowledges the prospect of state violence but keeps the topic at a suitable emotional remove. As she interviews her neighbors, the protagonist of *Islandborn* learns about Rafael Trujillo's dictatorship from the building's superintendent, Mr. Mir. His account of a national uprising against this tyrannical rule discusses Trujillo metaphorically as "the Monster," and tells young Lola:

> Heroes rose up. Strong smart young women just like you, Lola, and a few strong smart young men, too. They got tired of being afraid and fought the Monster. What a titanic battle that was. The whole Island shook from their struggle—the Monster tried all of its evil tricks but in the end the heroes found the Monster's weakness and banished it forever. (n.p.)

The double spread in which this passage appears features an interesting contrast between Díaz's ominous words, which hint at the toll such an uprising took, and Leo Espinosa's cheerful illustrations, which strike a celebratory tone. A multi-pigmented group of women, children, and men appear across the spread, holding hands at the beach, facing away from the reader, and glancing at the sun setting in the horizon. In the water in front of the figures are the last visible remnants of the green monster—one claw and the tip of its tail—as it sinks into the ocean. Tropical foliage and flowers in bloom frame this scene in the foreground, while floating musical notes imply that the group is celebrating their victory with song. The discordance can be explained by remembering that the images represent Lola's thoughts as she hears about the Island's history of political turmoil rather than Mr. Mir's own memories; given her limited experience of the world, Lola cannot imagine even an iota of the atrocities of the Trujillato. But adult readers familiar with the rest of Díaz's books, on the contrary, are aware of the dictator's serial rapes and sustained campaign of political assassinations as well as the literature surrounding the "heroes" who opposed this corrupt regime. If we push the notion of "the Island" as referring to Hispaniola as a whole, rather than either the Dominican Republic or Haiti, then Papa and Baby Doc Duvalier emerge as possible alter-egos for "the Monster," whom Mr. Mir so reviles. Regardless, Lola includes references to "the Monster," along with her neighbor's recollections of the culture and resilience of the Dominican Republic in the illustrated report she turns in as her homework project. That conclusion emphasizes the book's meta-fictive qualities—we have seen Lola's project twice, once as the images take shape in her head, and the second time when we see a glimpse of what she turns in.

In contrast, the meta-fictive quality of Sonia Sotomayor's book autobiographical narrative is evident from the start since *Turning Pages* is both an adaptation for early readers of her critically acclaimed memoir, *My Beloved World,* and a distillation of her impressive achievements into the most defining part of her personality: her love of reading. This not only makes her seem relatable to the book's target audience, who is, after all, getting to know Sonia by having her story read to them, but it also gives these children a model for how to pursue their own curiosity and seek comfort in reading when facing life's difficult situations. A case in point is Sotomayor's discussion of her diabetes diagnosis at age seven. Facing the prospect of having to self-inject insulin for the rest of her life, Sonia explains how her love of reading helped her overcome her fear of needles:

> I found my courage in an unlikely place—comic books. After reading stories of regular people who had secret superpowers that could save the world, I imagined being as brave and powerful as they were. Then I learned how to give myself the shots, and in time I got used to it.
>
> Books, it seemed, were magic potions that could fuel me with the bravery of superheroes. (6)

Lulu Delacre's illustration on the page features an insert of a five-panel sequence of "Justice League of America" that simultaneously puns on the adult Sotomayor's occupation, as one of nine Supreme Court Justices, and also visually develops the idea of courage being a magical quality in a mini-issue called, "The Magic Potion." The first panel in this imaginary sequence depicts a large and menacing syringe at the foreground, with a cowering Sonia in the background. The next panel shows Sonia at scale injecting herself in the arm with a much smaller syringe. The next two show Sonia, now sporting a cape, raising her hands in victory and then taking flight over the city. Reading books helps Sonia feel at home in the English language, and then later cope with the death of her father. And it is in the books she reads as a college student at Princeton that Sonia learns about the history of how Puerto Rico became a part of the United States. This reading helps her appreciate the hardship her grandparents faced on the island, as well as her parents' struggles to make it in New York City. *Turning Pages* suggests that children can read (and write) their way into finding their place within American society and culture and also share these stories with others to establish a Relation identity.

Although Sotomayor's *Turning Pages* is an autobiographical account, Edwidge Danticat refers to her own family's story of immigration and separation only in the author's note to the fictional tale of *Mama's Nightingale*. Danticat's parents were undocumented immigrants to the United States who eventually regularized their status and then sponsored Edwidge and her brother Bob to join them in New York. Danticat refers to her own pro-immigration activism as an adult parent and links it to the plot of the story she tells: "I meet a lot of children who are separated from either one or both of their parents because their parents are undocumented, or as Saya says, are 'without papers.'" She concludes the note by explicitly addressing her target audience: "this book is dedicated to those children, who, like Saya, are dreaming of the day when their mother, or father, or both parents will come home" (28). This dedication is the second one in the book; the first is located opposite the copyright information, and it reads "For Nara and Liz, with love and gratitude —ED." Sotomayor likewise distinguishes between the family members to whom she explicitly dedicates the book in the front-matter, "To Abuelita Mercedes, Mami Celina, and all the role-model women in my life," and the nameless children who inspired the tale by teaching the judge a fundamental life lesson: "I owe much to the children who taught me that hugging is important to being happy" (32). By explicitly discussing how their personal life stories and picture book narratives overlap, Sonia Sotomayor and Edwidge Danticat offer themselves up as role models to children, validating reading and writing as activities that have the power to teach and persuade others.

Turning Pages and *Mama's Nightingale* depict American-born children who speak more than one language at home through first-person narratives that define the Spanish or Haitian Creole words in context. Saya's account of family separation also acknowledges the power of oral storytelling to keep Haitian American families connected vertically across the generations, and horizontally across the immigration-enforced separation. While her mother is held at the Sunshine Correctional Facility, Saya hears her voice first, by listening to the answering machine tape and later, when that breaks, by playing stories her mom records and mails to her in a cassette tape: "Suddenly the room is filled with Mama's wind-chime voice singing about the soursop and the nightingale. At the end of the song, Mama tells me a new bedtime story, one she made up herself. It's about a mommy nightingale who goes on a very long journey and is looking for a rainbow trail in the sky so she can return home to her baby nightingale." Leslie Staub's illustration in the double spread where this passage appears quite literally shows Mama hovering over the sleeping Saya as she cuddles her stuffed monkey. A pink ribbon connecting two caged nightingales surrounds Mama's right arm, while her left hovers protectively over Saya's head under the image of a free nightingale singing at the moon while perched on a red flower. The iconography at work here recalls the imagery of the sequin-covered Haitian art flags or *Drapo Vodou*.[1]

Mama's Nightingale incorporates metafiction as it celebrates the child's power to express herself and tell her story orally as the mother does and the first-person narration imitates, and also through writing, a medium Saya's father prefers in order to reach out to public officials who might help his wife's case. The mother's stories archive comforts her family, while the father's constant correspondence to judges, state and local government officials, and journalists appear to fall on deaf ears as Saya observes, "No one ever writes him back." Young Saya decides to collaborate with her father by writing her family's story in her own words. The father includes her story with his own appeal to the newspaper, which publishes it along with an interview with the family. The publicity that ensues, "all the phone calls and the letters to the prison from people who read about us in the newspaper and saw us on TV," results in an expedited review of Saya's mother's case. Ultimately, the judge releases her to await the processing of her papers at home with her family. The book concludes with Saya and her mother at bedtime, dynamically discussing the new ending of story about the nightingales.

However, Mama's plight has not been fully resolved within the pages of this picture book: she is still undocumented at the end of the story, thereby leaving open the possibility that the family could be separated again. Amy Fish, explains the political stakes of *Mama's Nightingale* as a direct challenge to US immigration policies:

> Rather than drawing attention away, Saya calls public interest toward her mother's story in an apparently straightforward act of visibility politics. Even as Saya uses her position as a child of migration to practice advocacy, however, her connection to the trickster nightingale's tactic of distraction lends a shadow of fugitivity to her spotlight. Behind Saya's narrative success stands the unsettling sense that Mama's humanity could be recognized by U.S. power only when refracted, or distracted, through an idealized construction of innocent, depoliticized childhood. (10)

This reading suggests that a US-born child narrator, like Saya, only earns the power to speak publicly at the cost of silencing her immigrant parents. This dynamic is at work within Saya's family (daughter/father) and it also works between Saya (the character) and Danticat (as author) because she leverages

---

1. Leslie Staub's illustrations echo or invoke the art, rather than the religious, flags of the Haitian Drapo Vodou tradition as described by Anne M. Platoff.

her own public platform as an immigrant writer to tell the story of a Caribbean American child. Yet, as we saw in the author's note, Danticat adds an account of her own experience of immigration into her poignant critique of America's inhumane immigration policies.

Whereas family separation is resolved happily in *Mama's Nightingale*, LaTisha Redding's *Calling the Water Drum* focuses on a more permanent type of family separation due to irregular immigration from Haiti to the United States. Rather than lay the blame squarely at the American immigration system, Redding instead highlights the enormous risks Haitian families brave as they seek greater safety and the promise of economic opportunity in the United States. The titular action of "calling the water drums" refers to the young protagonist's active mourning for his mother and father, who perished at sea during their crossing. Rescued by the occupants of a different immigrant boat, Henri now lives in New York with his uncle, the person who had sent money and asked his family to come join him in the United States. Though the tale is narrated in first person, what we hear is Henri's internal monologue, the words he does not say in response to the efforts of those around him to engage in dialogue. For example, when his neighbor, Karrine, asks Henri why he plays the drum, the boy does not respond to her but instead tells the reader a few pages later that "my drum is really an old bucket. It's what I used to help Manman carry water when we lived in Haiti." Thus, the drum playing physically connects young Henri to both his lost parents and his homeland; by drumming Henri establishes a sonic connection to home.

We learn Karrine's backstory toward the end of the book. It turns out that she enjoys listening to Henri mourn with his drumming because she has lost her own father in Louisiana during Hurricane Katrina. The exchange that follows this revelation is one of the few times Henri speaks out loud during the narration:

> But today there are no crowds around, and Karrine says softly, "I miss my daddy, Henri. Do you miss your parents?"
> I stop playing, and a sound rises like a wave in my throat. I open my mouth, and one word spills out. "*Wi.*" Yes.

This admission constitutes the friends' solidarity in mourning—by discussing their own bereavement openly with one another, the burden of grief appears less hard to bear. It also marks a distinct difference between the scope of all three of the prestige children's books, which follow a single child from a particular Caribbean background (Dominican in *Islandborn*, Puerto Rican in *Turning Pages*, and Haitian in *Mamma's Nightingale*), and the more dynamic social interactions across Caribbean and other populations that characterize the textual worlds of professional picture book authors. Through Karrine and Henri's friendship, *Calling the Water Drum* portrays their family backgrounds as forming part of a Relation identity, the Greater Caribbean diaspora with a center in New York City. Both child protagonists are also climate migrants, since their families' losses are distinctly tied to natural phenomena that resulted in their displacement.

The author's note is the most surprising element of a book that creates such an open and dynamic vision of Caribbean American belonging forged by trauma. Like Danticat, Redding uses this space to situate her own family's migration story in the context of the tale she tells. However, there is one big difference: Redding does not trace her background back to a specific Caribbean island but rather to the American South, though she does not specify which state. As a child new to New York City, she bonded with school friends who traced their heritage to Haiti, Sweden, Puerto Rico, Barbados, China, Germany, Jamaica, Russia, Trinidad, and Spain, whose accents made her feel more comfortable with her own. Redding openly acknowledges her own background to explain why she identifies strongly with her Haitian American friends' accounts of the harrowing sea voyage that brought them to the United States: "It is these unsettling memories, images, and facts that spurred me to write this story. I want readers of *Calling the Water Drum* to know that I formed Henri's story to reflect both the uncertainty and the hope that exist side by side with sacrifice and courage in forging a new life." Thus, Redding occupies a subject position very similar to Karrine's with respect to Henri. She is the Black, Southern friend to the silent Haitian protagonist who bears witness to his suffering and revels in his joy. Redding and Karrine both engage in Relation identity with their Caribbean friends. As readers, we are privy to a tale of tragedy and loss we would never have occasion to hear about directly. This distance between the bereaved children and the book's readers comes across most clearly in the double spread where Karrine and Henri's conversation takes place. Both children are pictured in the left-hand corner of Aaron Boyd's illustration; Karrine stands by a fountain pool while Henri sits at its rim, their reflections refracted in the water. The words appear on the right-hand page with a background of the almost deserted park surrounded by trees and a few pigeons searching for food on the floor.

In contrast, *Rice & Rocks* showcases the healing power of children's friendships to help mitigate their insecurities by showing them happily eating Sunday dinner together at Giovanni's house. Like *Islandborn*, *Turning Pages*, *Mama's Nightingale*, and *Calling the Water Drum*, this narrative centers the migrant/immigrant experience and does not include characters from dominant white society. The protagonist is Jamaican American, and the book's title refers to the nickname he has given to his grandmother's signature dish, rice and peas. Giovanni does not like the peas and is somewhat ashamed of his culture. Having invited his school friends over for Sunday dinner, his biggest fear is that they will dislike the rice and rocks the family usually enjoys and therefore will stop liking him as well. Giovanni's aunt and a magical pet parrot take the child on a quick jaunt through his friends' birthplaces, Puerto Rico, New Orleans, and Japan, to illustrate how each of these cultures has its own version of rice and rocks: *arroz con gandules* or rice with pigeon peas, red beans and rice, and Sekihan or sticky rice boiled with red azuki beans, respectively. By the end of the tale, Giovanni has learned to negotiate his social anxiety about appearing too exotic for his school friends. His aunt helps the boy realize that by learning more about his Jamaican heritage and feeling proud of it, he can effectively connect with the children whose own stories of migration make them more open to appreciate it. The book ends with a drawing of a photograph commemorating the successful meal, thereby affirming its message that a culture's cuisine is among the most accessible way to extend hospitality and make community or enact a Relation identity.

While the final picture book under discussion, *A Shelter in Our Car,* also celebrates childhood friendships as the balm that helps soothe hardship, it is the only one of the six that includes a child who is white. The protagonist, Zettie, and her mother are a Jamaican American family experiencing homelessness. This book is unusual in that the visual narrative sets the scene before the first word appears on the page. In the double spread that includes the copyright information and the author's and illustrators' dedication, we see on the left-hand page an image of Zettie and her mother lying down in each other's arms in the back of their station wagon. On the right-hand page Elaine Pedlar depicts the same scene from a different vantage point, zooming back further to reveal that the wagon is parked under a streetlight and two police patrol cars are approaching. Though this is an ominous beginning, the encounter with the police results in nothing more serious than a warning to move the car someplace else. Unlike Giovanni, whose fear of rejection was anticipated and did not actually take place, Zettie is the victim of school bullies who call her names and pull her braids. Their race or ethnicity is not evident since they are depicted as shadowy figures. Zettie finds comfort in talking with her best friend Benjie, an unhoused white child, thereby affirming class solidarity rather than ethnic or racial identity as the basis for affective ties.

Zettie has a complicated family history. She immigrated with her parents from Jamaica to the United States. Her father passed away at some indeterminate time prior to the story's opening, and her mother has temporary employment doing low-skilled labor while also attending community college. Mother and daughter reminisce about their time in the Caribbean while eating their dinner in an example of Root identity: "'Do you remember the sun in Jamaica?' Mama asks. 'How brightly it shone after a shower of rain?' I do remember. Especially on cold, cloudy days like today." While this affirms their joint identities as immigrants, the contrast between the cold reality of their dire socio-economic precarity and the more pleasant memory of the past calls into question whether immigrating to the United States was a good idea. By the end of the book, however, the family learns that Zettie's mother has earned a spot at a transitional living housing complex thanks to her job handing out leaflets for a nonprofit agency. The family decides to rent a motel room for the night as their celebration. What goes unremarked, however, is that this family's good luck means they will no longer be close to Benji and his mother. As readers, we can anticipate how much heartbreak this realization will cause Zettie since the children had established their own Relation-identity community.

The bleak realism of *A Shelter in Our Car* and *Calling the Water Drum* convey their authors' shared belief that representation matters especially to those children whose life circumstances are less than stable. In addition to the autobiographical author's note, Monica Gunning, a former teacher, includes an explanation about homelessness in the United States that concludes by listing concrete steps her target audience can take to help: "Research the problem in your community and share what you learn with other people; find out about organizations that work with persons without homes and ask what you can do to help; work with your school to organize a clothing drive." The implication here is that learning that homelessness is a problem that affects both immigrants and US-born Americans may spur children on to raise their families' consciousness and bring about some change. For her part, in *Calling the Water Drum*, Redding creates a space in which bereaved children can express their grief without having to explain their trauma. By making mourning practices visible to larger audiences, Redding, Sotomayor's *Turning Pages*, and Danticat's *Mama's Nightingale* call attention to the psychic toll that the childhood trauma of parental loss or separation can take on these children's development. Díaz's *Islandborn* and Richards's *Rice & Rocks* also acknowledge children's social anxiety when school-mediated social situations require them to discuss or disclose their family heritage publicly.

These six texts portray Caribbean American childhoods as both difficult and joyful. Reading them together affirms that children from Caribbean backgrounds have some shared experiences with one another and with children whose own families remember their arrival to the United States. By sharing their stories with audiences who are not like them, these picture books portray their child protagonists as ambassadors for immigration but also for diversity of experience. Their joint emphasis on finding a place and way to belong within the United States as members of their overlapping communities gives children at least the illusion of agency by endorsing their efforts to take charge of their own narrative rather than submit to the way others see them and/or their situations.

CHAPTER 4

Education, Love, and Belonging in Young Adult Fiction

On a fall evening in October 2019, Cuban American novelist Jennine Capó Crucet took the stage at Georgia Southern University to discuss her novel, *Make Your Home Among Strangers*, which the university's office of first and second year experiences had chosen as its required reading for incoming students.[1] The novel tells the story of Lizet, a high-achieving first-generation Cuban American young woman who struggles academically during fall semester of her freshman year at a selective liberal arts college in the Northeast while also facing family disapproval for moving away and trying to improve her circumstances. An article from *Inside Higher Ed* reports that during the event's question and answer period, a group of angry GSU students challenged Capó Crucet's discussion of white privilege both during her remarks and in the novel's portrayal of a few white secondary characters (Anderson). Students also reportedly challenged the writer's credentials to be a speaker at Georgia Southern, seemingly unaware that Capó Crucet is both a novelist and a former professor of English at the University of Nebraska, Lincoln. Tense interactions ensued, and later in the evening a group of students burned their copies of the novel in a bonfire, an act that was caught on video and shared in a tweet

---

1. Throughout the chapter, I will follow Latinx naming conventions by using both of Jennine Capó Crucet's last names rather than defaulting to "Crucet" as do other Anglophone publications. The bibliography lists her work under Crucet, however, in accordance with the Library of Congress's filing system.

that went viral (@elainaan). The student who posted the video apologized to Capó Crucet on behalf of her university, but the institution's official responses were not so clear cut. While no administrator supported the book burning itself, Georgia Southern University's official spokesperson, the vice president for strategic communications and marketing, defended the action as an example of students' "freedom of expression," while the chair of the Department of Communications and Linguistics proclaimed that unit's support of Capó Crucet and called upon the student body to find more productive avenues through which to channel their frustrations (Anderson).

This brief discussion of the controversy surrounding some students' negative reactions to *Make Your Home Among Strangers* illustrates two important things about the current state of institutional approaches to diversifying college campuses in a top-down way without providing adequate academic support for symbolic efforts such as assigned first-year readings. First, the description of the students' belief in the Great Replacement theory and the circulation of the book-burning video centered the students' white fragility while effacing the novel's thoughtful examination of the culture shock that high-achieving first-generation students of color experience both at home and at the colleges or universities to which they gain admission. Second, social media posts about the book-burning at Georgia Southern went viral and dominated the national narrative about *Make Your Home Among Strangers*, giving almost no recognition to the critical acclaim and accolades it received upon publication.

The students' negative reaction at Georgia Southern is decidedly out of keeping with how popular a choice *Make Your Home Among Strangers* has been among first-year experience reading programs: more than thirty-five colleges and universities have assigned it without incident and Macmillan, the publisher, proudly features it and Capó Crucet's follow-up essay collection, *My Time Among the Whites*, as part of its branded initiative, "McMillan Books for the First Year Experience." An article recounting Capó Crucet's appearance at the Southern Festival of Books in Tennessee a few days after the GSU visit rehearses the controversy even as it also informs its more literary readers of the many accolades the work has earned: "Her novel, 'Make Your Home Among Strangers,' was a New York Times Book Review Editors' Choice book, the winner of the 2016 International Latino Book Award, and was cited as the best book of the year by NBC Latino, the Guardian, and the Miami Herald" (Bliss). This article breaks from others by emphasizing Capó Crucet's nationality rather than her ethnicity: "In the collection of essays Crucet—a critically acclaimed writer and a first-generation American raised in Miami—explores what it means to feel like a stranger in the country in which she was born."

McMillan, the novel's publisher, lists the book under literary fiction rather than as a part of its young adult (YA) fiction line-up. Regardless, the combination of critical acclaim and its college subject matter made the work appealing to colleges and universities who sought to meet both their diversity and first-year experience mandates by assigning a book by a Black, Indigenous, or Person of Color (BIPOC) writer.

David Shih, yet another English professor, took to *Inside Higher Ed* to reflect on the aftermath of this confrontation at Georgia Southern and how it might be emblematic of the larger problem of the institutional tokenization of literature to carry out the twin functions of decolonizing the curriculum and doing diversity and inclusion training on the cheap. He wonders about what sort of class discussion about the novel the students who burnt the book participated in before attending the author's visit and then clarifies:

> My point isn't to single out the pedagogy of individual instructors but to identify what appear to be the assumptions behind the organizational structure of the first-year experience common-text initiative. I suspect that one of those is that texts, to a large extent, "teach themselves." Only with this assumption might such an academic program authorize a cadre of instructors—with varied sets of credentials and social identities—to oversee first-year students' readings of a Latinx woman's encounters with whiteness and class privilege. (Shih)

The paratext of the paperback edition of *Make Your Home Among Strangers* includes both a brief interview with the author and a separate section including ten discussion questions (without an answer key) at the end of the novel and thus could be said to be complicit in fostering the perception that the book could "teach itself." However, Shih critiques the institutional assumption that anyone can successfully lead meaningful discussions of literary texts because such thinking devalues the humanities scholars' specialized training honed through course work and research. When this attitude overlaps with an institution's desire to check off the box outlining simplistic diversity learning outcomes like "'discuss diversity and inclusion'" without providing students any historical context, defining key terms in the novel under discussion, or outlining the goals for undertaking such discussions in the first place, the situation amounts to professional malfeasance (Shih). Such an approach has the potential to do more harm than good to the university's overall race relations and sense of community. As the book-burning incident illustrates, not only can literary works support multiple interpretations, but they can also be willfully mischaracterized and discarded symbolically. By burning *Make Your*

Home Among Strangers in the name of denouncing critiques of white privilege, a few angry white students symbolically rejected Caribbean American literature wholesale because it does not center whiteness either.

I discuss *Make Your Home Among Strangers* alongside other recently published Caribbean American novels that also thematize the academic and social struggles young adult protagonists face as they transition from high school to college. Despite all the attention given to Capó Crucet's depiction of white privilege at Rawlings, the fictional small liberal arts college the protagonist attends, the bulk of the novel examines how Lizet's family simultaneously celebrates her academic achievements in the abstract and nonetheless repeatedly berates her for how her education has made her more professionally ambitious than her relatives. Lizet ultimately breaks with her family for good and takes advantage of the mentorship opportunities her white European (German) faculty mentor made her aware of. In foregrounding a young woman's coming of age story against a set of complex transitions between high school, childhood, and domestic life and college, adulthood, and public life, *Make Your Home Among Strangers* presents the emblematic journey Caribbean Americans make between the communal nature of social organization of their heritage to the more independent American style of individualism that is open to accepting the help offered by the titular "strangers," those who are peers, mentors, or colleagues but do not share the same cultural or ethnic background as the protagonist's. This is a pattern we will see repeated throughout the rest of the novels discussed in the chapter though Aaron Barlow cautions that, "Individualism, for all 21st-century Americans, has become an abstraction and, in its purest form, an unattainable ideal. That has not reduced its impact, however, or the necessity of trying to understand the American genesis of faith in individualism, no matter how it is defined" (52). In broadening their social networks beyond their familial or ethnic circles, Caribbean American young adult characters develop affective ties to their compatriots as fellow Americans in the novels under discussion.

The rest of the archive I have assembled for comparison here all belongs to the genre of YA fiction because these texts' target audience is much broader than that of literary fiction. Thus, they fill in the gap between the institutional appropriation of literary fiction by BIPOC used to fulfill a "diversity and inclusion" mandate, and teenagers' and young adults' need to see themselves and their circumstances reflected in easily accessible and popular stories. Though novels to which I will compare *Make Your Home Among Strangers* do fit into this publishing niche, they are extremely well crafted and present complex portrayals of Caribbean American teenagers and young adults as multidimensional characters aware of the intersectional oppressions to which they have been subjected and the potential affective traps that their friends and family try to impose on them.

Gabby Rivera's *Juliet Takes a Breath* (2016) follows the titular lesbian Puerto Rican college student during the summer she first comes out to her family and then leaves for the West Coast to intern with a white feminist writer. Elizabeth Acevedo's *With the Fire on High* (2019) tells the story of Emoni Santiago, a half-Black, half-Puerto Rican teen mother as she struggles to finish high school and turn her talent for cooking into part-time college studies at Drexel University's culinary arts program and a job cooking at a fine dining restaurant. *American Street* (2017) by Ibi Zoboi, chronicles Fabiola Toussaint's first few months adapting to life and high school in Detroit with her aunt and cousins after flying in from Haiti. When they land, Fabiola's mother is apprehended by immigration officials because she had overstayed her visa during a previous visit. She and Fabiola, who was born in the United States but raised in her mother's homeland, remain separated for the duration of the novel. The threat of deportation also looms large over Natasha Kingsley's mixed-status Jamaican American family in the romantic adventure *The Sun Is Also a Star* (2016) by Nicola Yoon. When her father is arrested for driving under the influence in New York City, the Kingsleys have to agree to a voluntary removal or self-deportation to avoid facing the same fate as Fabiola's mother in *American Street*. The weight of their departure looms over Natasha on the one day the novel's actions take place, thereby dashing her plans to attend college in the United States and study data science. Finally, Sofia Quintero's *Efraín's Secret* (2010) chronicles the titular character's ambition to prove himself worthy of admission to an Ivy League university despite attending an under-resourced public high school in the South Bronx. After getting shot and arrested while doing a favor for his drug dealing best friend, Nestor, Efraín's legal troubles interfere with his plans to retake the SAT during senior year. By the end of the novel, the half-Dominican and half-Puerto Rican protagonist is on track to attend the University of Puerto Rico the following fall.

Elizabeth Acevedo and Nicola Yoon are the most accomplished Caribbean American YA novelists of the group. Acevedo, who is Afro–Dominican American, won the National Book Award in 2018 for her first novel, *The Poet X*. Emoni, the protagonist of her second novel, *With the Fire on High*, has a complex family back story: her Black mother from North Carolina died in childbirth and her Puerto Rican father was so bereft by this loss that he relinquished custody of his daughter to his US-based mother and returned to the island to mourn. Jamaican Nicola Yoon's *The Sun Is Also a Star* was a National Book Award finalist in 2016. Both it and her debut novel, *Everything, Everything* have been adapted into Hollywood films. Haitian-born Ibi Zoboi's

American Street was also a National Book Award finalist the following year. She has published many other books for young adults and middle readers and holds an MFA in Writing for Children and Young Adults from the Vermont College of Fine Arts.

Sofía Quintero's family is both Puerto Rican and Dominican. She has published hip-hop and crime fiction under the pen-name Black Artemis. *Efraín's Secret* is her first young adult novel; it was an American Library Association's Best Book for Young Adults Award finalist. Gabby Rivera's *Juliet Takes a Breath* has gained growing acceptance within the American publishing establishment. The novel was first published independently in 2016 and then was re-released by an imprint of Penguin Random House, Dial Books, in 2019 (gabbyrivera.com). Given Rivera's success as a comic book writer for Marvel, the novel was rereleased as a graphic novel by independent comic book and graphic novel publisher BOOM in the fall of 2020 (Grunewald). *Juliet Takes a Breath* has earned the respect of fellow queer Caribbean American writers, such as Haitian American novelist and scholar Roxane Gay. In her review of *Juliet Takes a Breath* on GoodReads.com, she calls the novel "fucking outstanding." Quoted in Powells.com's page about the novel, Elizabeth Acevedo's review is equally enthusiastic; she says of the eponymous protagonist: "This is the homegirl I've always wanted to see in literature, made flesh by Rivera's pen."

The YA novels examined here eschew easy answers to the intractable social problems that surround their adolescent protagonists—*Juliet Takes a Breath*, *With the Fire on High*, and *Make Your Home Among Strangers* feature narrative closure and depict the protagonists as reaping the rewards of having learned valuable life lessons. Others like *American Street*, *The Sun Is Also a Star*, and *Efraín's Secret* have more ambiguous endings that acknowledge the main characters' fates may not rest in their own hands. While not explicitly didactic, these novels all include the Caribbean immigrant parents' firm conviction that a good education will allow their children to have access to more economic opportunities than those available to the older generation. The plotlines literalize this assumption and depict how structural barriers such as poverty, the local government's disinvestment in education, structural and interpersonal racism, sexism, and language difficulties all diminish or at least curtail the protagonists' chances of meeting their parents' expectations of academic success and upward mobility. These novels' dedication to highlighting their protagonists' struggles to overcome their cultural and socioeconomic challenges provide mini-civics lessons by showcasing how fundamentally uneven Caribbean American adolescents' access to good public education can be.

The emphasis on education as the novels' leitmotif is intentional—I want to examine how contemporary YA Caribbean American authors discuss formal education in light of two combined pressures. First, the external social expectation that immigrants and their families assimilate to dominant American cultural expectations by speaking unaccented and idiomatic standard English, not missing class, and participating in extracurricular activities. Second, the internal familial expectation of success, an added pressure imposed on their children by immigrant parents whose own lack of formal schooling narrow their professional horizons in their chosen homeland. This balancing act corresponds to a larger American foundational story that is shared by earlier waves of European immigrants who arrived through Ellis Island and settled in ethnic enclaves throughout the East Coast in the nineteenth and early twentieth centuries. During the Progressive era, compulsory education legislation curtailed the possibilities for child labor and children entered the school systems in large numbers. As a result, dedicated activists hastened the process of acculturation through a rigid system of indoctrination. To those reformers we owe the invention of such hallmarks of Americana as Thanksgiving school pageants and similar secular observations that introduce the core values and central historical highlights of the American project as part and parcel of the larger goal of bringing about the transformation that would result in e pluribus unum, out of many one. As historian Elizabeth Plenck reminds us: "Public school teachers and settlement house workers hoped to assimilate immigrant children to America and use children as Americanizers of their parents. They wanted the children to become patriotic citizens who demonstrated their love of country through celebrations of cherished American holidays" (778). Though subsequent immigration reform efforts eventually eliminated the quota system and opened immigration to people from countries other than Europe, the assumption that children would continue "Americaniz[ing]" their parents remains woven into the American public-school curriculum.

The cherished American tradition the young adult novels under discussion hold up as aspirational is not the Thanksgiving meal, but the expectation of a college education. Scholars refer to immigrant parents' expectations about their own children's academic success as "educational optimism" and use the term, "college aspirations" to indicate when parents expect their children to continue their education beyond high school. According to sociologists Elizabeth Raleigh and Grace Kao:

> educational optimism is generally high for minority parents, especially once socioeconomic status and family background is taken into account. Immigrant parents have even higher likelihoods of forming and maintaining college aspirations for their children, compared to native-born parents. This

suggests a strong degree of "immigrant optimism" among foreign-born parents of young children. (1098–99)

Raleigh and Kao also point out that the consensus among other sociologists of education is that "blacks and Hispanics have higher levels of aspirations compared to their white counterparts" (1085). These expectations reflect on the one hand the familial pressure imposed upon children and teenagers within an immigrant household perform well academically and, on the other, the assumption that a college education will lead to their adult children's acceptance into dominant American society. However, these studies do not account for the concomitant pressure that immigrant parents also put on their school-age children to maintain a Root identity through preserving the cultural ties that connect them to their parents' countries (or cultures) of origin. Thus, immigrant parents simultaneously place assimilationist and anti-assimilationist pressures upon their US-born or US-raised children and expect them to manifest their adherence to these mutually exclusive pressures through their academic success as the Caribbean American memoirists discussed in the first chapter of this book can attest. The novels under discussion here portray how the young Caribbean American protagonists navigate these contradictory expectations by articulating their own criteria for what their studies should help them achieve both personally and professionally.

Through a careful reading of select examples of contemporary YA fiction written by and about people of Caribbean descent, this chapter examines how these coming-of-age narratives depict educational spaces—whether formal, like high schools and college campuses, or informal, like community centers or the domestic space—as sites where young people learn about what it means to belong to the nation through exposure to a history of activism and/or ideas. This chapter examines how YA literature by Caribbean American authors works as a supplement of sorts to formal K–12 education in the United States. The novels assembled here have found commercial success within the YA niche in publishing. They are also complex and artful depictions of the struggles that teenagers and young adults of Caribbean heritage face as they try to find where and how they belong to American society.

With the Fire on High, Efraín's Secret, and *Make Your Home Among Strangers* chronicle the process through which the protagonist learns to navigate the formal schooling opportunities available to him or her within institutions, while *Juliet Takes A Breath, The Sun Is Also a Star,* and *American Street* focus more on the important mentoring role that family members play for students who try to make sense of their academic ambitions as part of larger personal problems. These two approaches, formal and institutional on the one hand

and informal and familial on the other, frame how these texts portray what I contend are three main aspects of the Caribbean version of the YA genre:

- claiming one's sexuality,
- pursuing one's academic ambitions, and
- claiming one's Caribbean heritage as a personal choice rather than as either a duty or a legacy passed down by the parents.

This latter aspect is distinct from, and yet often tied to, a greater understanding of how structural barriers prevent members of minority communities from having equal access to the privileges and benefits of full citizenship in the United States. The teenage and twenty-something protagonists undergo primarily internal transformations: they change their outlook on the options available to them and leverage their networks of peers, friends, and mentors to better navigate structural barriers. Most importantly, these texts validate the protagonists' unique Caribbean American experience as distinct from, yet just as defining as, the parents' immigrant experience.

CLAIMING ONE'S SEXUALITY

Becoming a young adult involves taking ownership over one's own desire, sexual preferences, and sexual encounters. This process is fraught because it is one of the developmental areas for which parental guidance is only of limited use. Figuring out how to balance sexual desire and identity formation is a key through-line in *Juliet Takes a Breath*, *With the Fire on High*, *The Sun Is Also a Star*, *American Street*, and *Make Your Home Among Strangers*. These texts avoid the cliché of fetishizing the loss of virginity and, instead, feature female protagonists making conscious and thoughtful decisions about their lives as women with sexual needs, desires, and considerations beyond pleasing their partners. As these young women consider their options, they do so fully conversant with American sexual mores rather than simply following the conventions and expectations of their Caribbean cultural heritage.

In *Make Your Home Among Strangers*, Lizet was a model student throughout high school even though nobody in her family expects her to pursue her studies beyond graduation. Unlike her older sister, who miscalculates her boyfriend's interest in marriage and becomes a single mother living at home, Lizet uses birth control when she has sex with her high school boyfriend. She wants to control her own destiny. The collapse of her family unit coincides with Lizet's announcement of her acceptance into Rawlings, further undermining the young woman's faith in romantic love as the foundation for anything lasting. Her first semester at the liberal arts college allows the Cuban American young woman to heal from the chaos of her parents' divorce and begin envisioning a future for herself as an independent woman. This helps Lizet distance herself emotionally and break up with her high school boyfriend and, in effect, with her mother and sister as well since none of the three understand or support Lizet's ambitions as legitimate.

Both Lizet's sister and her mother lean into biological determinism by embracing the trope of motherhood, personally and communally, as their defining identities during the time Lizet has been gone. The mother dedicates herself to activism within the Cuban American community to redefine her self-worth after the divorce. Ironically, her emotional detachment allows Lizet to connect with her father and see him simply as someone who had the courage to walk away from an unhappy circumstance. In keeping with the novel's feminist ethos, Lizet befriends a young white man of limited socioeconomic means who works as a resident assistant. Their platonic friendship teaches Lizet to be more American in her pursuit of individual opportunities that come her way.

Make Your Home Among Strangers keeps immigration at a distance by including a secondary storyline focusing on a fictionalized version of the custody battle over the young Cuban refugee, Elián González, between the United States, the Cuban American community in Miami, and the Cuban government. In contrast, *American Street* and *The Sun Is Also a Star* depict the topic more directly by portraying their teenage protagonists' sexual awakenings against the backdrop of their parents' immigration troubles. In the author's note, Zoboi explains that some of her inspiration for Fabiola came from current events:

> When Trayvon Martin was killed in Florida in February of 2012, he had been on the phone with Rachel Jeantel, the daughter of a Haitian immigrant. During her testimony in the George Zimmerman trial, I recognized a little bit of myself in Rachel, and in many Haitian teen girls I've worked with over the years. We fold our immigrant selves into this veneer of what we think is African American girlhood. The result is more jagged than smooth. This tension between our inherited identity and our newly adopted selves filters into our relationships with other girls and the boys we love, and into how we interact with the broken places around us. (325–26)

As the US-born daughter of a Haitian woman, Valerie, Fabiola Toussaint is one such teenage girl trying to fit in to the model of African American girlhood in Detroit. Soon after their plane lands in the United States from Haiti, immigration officials separate the family by apprehending Valerie for overstaying her visa when she was pregnant with her daughter.

Fabiola's coming of age story is tragic in an iconic Caribbean American way, where her romantic life takes a backseat to her filial duties. Her longing to be reunited with Valerie makes Fabiola vulnerable to a local police detective's manipulation: she offers Fabiola the chance to speak to her mother if the teenager informs on her cousin's boyfriend, Dray, a known drug dealer. The teenager feels torn between her conflicting familial duties to her mother and her cousin, Donna. *American Street* introduces the theme of claiming one's sexuality through Fabiola's attraction to Kasim, a hard-working young man who is Dray's best friend. Donna and her sisters encourage Fabiola to pursue a relationship with Kasim, but every step she takes in her courtship makes her mother's absence more unbearable. Eventually, the moral compromise she reaches costs Fabiola her love: Kasim is shot and killed during the drug raid. Detective Stevens keeps up her end of the bargain and gives the family both enough money to leave Michigan and the name of a contact person in ICE so they can reconnect with Valerie: "'She's already started the termination of proceedings,' Detective Stevens says. 'ICE will drop the charges and release your mother into the United States'" (319). The promised family reunion does not take place within the novel's time frame, but it lies ahead in the not-too-distant future and involves further family uprooting to a different state.

Whereas the tragic price Fabiola pays for her sexual awakening parallels Puerto Rican Maria's loss of Tony in the musical *West Side Story*, the resolution to Natasha Kingsley's love story takes on the quality of a fairy tale in *The Sun Is Also a Star*. As teenagers in love, Natasha and Fabiola feel that their parents' irregular immigration status negatively impacts their ability to fully explore fulfilling relationships with American young men. Natasha resents sharing her family's fate as they prepare to self-deport from the United States after the father's DUI arrest. Like Valerie and Fabiola Toussaint were in *American Street*, the Kingsleys are also a mixed-status family, though only her younger brother is a US citizen in *The Sun Is Also a Star*. Natasha left Jamaica as a child and no longer has distinct memories of her life in the island. She experiences a whirlwind one-day romance as she runs around New York City trying to secure a stay order for her family to remain in the United States. Her Korean American suitor, Daniel Jae Ho Bae, pursues her to while away the hours before his entrance interview with an Ivy League university he does not want to attend. Daniel asks Natasha questions from an online quiz designed to help people fall in love and, though she initially rebuffs his efforts, he gradually wins her over. Both teens have to remind themselves, "we cannot have sex in the *norebang,*" the private song room in a Korean karaoke bar where they have lunch (173). Though the couple try to maintain a long-distance relationship after Natasha's departure, it does not last. The novel's fairy-tale dimension becomes evident in the last chapter, which takes place many years after their meeting and separation. Natasha and Daniel recognize one another while on board a flight and the novel closes with the suggestion that their sexual tension was still strong. Through the trope of teenage romance, *The Sun Is Also a Star* suggests that there is potential for Asian American and Black allyship in the United States, even as it acknowledges the lingering tensions and distrust between these two communities in social contexts such as the Black haircare store that Daniel's family runs.

Unlike their Cuban, Jamaican or Haitian American counterparts, the Puerto Rican protagonists of the next three novels under discussion do not have to contend with questions about their families' immigrant status because Puerto Ricans have birthright US citizenship. However, like Fabiola in *American Street* and Natasha in *The Sun Is Also a Star*, the teenage protagonists of these novels fall in love with people from cultures different from their own and thus learn to negotiate cross-cultural dialogue between Black and Caribbean communities as the backdrop to their romantic relationships. The titular character of *Efraín's Secret* narrowly escapes Kasim's fate in *American Street*. After getting shot during a turf battle between rival gangs, Efraín agrees to testify against his assailant and his family sends him back to Puerto Rico for his own safety. This arrangement entails Efraín's separation from his friends, family, and his Black girlfriend, Candace, whose family moved to New York after being displaced from New Orleans during Katrina. However, much like *The Sun Is Also a Star*, the novel ends with the possibility that the couple will reunite during Christmas break, when Candace will visit Efraín in Puerto Rico. Fairytale endings notwithstanding, Efraín's view of manhood in general and romantic relationships is complicated long before he gets mixed up with gangs and agrees to run drugs to save money for college. The burden of keeping his Dominican father's infidelity hidden from his Puerto Rican mother eventually leads to the two men's estrangement, a conflict that is only briefly repaired when the teenager's life is in jeopardy.

Throughout the novel, Efraín's primary focus is on his academic achievements, his GPA and SAT scores, as he tries to gauge how likely he is to gain admission to any of the Ivy League Schools. The chapters in the novel are titled after a list of SAT words Efraín is trying to memorize. This obsession comes to a head in a heated exchange he has with Candace. The argument that temporarily ends their relationship has to do with their conflicting views of excellence in higher education, a distinction Candace encapsulates in one brief sentence: "Because just as much as you want to go to an Ivy League school, Efraín, it's important to me to go to an HBCU" (127). The underlying tension in this statement reflects the couple's conflicting views of belonging. Efraín, whose Puerto Rican / Dominican family is of mixed race, thinks academic and social success is only possible through the accreditation offered by the most elite bastions of white privilege such as Harvard University. According to her brief book jacket bio, this resonates personally with Quintero, who describes her own experience as a "Ivy League homegirl." For her part, Candace values the culture-affirming space that HBCUs offer for ambitious Black professionals in the making, such as Kamala Harris. Candace sees college as a chance to learn in an environment in which she is not in the minority. Both Candace and Efraín are too proud to back down from their respective views of excellence and, thus, they never quite reconcile. By testifying, however, Efraín does right by his dead best friend even though it costs him a chance to mend his broken relationship. Ironically, however, Efraín ends up getting the very same type of educational experience Candace had wanted for herself: by pursuing his university studies in his mother's island of origin, Efraín will learn in an environment surrounded by people who share his ethnicity but not his first language. Both culturally and linguistically, Efraín has more in common with the dominant white society of the US mainland he left behind than with island Puerto Ricans, so his process of identity formation and belonging will be interrupted by an uncertain outcome.

Puerto Rico is also where Emoni Santiago's father, Julio, goes to mourn the loss of his Black American wife after she dies in childbirth. At the start of *With the Fire on High*, we learn that Julio makes yearly visits to Philadelphia so he can spend time with his daughter and granddaughter. By the novel's end, Julio finally relocates to the mainland full time to babysit his granddaughter while Emoni attends Drexel University part time and works in a restaurant to pay the bills. Emoni was raised by her Puerto Rican *abuela* or grandmother who then also helps the teenager care for her own daughter, Babygirl, while she finishes high school. Emoni has experienced one of the more burdensome outcomes of exploring one's sexuality of all the teenage protagonists under discussion. She is a teenage mother with a child in preschool and a somewhat contentious relationship with her daughter's father, Tyrone. While Emoni recalls feeling pressured into having sex before she was ready, when she realizes she is pregnant, she chooses motherhood over an abortion and subsequently prioritizes learning to become a responsible parent over exploring other romantic possibilities. Despite this, Emoni supports other teenagers' romantic lives. She even prepares a delicious meal for her best friend, Angelica, to woo her girlfriend.

The novel's arc sees Emoni learn to balance her desire to be a good mother with the need to trust Tyrone to spend time with Babygirl. Along the way, she also learns to relax and let herself get to know and feel attracted to Malachi, a new kid in school who moved at the start of senior year to get away from his brother's murder. Having raised three generations of Santiagos, Emoni's *abuela* has fallen in love and is ready to prioritize her relationship over her parental duties once Emoni graduates from high school. Acevedo's savvy choice to have the grandmother model a sexually desiring woman willing to take a chance on love late in life makes it possible for Emoni and her new love interest, Malachi, to not rush into bed since they each clearly have emotional trauma to work through. A sweet example of this comes in the chapter called "Prom," which opens with the following observation: "Although Malachi and I talk every day and see each other in school, we've been more chill since Spain. We've fallen into an easy rhythm of friends who kiss and talk all the time, but there's no pressure for much else" (373). Although *With the Fire on High* shows a multi-generational family in which sexuality has brought its share of heartbreak and hardship related to pregnancy, it also affirms each generations' love for the others and holds up the possibility that sex and romance may happen later in one's life.

In contrast, Gabby Rivera's *Juliet Takes a Breath,* features a central conflict that threatens to shake the Palante family's foundation: Juliet postpones coming out to her family until the evening she leaves for Oregon to pursue her summer internship. She wants her mother to accept her as a queer woman but fears rejection. Privately, she has already come to terms with her lesbianism and had her first girlfriend while studying away at college. This is an important step in her development since Juliet has found an LGBTQ+ community away from her neighborhood and been accepted as a member. Her romantic relationship, however, did not work out and she has suffered her first heartbreak much like Efraín and Natasha in their respective narratives.

While at college, Juliet takes the initiative to arrange and pursue her own paid internship as a research assistant for Harlowe Brisbane, a white feminist lesbian author based in the Oregon. This shows Juliet is savvier at navigating the somewhat byzantine world of college career centers and success coaching than Lizet in *Make Your Home Among Strangers.* Whereas the Cuban American freshman almost lets her impostor syndrome cost her the internship opportunity one of her professors had recruited her for in Capó Crucet's novel, the Puerto Rican sophomore of Rivera's book emails the author of her favorite book, *Raging Flower,* and arranges to spend the summer in Portland. Despite her initiative, young Juliet has much to learn when she arrives in the West Coast, from being asked about her pronouns, to meeting women in polyamorous relationships, to trying to reconcile her expectations of East Coast white people with the hippies of Portland, Oregon. Thus, Juliet's summer internship becomes an in-depth education in how adult, politically committed, multiracial lesbians live, argue, and love in community. But, because this learning process takes place within the confines of a majority-white city, Juliet finds it difficult to figure out how the lessons she learns there could apply to her own life.

Juliet's bisexual cousin, Ava, teaches her how to incorporate her feminism and queer identities with her *latinidad* by introducing her to the queer party scene in Miami, "the Clipper Queerz," which incorporates hair grooming and LGBTQ+ acceptance at a libidinal level (202). At one such gathering, Juliet decides to get her first undercut despite not having cut her hair since elementary school. She makes this decision only after confiding in the nonbinary hairdresser she thinks of as "Blue Lips," about her mixed feelings about having her hairstyle reflect her sexual identity:

"You gonna get a cut?" Blue Lips asked.
"I'm afraid of looking like a dyke," I said.
"Are you a dyke?"
"I think so."
"Then no matter what you do with your hair, you're gonna look like a dyke," Blue Lips said. They smiled at me and patted the chair.
I said a quick prayer to La Virgen.
"I hadn't thought about it like that," I replied. (211)

This is an interesting moment because it marks the first time Juliet has voiced such doubts about the possibility of aligning her physical appearance with her self-identity. Despite having come out to her family, survived her first relationship and break-up with a woman, and spent half the summer working for a lesbian author, Juliet's impulsive choice to cut her hair symbolizes her willingness to stop living according to the rules she had set for herself as a ten-year-old. Chronologically, Juliet's epiphany about being ready to live by a new set of rules comes on the heels of her aunt's disclosure of her own past same-sex relationship as a teenager. This is the third female coming out story within the family within the novel (first Juliet's and then Ava's); whereas the young women's declarations were self-affirming acts of discovery and ownership, the aunt shares her story with Juliet to reassure her that her mother will eventually accept her as a complex human being. This becomes an interesting trope in this novel where family members introduce our protagonists to the importance of recognizing their own complex reality as women who are both Caribbean and American, mixed-race, multilingual, and desiring whether queer, straight, or bisexual, feminist, and unwilling to live by *machista* or patriarchal gender roles.

ACADEMIC AMBITIONS

The novels under discussion acknowledge the tension between actual learning and the outward trappings of academic credentials. During her internship, Juliet Palante learns how feminism can be a praxis for living as well as for one's research practice. Professionally, the research Harlowe Brisbane asks her to conduct on the biographies and life writings of Puerto Rican and other women of color make the protagonist suddenly aware of Caribbean American foremothers from whom she could learn. On a personal note, she discovers her own voice and gains clarity about her desire to become a writer, an epiphany that will presumably guide her subsequent studies. *Juliet Takes a Breath* illustrates this progress structurally by opening with the fan letter Juliet writes to Harlowe Brisbane and closing with the combination poem / affirmation letter that the young Puerto Rican woman writes to herself. This later document, then, suggests that the pages between these two bookends, which constitute the bulk of *Juliet Takes a Breath,* are the result of Juliet's efforts to write her truth and her journey into being rather than the work of the novel's actual author, Gabby Rivera.

In a similar way, the structure of *Efraín's Secret* shows its protagonist's progression through its use of the word definition mechanism. The first chapter features the definition of "imperative," and reflects the self-imposed pressures that Efraín contends with in his academic and interpersonal interactions. The last chapter, "fervent," signals that the more mature Efraín regards the chance to pursue higher education in a context free from the threat of gang retribution is now a guiding passion rather than an obligation. His obsession with SAT scores and schemes to gain admission to Harvard University illustrates that Efraín has given more thought to the prestige that an academic credential can give him professionally than to the opportunity higher education in any setting presents for pursuing a course of studies that would be intellectually stimulating or, more practically, that would lead to a well-paying career.

While she imagines the educational opportunities available to her in the United States, Natasha in *The Sun Is Also a Star* feels duty-bound to pursue a practical course of studies to help her undocumented family financially. Prior to the immigration proceedings, Natasha had put pressure on herself to succeed academically because she loves to learn but also because she is living in a world where DACA-mentation is not an option. Her undocumented mother saves and scrimps so that she can afford to buy her daughter a "good" fake birth certificate or social security card so that she has a shot at being admitted to college. Natasha disapproves of her father's profession as an actor because it does not result in a reliable income and thus, despite loving and doing well in physics, however, Natasha has already decided to compromise her dreams and pursue a major with more reliable employment options: data science. She tells Daniel, her Korean American love interest, the story of how she determined her future field of study: "This isn't destiny. I chose this career. It didn't choose me. I'm not fated to be a data scientist. There's a career section in the library at school. I did research on growing fields in the sciences and, ta-da. No fate or destiny involved, just research" (98–99). The novel presents Natasha as an organized and ambitious young woman on the brink of realizing her dreams of pursuing higher education in the United States.

Though the family ultimately complies with the immigration order and returns to Jamaica voluntarily, this outcome is far from the failure Natasha would have anticipated during her efforts to stay in the United States. The concluding section informs readers on how her life went after settling down in Jamaica and attributes its positive direction to her interaction with Daniel, who had told her of his plans to defy his family's expectations that he become a doctor by studying English literature instead: "One good thing did come from her time with Daniel. She looks for a passion and finds it in the study of physics" (339). The narrator's editorial remark here aligns with Daniel by valuing the pursuit of knowledge above the unimaginative self-sacrifice Natasha had contemplated earlier. This statement suggests Daniel's influence helps Natasha to act more like an American—by being true to herself—than would have been possible for her if she had stayed in the United States.

Two other novels provide clear illustrations of how a Caribbean American character's perceived obligation to her family comes at the expense of her own academic ambitions. The first is *American Street* where Chantal, Fabiola's oldest cousin, forgoes the chance to study at a research university so she can stay close to her family and help them. Like Natasha, Chantal is not a United States citizen; the difference, however, is that she does have "resident alien" status (Zoboi 116). Both the Haitian and Jamaican matriarchs expect their daughters to shine academically, much like Karine Jeane-Pierre's parents expected their daughter to become a doctor. The interior monologue in the chapter "Chantal's Story" reveals the young woman's pragmatic choice to honor her filial duty rather than take a chance exploring her own potential: "Ma wanted me to go to a big university. She told me not to worry about her and my sisters, to just do my own thing. But how could I? This is home. My mother is home. My sisters are home" (117). The drama plays out in full circle as Chantal's mother, Matant Jo, constantly reminds her oldest daughter of how disappointed she is in her: "'You were my only hope. You think it was my dream for you to end up at community college? All those good grades? That big SAT score, and Wayne County Community College is all you have to show for it?'" (17). Though her mother has great expectations, these do not accord with how dependent she and the other two girls are on Chantal's resourcefulness and innate sense of responsibility. On the few instances where Fabiola gets to speak to her mother at the detention center, Valerie also puts similar pressure to succeed academically on her only daughter: "'How is school? Fab, tell me that you're studying lots?'" (159). Unfortunately, both the difficulty of being separated from her mother and learning to communicate in English rather than Creole at school combine to make Fabiola struggle to live up to her mother's expectations.

The second novel that illustrates how stifling a Caribbean American character's sense of obligation to her family can be is *Make Your Home Among Strangers*. The first chapter is narrated by present-day Lizet, who lives on the West Coast and works as a lab manager for a marine biology research institute. She describes amusing her boss by mining her past for stories about what her parents would throw into the canal across the street from her childhood house in Miami, Florida, including, among other things, "any obvious junk mail, before I knew to grab the brochures from colleges from out of her [mother's] hands lest she send them sailing from her grip" (Capó Crucet, 2). The battle for control about information of educational opportunities available to Lizet encapsulates the conflict between her and her mother ten years earlier during her freshman year at Rawlings, a prestigious liberal arts college on the East Coast. Where Chantal felt unable to seize on her mother's encouragement, Lizet feels almost crushed by the opposite familial reaction: the insulting burden of low expectations. Like Efraín, Lizet's academic success is due primarily to her own initiative and ambition to succeed. She only tells her family that she has applied to colleges after she:

> faked my mom's signature on the deposit waiver the school had mailed along with my letter and returned with it the card saying I accepted my spot in the class of 2003. I eventually mustered the ovaries to show them the folder full of papers Rawlings had sent me with my financial aid package, using the

official-looking forms to confuse them into thinking it was too late to fight me about it. (35–36)

Lizet's deception, coming on the heels of her older sister becoming a single mother, destabilizes the family so much that the parents end up divorcing and the father sells the family home. However, Lizet's scheming effectively give her the means to escape this otherwise paralyzing scenario.

Even though her father's initial reaction to the news of Lizet's acceptance was to tell her he felt betrayed by her actions, he eventually reconciles with his daughter and supports her ambition once he sees that she is determined to make something of herself in a predominantly white institution. Lizet's mother and sister, however, almost enjoy hearing about Lizet's precarious academic standing at the end of the first semester, accusing her of thinking she was better than either of them. Her desire to leave home and pursue a career instead of settling for marriage and a job threatens both the women in Lizet's family because these choices seem like an indication that Lizet has turned her back on her heritage in favor of assimilating into mainstream white American culture. Soon after she returns home after freshman year, Lizet takes a chance and accepts the internship that one of her biology mentors had arranged for her. Thus, for both Lizet in *Make Your Home Among Strangers* and Juliet in *Juliet Takes a Breath,* paid academic internships give them a convenient way to escape their respective families' disapproval as they test out their own future career pathways.

Emoni Santiago experiences a similar professional epiphany in *With the Fire on High* but through a high school class on culinary science rather than via a formal internship opportunity. One unusual element of this class was its travel component: students are expected to fund-raise the cost of their airfare to Spain, where they would spend a week learning about the restaurant industry first-hand and helping in a restaurant kitchen. Like Lizet, Emoni suffers from impostor syndrome due to the scrutiny she endured while pregnant during freshman year. However, Emoni's family strongly supports the teenager, who has proven herself to be a dedicated mother, dutiful granddaughter, and good student. Her *abuela*, the teacher, the school counselor, and a local restaurant owner all work to convince Emoni that her cooking talent could not only earn her a chance to travel internationally, but also to pursue a professional education through Drexel University's culinary program. They encourage her to cook in exchange for donations toward the cost of the trip. While this extraordinary level of support might seem the novel's most obvious flight of fancy, it also calls to mind the opposite scenario where Emoni's self-doubt could have cost her the chance to graduate from high school, and thus the ability to find a career path that would provide economic security for herself and her child. Both *abuela* and Julio take up the mantle of family responsibility and self-sacrifice to allow Emoni to succeed in *With the Fire on High*, unlike Chantal's mother in *American Street* or Lizet's family in *Make Your Home Among Strangers*.

RECLAIMING HERITAGE

Emoni's trip to Spain as a Black and Puerto Rican teenager has inescapable colonial overtones. After all, slavery did not end in Puerto Rico until 1873 and the island remained a Spanish colony until the end of the Spanish-American War of 1898. However, *With the Fire on High* acknowledges the different valences that the trip presents for Emoni, as an American student, and her father Julio, as a United States-born Boricua who returned to the island and became a born-again activist for independence. Emoni describes her father's reaction thus:

> My father is big [*sic*] fan of the island. And he is not a big fan of Europe. He has a lot of ideas about the way they treated Latin America and the Caribbean when they were in power and believes they (and the United States) are the sole reason why so many of those countries are struggling now. And in case I forget how he feels, he never hesitates to launch into one of his history lessons. (*With the Fire on High* 120)

In the same way that Julio lectures Emoni on Puerto Rican history, she gives readers many history lessons about Puerto Ricans, Philadelphians, and African Americans in her role as first-person narrator. Early in the novel we hear more about her neighborhood and its unique demographic profile as a backdrop against which to better understand Malachi's misperceptions when he first meets Emoni. She explains: "In Fairhill, we are mostly Spanish-speaking Caribbeans and Philly-raised Black Americans with roots in the South. Which means, in my hood everyone's parents or great-grandparents got some kind of accent that ain't a Philly one" (68). Puerto Rican neighbors criticize her for not speaking Spanish, while African Americans (including Malachi) question whether she is Black enough to be counted among them. Because of Julio and Abuela's influence, Emoni knows and values her Caribbean heritage, but she feels disconnected from her Southern roots due to her mother's death. Emoni does maintain a culinary correspondence with her aunt Sarah in North Carolina. They exchange recipes and Sarah tells Emoni about what it was like to grow up with her mother. By the end of the novel, Emoni makes plans to meet Sarah and her cousins in person while her daughter is on vacation with Tyrone. Because of how much she has matured as a woman and a co-parent during the novel, Emoni finally makes time to connect with her Southern family and claim a bit more of her African American heritage.[2]

The reference to Malachi and Tyrone in this context illustrates an interesting pattern within these YA narratives: the Black love interests' traumatic backstories in *With the Fire on High*, *Efraín's Secret,* and *American Street* serve as an acknowledgement of sorts that Caribbean protagonists share similar hardships and life experiences with their Black neighbors. *American Street* maintains an almost unbridgeable distance between the Haitian American cousins and everyone else. The Black young men who fall within the cousins' sphere of influence do not survive the encounter. Fabiola's love interest, Kasim, is doubly marginalized: first because he grows up Muslim, and second because he holds a regular part time job rather than dealing drugs with Dray, as Fabiola's friend Imani informs her: "'Nobody really liked Kasim 'cause he wasn't a baller. You could tell by his clothes and sneakers that Dray wasn't even trying to hook him up with dough, talkin' about everybody has to earn that shit. Looks like Kasim is doing just fine without Dray's dough.'" (Zoboi 122) Thus, even in being attracted to Kasim, Fabiola performs her outsider status because she can appreciate things about him that local girls disdain. Thus, the cultural differences between the Caribbean and Black romantic partners highlight each community's precarious claim to inclusion within American mainstream society.

Fabiola was born in the United States but raised in Haiti, so when she arrives in Detroit to live with her aunt's family, she occupies a complicated subject position: she is simultaneously a cultural outsider unfamiliar with the English language and with American customs and a legal insider as a United States citizen, a type of legitimacy that Chantal lacks. Thus, she experiences a kind of culture shock that is somewhere between Natasha's in *The Sun Is Also a Star* and Juliet's in *Juliet Takes a Breath*. *American Street* centers Haiti's African-descended religious traditions as it adds an element of the fantastic to the basic story arc of intergenerational folkloric knowledge transmission. Because she had grown up watching her mother, a mambo, perform vodou

---

2. I specifically use "African American" here rather than Black because Emoni makes the point repeatedly throughout the novel that she is Black on both sides of her family. Since she was brought up by a Puerto Rican grandparent in a Caribbean ethnic enclave, the experience of going to North Carolina will allow her to experience her own Blackness through a different prism, that of a historically Black community. This distinct experience can best be understood through the framework of African American as a different diasporic community.

religious traditions, maintain an altar to their *loas*, and be mounted by the spirits, she is the only character who recognizes the local bum as being an incarnation of Le Baron Samedi. This novel, however, features two instances in which family members try to introduce one another to different parts of their heritage: Fabiola's efforts to instruct her cousins on the logic and heritage of her vodou faith fail, whereas the cousins make more inroads by serving as cultural translators and explaining to Fabiola how the social norms followed in the private American high school they attend serve as a guide for understanding American and Detroit culture. The novel's conclusion sees the entire family on the move away from Michigan and head toward the East Coast to start a new life, and the suggestion is that they will all need to undergo further acculturation once more.

American Street, Efraín's Secret, Make Your Home Among Strangers, Juliet Takes a Breath, and *The Sun Is Also a Star* all envision deterritorialization as part of their young Caribbean American protagonists' life experience. Partly, this works metaphorically, as the characters' transition away from childhood and toward adulthood. However, I would advocate a more geographic context against which to understand this narrative. When Caribbean American protagonists like Juliet or Lizet want to escape their family's restrictive interrelationships, they leverage the sheer size of the United States to physically get beyond their reach. This is the same logic the police use to put Fabiola's family beyond the sphere of influence of the gangs whose secrets they betrayed. In contrast, a Caribbean family's insular mindset can best be understood when they opt to turn back to their islands of origin rather than relocate within the United States as they seek to put distance between themselves and/or situations of emotional or physical danger. Such is the case in Julio's choice to go live in Puerto Rico after the tragic death of Emoni's mother in *With the Fire on High,* or Efraín's mother's decision to send her son to Puerto Rico after testifying at his shooter's trial in *Efraín's Secret*. On purely economic terms, Puerto Rico is a more practical option than sending Efraín to a different state because paying for out of state college tuition would have been beyond the family's limited means. This insular mindset, however, is what keeps the Kingsleys from more actively fighting their deportation order in *The Sun Is Also a Star.* Natasha thinks that the reason they are resigned to go back to Jamaica after the father's DUI arrest is due to their lack of familiarity with the American legal system.

Natasha's experience growing up as the child of undocumented migrants failed to integrate her and her American-born younger brother into Jamaican or Caribbean American diasporic society since her parents refused to discuss life back in Jamaica. Thus, the Kingsley siblings in *The Sun Is Also a Star* navigate their American life through the prism of race, as Black, but always with the dread of being found out as Others and outsiders to the national polity. Natasha's attraction to Korean American Daniel works along similar lines to the dynamics of Caribbean protagonist and their Black love interests but with some marked differences. *The Sun Is Also a Star* acknowledges and repudiates the profound anti-Blackness of those Korean Americans, like Daniel's family, who have gone into the business of selling items for Black hair care. He and Natasha find common ground in being the more Americanized children of immigrants. In addition, Daniel struggles to free himself from his parents' and his teachers' expectations that he live up to the model minority myth by mindlessly seeking out opportunities for elite credential success rather than pursue his love of writing in earnest. His courage in defying his parents' wishes inspires Natasha to follow her own heart in her new life in Jamaica, one of the clearest ways in which she lives up to the American aspect of her Caribbean American identity.

For her part, Juliet's Caribbeanness is closer to Emoni's and different from Natasha's—whereas the Jamaican teenager has grown out of her island accent and now appears to be Black for all intents and purposes, Juliet's English comes by way of her Puerto Rican family's Spanglish. In *Juliet Takes a Breath*, the protagonist's Puerto Ricanness gives her access to something Natasha desperately wants but cannot legally obtain during her adolescence: United States citizenship. Juliet's college education has made her feel out of her comfort zone during the time she spends back at her parents' apartment, but it has also given her the critical thinking tools to crack the ranks of professional researchers (as a research assistant and beginning writer). Her coursework on feminism and queer theory gives her a useful context against which to understand her own lesbian identity, though this intellectual and academic training does not prepare her to handle breaking up with her first girlfriend nor navigating the complex intersectional kinship ties of West Coast intellectual lesbian activists with whom she spends the summer. Much like Natasha learns from Daniel, Juliet learns from the white feminist Harlowe Brisbane about the importance of researching more about her Puerto Rican heritage. In this way, the family at the heart of *Juliet Takes a Breath* is different from the more politically self-aware Puerto Rican father Julio in *With the Fire on High*. So, not all Puerto Rican families place the same premium on being aware of their heritage.

The protagonists fail to either achieve the incredibly high academic goals they had set for themselves (due to injury related to drug dealing in *Efraín's Secret* or deportation in *The Sun Is Also a Star*) or else they become morally compromised in ways that do not bode well for their future trajectories as adults in their respective social spaces (cooperation with police and/or the cosmic order leads to two murders—both African American young men in *American Street*). Fixing the protagonists' plight is beyond the ken of these novels; however, some signal at a solution arrived at by adults, like sending Efraín to Puerto Rico, while others hint at a resolution, such as the promised reunion between Natasha and her love interest aboard a plane in the somewhat distant future in *The Sun Is Also a Star*. Finally, others end abruptly, like *American Street*, because they reach the natural conclusion of plunging the protagonists into a cycle of unending violence.

These novels' endings are valuable not only as object lessons about what pitfalls to avoid but also because they subvert the popular bootstrap myth by illustrating that sometimes individual effort and ambition are not enough to help characters pull themselves up the socioeconomic ladder and change their prospects. At the same time, these novels highlight and make visible the various social networks accessible to the Caribbean American protagonists through interactions with school mentors, government or law enforcement officials, flawed role models, and even friends and family. Each in their way, these people model different ways of belonging within the larger American culture against which the protagonists can expand their own limited imaginations. By learning about how others make their way in the world and navigate their own circumstances, Caribbean American young adult novels showcase their target audience's own agency to effect some change to their circumstances and take advantage of opportunities for themselves. They expand our shared set of assumptions and expectations about the struggles the next generation has had to overcome on their way to claiming their full place within the imagined community of the United States.

CHAPTER 5

Miles Morales as Multimodal Caribbean American Superhero

As the only child of a Black father and a Puerto Rican mother, young Miles Morales is the third of the various Latinx-inflected variations on the Spider-Man superhero in the Marvel comics universe. Prior to his first appearance in the fourth issue of the comic book series *Ultimate Fallout* in 2011, Marvel had already introduced two mixed-ethnicity variations on the Peter Parker original: 1992 saw the arrival of Miguel O'Hara, from Marvel's *2099: Manifest Destiny,* whom Kathryn M. Frank describes as a "half-Irish, half-Mexican" (*Graphic Borders* 243), and *Araña*/Anya Corazon, who debuted in 2004 in *Amazing Fantasy* and eventually earned her own self-titled series.[1] Latinx comic book scholar Frederick Luis Aldama finds *Araña* to be one of the more fully conceptualized Latina comic book characters: "she stays connected to her cultural roots via the memory of her Mexican mother, Sofia, and she learns much from her smart, sensitive, and strong Puerto Rican father, an investigative reporter for the *New York Herald*" (Aldama 2009, 38). The shift in gender here is notable, as is the female character's choice to identify herself via Spanish-language moniker, *Araña,* rather than embracing the English language possibilities of Spider-Girl or Spider-Woman during the series writ-

---

1. I follow the comic books' naming conventions in terms of leaving out or including accents in the Latinx characters' names. I do not hypercorrect to make them come into compliance with standard Spanish grammar.

ten by Fiona Avery and featuring art by Mark Brooks.[2] As bicultural characters, Anya Corazon and Miguel O'Hara share their Mexican heritage and their whiteness and its concomitant privileges. They may be Latinx, but they are white or white-passing Latinx characters. Both O'Hara in the 90s and Corazon more recently have enjoyed success within the comic book world, becoming popular characters who show up in other characters' story arcs. Despite this popularity, neither has broken through to other media in the same way that Miles Morales has.

Morales's success as a comic book superhero far outstrips that of his Latinx precursors. *Miles Morales: Spider-Man*, the novelization by Jason Reynolds, was a finalist for a National Book Award. And Morales is the undisputed star, though far from the only alternate Spider-Man, in the 2018 Oscar-winning film *Spider-Man: Into the Spider-Verse*. The character made his much-anticipated title video game release from Insomniac for PS5 in 2020, *Marvel's Spider-Man: Miles Morales*. It is perhaps this unique subject position as both a mixed-race and bicultural superhero that resonates so much with American audiences of all types.[3] The rest of this chapter will discuss how Miles Morales' origin story involves mixed media (comic books, films, and television); critically analyze Miles' mixed-race and bicultural subject position within the larger context of race and Caribbean identity; and finally trace how the character performs his Caribbean American identity in different media modalities. My overall argument is that Miles Morales's success in connecting with audiences across such a wide variety of platforms and demographics has to do with his appeal to an ideal of collaboration and mutual understanding between Black, Latinx, and Caribbean Americans as a triangulation of how both Hispanophone Caribbean Americans and bicultural Blacks problematize the traditional American conceptions of the color line.

---

2. The later versions of *Araña* as an older teenager change the visual and linguistic depiction of Anya Corazon. According to Frederick Luis Aldama, the series *Spider-Girl: Family Values*, written by Paul Tobin and with art by Pepe Larraz, debuted in the same year as Miles Morales. This comic series sees Anya adopt the Anglicized identity of "Spider-Girl" and, according to Aldama, "she's dark skinned and visually shown battling evil in and around a vibrant urban environment" (*Latinx Superheroes*, 68).

3. I use the term "mixed-race" with relation to Miles Morales advisedly. In the comic book version images drawn by Sara Pichelli (#1–5, #8) and David Morales (#9–12), Miles's Puerto Rican mother, Rio Morales is depicted as having light brown skin and mostly straight brown hair with a bit of a wave to it. In the film version of *Into the Spider-Verse*, Rio's skin tone stays light brown, but her hair has more curl to it. The award-winning actress voicing her character is Luna Lauren Velez, who identifies as Afro–Puerto Rican (Conde). In the video game versions of the character, both *Marvel's Spider-Man* for PS4 and the new *Marvel's Spider-Man: Miles Morales*, set to debut in time for the release of the new Play Station 5 console, Rio's race has definitively changed. She is white skinned, her eye color is lighter, and her brown hair is almost straight in texture. The actress who voices her for the 2018 game is Jacqueline Pinol, who identifies as white with "Latin parents."

ORIGIN STORY AND MIXED MEDIA

Miles Morales's origin story is multimodal and involves television in a fundamental way, thereby distinguishing him further from his Latinx Spider-forbears. Though the teenage Miles Morales has a Black American father and a Nuyorican mother across all the iterations of his story, the character's own origins can be traced back to the season two premiere episode of the television sitcom *Community* in which actor Donald Glover, playing Troy Barnes, appeared wearing a Spider-Man costume. A *USA Today* story touting the forthcoming publication of *Ultimate Fallout 4*, which would feature Miles Morales for the first time, explains that Glover had been publicly campaigning for film producers to cast a Black Spider-Man in the upcoming reboot of the Spider-Man franchise. The article quotes Michael Bendis, the comic book writer, discussing how the actor's appearance on the show inspired him:

> "He looked fantastic!" Bendis recalls. "I saw him in the costume and thought, 'I would like to read that book.' So I was glad I was writing that book."
>
> The writer gives Glover "mucho credit" for the way Miles Morales looks in *Ultimate Fallout* issue 4, which is out Wednesday and marks the first appearance of a new Spider-Man. His adventures will continue in September's *Ultimate Spider-Man* No. 1, written by Bendis and illustrated by Sara Pichelli. (Truitt)

By crediting Glover, Bendis acknowledges iconicity's collective power as a generator for self-identification and reimagination of original texts or characters. This collaborative understanding of the creative process is something Aldama values about the Miles Morales franchise as this anecdote about his daughter's affinity with the character illustrates:

> When Brian Michael Bendis (writer) and Sara Pichelli (artist) choose to re-create Spider-Man as the Puerto Rican/Black Miles Morales, they bring to it a willfulness (writing, visuals, and whatever research might be required) that engages fully our co-creative processes as Latino and African American readers; they invite us to fully co-create ourselves as Spider-Man. However, it also invites non-Latinos and non-African American readers to co-create themselves as a teen, male Blatino Spider-Man. My ten-year-old daughter, Corina, identifies as Mexipina, yet she can and does delight in imagining herself as a mixed-race Puerto Rican and African American teen wall crawler and web spinner. (92–93)

Though she is not the comic book's ideal reader, whom Aldama defines as "Latino and African American readers," Corina's mixed-race identity as an American girl of Mexican and Filipina ancestry presents no barrier to her identification with Miles Morales. The potential downside of placing so much emphasis on the "co-creative processes" that take place between writers, artists, and readers, is that the final product also runs the risk of appropriating other people's ideas, such as Donald Glover's quest for a Black Spider-Man in using the actor's likeness as a point of reference.[4] However, Glover's endorsement of, and more active participation in, co-creating the Miles Morales franchise encompasses his stint voicing the character of Miles Morales for the television version appearances in the third season of the animated series *Ultimate Spider-Man* and his cameo appearance as Miles's criminal uncle, Aaron, in the 2017 film *Spider-Man: Homecoming,* which introduced white British actor Tom Holland as the titular superhero (Schaeffer).

Given the positive response to basing Miles Morales's image on Donald Glover, the character's Blackness was a given. What was not publicly disclosed until it was explicitly mentioned in the comic books was what type of Latinx or Hispanophone Caribbean American identity would make up the other half of his background. In an interview with the web publication *LatinRapper.com* in August of 2011, then editor in chief at Marvel, Axel Alonso, teased the following when asked whether the character was "urban": "He's born and bred in Brooklyn. African-American father, Hispanic mother. We'll be getting exactly which Hispanic later—Puerto Rican, Mexican, Dominican . . . Because he's been referred to as 'Latino' a few times in the press (laughs)" (Alonso, ellipsis in original). Alonso has some strong views on nomenclature and prefers the term "Hispanic" over "Latino." The nameless interviewer then chimes in to share how Blackness and *latinidad* are intertwined in some Hispanophone Caribbean ethnicities, but not others: "It's interesting because he's being billed in some of the news stories as Black and Latino, but if you're Cuban or Dominican, the two aren't mutually exclusive" (Alonso). The assumption that Dominican and Cuban Americans embrace African ancestry as part of their national and cultural heritage is interesting but seems to imply that the intermarriage between a Black American and a Cuban or Dominican would not,

---

4. According to Schaeffer, the tradition of publicly acknowledging Glover's role in inspiring the look of Miles Morales in the comic books was continued by the film's producers: "*Spider-Verse* producer Chris Miller and co-writer/producer Phil Lord technically confirmed Glover's cameo in the film a couple weeks ahead of its theatrical release. Lord in particular noted that the movie's creatives wanted to *"tip our hat to Community and the groundswell of support for the Spider-Man of color that came out of that, and we just thought it was a neat little nod."*

in and of itself, result in the character having a mixed-race identity. By not listing Puerto Ricans and Mexicans among the group of Afro-Latino populations, the interviewer is thereby implicitly assigning these two groups a white or white-passing identity that would then result in a mixed-race identity for Miles Morales. To complicate things just a bit further, the *Hollywood Reporter* ran a quote from Shameik Moore, the African American actor who voices Miles Morales in the film, in which he incorrectly describes his character's ethnicity: "He's a black Spider-Man. Black and Mexican—I think that's very powerful and iconic," Moore said to applause, before the sizzle reel played" (Couch). While his remarks inaccurately described Morales's Latinx heritage, the publication posted no correction likely because the point of the story was to convey audiences' excitement at the prospect of the film's premiere. His comments caused no major backlash online.

However, comic book fans who identify with any aspect of Morales's ethnic or racial identity found Marvel's choice to broaden its representation of an iconic superhero absolutely affirming of their own American experience. In a personal essay introduced by his editor at the *Washington Post*, reporter David Betancourt, whose beat includes race and comic books, shared his thoughts after Miles Morales's first appearance in issue *Ultimate Fallout #4*: "I—the son of Puerto Rican man who passed his love of comics to me, and a black woman who once called me just to say she'd met Adam West—will never forget that day" (Cavna). Unlike Aldama's daughter, mentioned earlier, Betancourt is indeed the comic book's ideal reader because of his Black and Puerto Rican heritages; he sees himself represented in the hero's mixed-race identity. However, his joy extends beyond the personal and includes nameless others who, Betancourt assumes, had not yet found their own lives reflected back at them in the pages of the comic books they loved: "a black kid in D.C., a Dominican kid in the Bronx, or a young Mexicano from California being able to read a comic and come away from it saying 'I can be Spider-Man'" (Cavna). This statement is important on two levels. On the one hand, the linguistic configuration here spans along a gradient of nonwhite subject positions from Blacks and Afro-Latinx Hispanophone Caribbeans (Betancourt as Black and Puerto Rican and the imagined Dominican American reader) to unmarked Mexican Americans (assumed to be Brown or possibly to claim an Indigenous identity). On the other hand, the fact that Betancourt can simultaneously celebrate the Super-Man franchise's inclusivity via Miles Morales without pausing to acknowledge either of the two Mexican American Spider precursors (Miguel O'Hara or Anya Corazon) confirms these characters' limited impact even within the small world of comic book critics who focus on race. I would suggest here that the only difference between O'Hara, Corazon, and Morales is that the white Mexican American dimensions of the first two render them invisible, and therefore neutral, rivals for Peter Parker's superhero status, whereas Miles Morales's Blackness stands as a radical challenge to Parker's embodiment of the American everyman: the "friendly neighborhood Spider-Man" is assumed to be a white male on the cusp of adulthood.

The online backlash against Marvel's endorsement of Miles Morales assuming the Spider-Man mantle shows that some members of the public at large could not imagine Black teenagers of any kind as either "friendly" or as belonging to their imagined neighborhood, an example of "digital redlining," to use Dr. Safiya Umoja Noble's term. In *Algorithms of Oppression,* Noble uses the term to criticize "digital decisions [that] reinforce oppressive social relationships and enact new modes of racial profiling" (1). Here it is important to pause and recall that Miles Morales first appeared as a comic book character during the first term of the Obama administration and that critics, including conservative personality Glen Beck, assumed that the Obamas were somehow to blame for this development. Digital redlining can also take on the flavor of good-natured territorial disputes, such as when Betancourt writes about his desire that Miles's Latinx identity in the comic books would be revealed to be Puerto Rican, rather than Dominican, because the latter had already beaten Puerto Rico in the finals of the World Baseball Championship (Betancourt). One of the characteristics of national or ethnic groups that fall within the Caribbean American label is that they hold on to regional differences most fiercely when it comes to competitions between their islands of origin.

Though he initially felt somewhat insulted by the prospect of the film *Spider-Man: Into the Spider-Verse* being an animated feature rather than a live-action adaptation of the comic book hero, Betancourt eventually felt the thrill of recognition once again upon watching Miles on the big screen:

> When Miles pulls down his mask, that was me, as a kid, pretending my winter caps were a Spider-Man mask. The besos Miles dodges from his Latina mother? Who hasn't had an abuela or tia do the same thing to them? A brown kid speaking English and Spanish? You don't see that on Univision or Telemundo. The movie only spends a moment connecting to the culture of who Miles is, but it is a strong, heartfelt and authentically crafted moment that washed my doubts and anger away.

This statement illustrates an important way in which Marvel as a global company provides a better backdrop against which to portray the specificity of Miles's own unique Caribbean American identity than would be possible for an ethnic media company like Telemundo or Univisión with a Latinx/

Hispanic viewership that values the universal elements of *latinidad* across national backgrounds at the cost of excluding or minimizing the visibility of Afro-Latinx communities.

RACE, CULTURE, AND MILES MORALES

African American studies scholar Adilfu Nama and artist Maya Haddad have reclaimed the term "Blatino" from gay pornography to serve as a signifier of the new ways of thinking through Blackness and Latinx ethnicity as subject positions in American culture in their chapter discussing how American popular culture maps the intersections between Black and Latinx communities in its visual imaginary across various pop culture media. Nama and Haddad define their use of the term as follows: "in this essay, 'Blatino' is used as a contemporary version of the term 'Afro-Latino,' with the former construed to address the intersection (and possibly the privileging) of black racial formation alongside Latino ethnicity" (253). The term Afro-Latino describes someone whose own experience of *latinidad* is marked through their Blackness. The benefit of the neologism over the more traditional term (Afro-Latino) in the context of describing someone of mixed parentage like Miles Morales is that in its use of a capital B and beginning the syllable (Bla) it acknowledges that a non-Latino Blackness can be part of someone's heritage and lived experience without being subsumed into their *latinidad*. One example of such a subject position is Emoni Santiago, the protagonist of the YA novel *With the Fire on High*, discussed in the previous chapter. Emoni's father is Puerto Rican and her dead mother was a Black woman from the South, thereby making "Blatina" a useful way to describe her bicultural heritage.[5]

Nama and Haddad use it in reference to Miles Morales: "'Blatinoness' as a phrase, representation, and identity crops up with the comic book 'Blatinoness' of Miles Morales, a comic book Spiderman that offers a striking racial contrast in meaning against the mainstream whiteness of the Spiderman franchise with Peter Parker" (254–55). Despite acknowledging that this new reimagined version of a Latinx Spider-Man marks a significant change for the franchise, neither Nama nor Haddad think the character or his interactions contribute meaningfully to an understanding of Black or Latinx experience, and conclude that as a whole, the series amounts to nothing more than increasing the

---

5. I did not use the term "Blatina" to discuss Emoni's heritage in chapter 2 because it is not how she refers to herself.

visual representation of the superhero's Blackness which, in their view, is only an "anticlimactic racial sensibility" (258) that pales in comparison to the more robust representation of Afro-Caribbean religions and cultures in a different Marvel comic series, *The Santerians,* a group of Afro-Cuban characters who wield the super powers of *loas.*

Frederick Aldama disagrees with this dismissal of the Miles Morales comic books as only providing superficial glimpses of either Black or Puerto Rican culture in the United States. He traces the character's evolution throughout the comic book series, pointing out how the nuclear family grows to include an intergenerational dimension based on Miles's academic difficulties:

> Miles is a super smart teenager living in an apartment with his loving Nuyorican mama, Rio, and his morally rigid African American father, Jefferson Davis. When Miles' grades at school start slipping because of his superhero work, Bendis (writer) and Pichelli (artist) introduce Miles' strong-spirited, bilingual *abuela,* Gloria Morales. (82)

The extended family of the Miles Morales franchise stands in marked contrast to the Peter Parker version of the Spider-Man narrative, which insists on Aunt May's influence over the teenager as his only surviving parental figure. In this way, the comic book version of the Morales/Davis family anticipates the shift in family structure from a single-mother household to a multi-generational one in the Cuban American reboot version of the sitcom *One Day at a Time* discussed in chapter 6.

In contrast, Jayson Reynold's novelization *Miles Morales: Spider-Man* focuses primarily on the nuclear family—parents and child—and complicates this somewhat idealized social unit by showing the parents' sacrifice to ensure that Miles obtains a good education: he attends boarding school during the week and only comes home on the weekends. Though this text does not contain any overt references to any previous Spider-Man incarnations, Miles's backstory suggests that there are more than a few parallels between Peter Parker's and Miles Morales's life experiences. The first is that they are both only children. The second parallel has to do with their similar socioeconomic backgrounds. Peter's Aunt May is on a fixed income, whereas Miles Morales is a son of working professionals, his father is a police officer and his mother a nurse. Both teenagers work after school to earn money or, in Miles's case, to defray the cost of room and board, and thus help their respective families financially. The third parallel is that both the Parker and Morales/Davis families have experienced an uncle's violent death. Whereas Peter's uncle Ben is murdered by unknown assailants, Miles's uncle Aaron "had accidentally killed himself while trying to kill Miles" three years prior to the start of the novel (12).

The video game versions of the Miles Morales story add yet another level of personal tragedy to the Morales/Davis household. Miles Morales plays a supporting role in Insomniac Games' *Marvel's Spider-Man* (2018). In that interactive narrative, Peter Parker works with Jefferson Davis, Miles's father, to fight against a gang called the Inner Demons, working for the henchman Mister Negative. Davis dies during a confrontation with the gang, and Parker reaches out to Miles, who gets bitten by a radioactive spider that Peter Parker's love interest, Mary Jane, unwittingly transports from the Osborn corporation. Jefferson Davis's death weighs heavily on young Miles. Parker serves as an intermediary between the teenager and his grief in the most recent version of the videogame franchise, *Marvel's Spider-Man: Miles Morales* (2020). In the game's trailer, Parker shares words of wisdom that Davis once told him: "A hero is someone who doesn't give up. Your Dad said that. He was right. Now it's your turn. Go be a hero, Miles." This trailer emphasizes the passing of the combined legacy of leadership and courage from dead father to son via Parker's intervention, made possible by the white man's decision to relinquish the role of superhero.

In contrast, the novelization maintains the integrity of Miles Morales's nuclear family and situates the traumatic death laterally: it impacts the paternal uncle. Young Miles is bitten by a radioactive spider that crawls out from a bag where his uncle Aaron had stuffed the tech he had stolen and planned to sell. *Miles Morales: Spider-Man* fully explores the irony of a Black character bearing the name Jefferson Davis via an excerpt from the lecture the history teacher (and arch-villain in disguise) Mr. Chamberlain gives in class: "'Jefferson Davis. The president of the Confederacy during the American Civil War. The man who appointed Robert E. Lee general of the Army of Northern Virginia, to lead the most important Confederate army'" (Reynolds, 114). Whereas the videogame Peter Parker promotes pride and understanding between the generations, the white intermediary here actively tries to sow dissension between father and the son in the novelization. Upon hearing his father's name spoken by his racist teacher, "Miles drifted in and out of the lecture, not only dealing with the sandalwood leaping from the back of Alicia's neck, but also the fact that his father's name was the same name as the man who was fighting to keep slavery alive" (115). *Miles Morales: Spider-Man* acknowledges Miles's mixed-race heritage but spends more time contending with what it means for Miles to be a Black man in America than it does imagining how his *latinidad* impacts his manhood or how society views him. This could reflect Reynold's own identity as a non-Caribbean Black man who has won multiple Coretta Scott King awards for his young adult fiction.[6]

The trope of Miles having difficulty behaving in his history class simultaneously illustrates the dynamic of the school-to-prison pipeline through the teacher's over-policing of Black students' speech and behavior and Mr. Chamberlain's willful conflation of a defense of slavery as a benign institution that was part of a genteel Southern heritage rather than a legacy of white supremacy. Though the novel ostensibly tells the superhero's backstory, the arc of the school subplot celebrates young people's activism rather than any feat of derring-do made possible by a mutant arachnid. The novel ends on an activist note with students lifting their voices to affirm their shared humanity by screaming, "WE ARE PEOPLE!" in opposition to their teacher's dehumanizing rhetoric and humiliating punishments (261). In showcasing regular young people's power to change the oppressive circumstances in which they live, *Miles Morales: Spider-Man* unapologetically demonstrates that Black lives do indeed matter. Given the book's target audience, this is a powerful message with which to end.

Miles Morales: Spider-Man also foregrounds race in two affective ways that highlight how the Caribbean American protagonist experiences belonging and Relation identity: through friendship and romance. Miles's best friend is Ganke, a Korean American fellow student at the Brooklyn Visions Academy. He enjoys spending time with the Morales/Davis family because he is still adjusting to his parents' divorce. Ganke is the only character besides Jefferson Davis who knows Miles's secret alter-ego. While original comic book writer Michael Brian Bendis created Ganke specifically to be Miles's best friend, the revamped Tom Holland version of Peter Parker in *Spider-Man: Homecoming* and *Spider-Man: Far from Home*, also has an Asian best friend, Ned Lees (played by Filipino American actor Jacob Batalon) to replace the comic book series' Harry Osborn (son of the Goblin). In an interview quoted in the MCU Exchange, Bendis expressed surprise and appreciation of fan theories that the film's writers may have turned to the comic book version for inspiration. Bendis is quoted as saying that he had not yet seen the film and was not involved in its production: "'But yeah, it's bizarre and flattering,' the writer continued. "I don't even know that Ganke was the inspiration, or that they got to this place on their own. It seems like it might have been, but no one's told me. . . . But Ganke wasn't part of Peter's story—he was part of Miles'" (Parker, ellipsis

---

6. According to the official website for the American Library Association, which gives out the Coretta Scott King awards, these prizes "are given annually to outstanding African American authors and illustrators of books for children and young adults that demonstrate an appreciation of African American culture and universal human values."

in original). The issue here is not Ned Leeds's origin story as a character but, rather, the decision to cast an Asian American actor like Batalon to fulfill the role of Peter Parker's best friend.[7] While the question of influence may never be fully answered, I have already mentioned that *Spider-Man: Homecoming* nods toward the Miles Morales universe in casting Donald Glover as Miles's uncle Aaron.

The second affective way in which race plays a part of Reynold's Miles Morales is through his crush on Alicia, a fellow classmate from a rich family who are "major donors to BVA, making it possible for kids like Miles and Winnie and Judge to attend" (Reynolds, 85). The class disparity between Miles and his love interest is in keeping with Marvel's overall depiction of Spider-Man as a product of working-class America. Unlike Miles and despite her Spanish-sounding first name, Alicia is not at all mixed-race; instead, the third-person narrator tells us, "She was Harlem royalty. Old black money. A descendant of artists who hobnobbed with people like Langston Hughes and Jacob Lawrence" (85). Miles's attraction to Alicia repeats a pattern we saw in the previous chapter, where Caribbean American teenage protagonists find themselves attracted to Black young men (in *American Street, With the Fire on High*) or young women (*Efraín's Secret*). Miles and Ganke's interracial friendship may also be read as a variant of Natasha and Daniel's attraction to one another in *The Sun Is Also a Star*. By connecting with someone from a more established Black family, Miles and the novelization as a text broaden the limited stereotypes that associate Black families only with poverty and/or crime. Like Efraín's girlfriend, Candace, Alicia is confident and proud of her heritage as a young Black woman. And both Miles and Efraín learn to speak up for themselves and to value their respective heritages from interacting with such mature Black female characters.

Thus, the Miles Morales intertexts portray Caribbean American belonging in multiple registers: interculturally, linguistically, academically, tragically, and supernaturally. As a mixed-race figure, the various incarnations of Miles explicitly forge allegiances between Asian Americans, whites, Blacks, and Puerto Ricans based on the affective ties they share (friendship, loss, supernatural abilities, and attraction) rather than on the differences that render their experiences distinct. Morales seems fated to join the permanent cast of the MCU superheroes, which means that new generations of animated film fans and comic book aficionados will see themselves and their lives (and maybe even their grandmothers!) represented within the pages of this main-

---

7. Ned Leeds was a character created by Stan Lee with art by Steve Ditko. At that time, he was depicted as a white man with blond hair. He first appeared in the 1964 edition of *The Amazing Spider-Man #18*, which has recently been reprinted within a compendium of Stan Lee's work called, *Amazing Spider-Man Epic Collection: Great Responsibility. Vol. 1.*

stream franchise. And, thus, this complex performance of Caribbean American belonging will reverberate across the ages and mediascapes to come.

PERFORMING CARIBBEAN AMERICANNESS

Though the announcement regarding Miles Morales's ethnic origins as Black and Puerto Rican comic book superhero was greeted with much excitement, none of the issues collected as the three-volume *Miles Morales: The Ultimate Spider-Man* leverages his Puerto Rican identity as a plot point in any degree. Neither he nor Rio ever speak Spanish, nor are the family's foodways featured as distinctive. To add insult to injury, the comic book version kills off Miles's mother Rio, rather than either his father Jefferson Davis or Uncle Aaron. The linguistic complexity of Miles's subject position, though hinted at in the comic books that originated the character, can only really be explored in longer formats such as the film adaptation and novelization by Jason Reynolds. These texts give Miles space to think through his personal and familial dynamic, a chance the original Peter Parker was denied twice over by the untimely deaths of both his parents and the tragic murder of his uncle. Thus, my analysis of this character's Caribbean American heritage focuses on those media story arcs that emphasize Miles' ethnic identity as a tangible part of what makes him Caribbean American.

Miles Morales: Spider-Man tackles the biggest question Latinx readers like me have had about this particular Spider-Man: why does this teenage boy bear his mother's last name rather than his father's, given what we know about his parentage and how both Latinx and American naming customs function? The answer comes in two stages: the first involves humor and takes place when Miles's roommate and best friend, Ganke, asks him why he doesn't use his father's last name before experiencing a minor epiphany: "Oh . . . snap. *Miles Davis!*" (20, ellipsis in original). Ganke's comment points out how awkward it would be for a nonmusical teenager to be the namesake of a jazz legend. However, Miles himself provides a second possible reason for bearing his mother's surname: "Back in the day, my pops and my uncle did enough dirt in their lives to make Davis a bad word in some circles. I look just like them both and live in the same neighborhood, so, I don't know, I wonder" (21). Miles's uncertainty about the accuracy of his explanation suggests that this topic is not one his family is comfortable discussing, especially given the circumstances of his uncle's death.

Ganke is also the audience's stand-in as we first see the Morales/Davis family perform their mixed heritage at the table. Sunday dinner is an important event in the household and the family eats using Mr. Davis's heirloom china, "passed down from his grandmother" (1). Ganke is a regular at Miles's house for Sunday dinner before the two of them return to Brooklyn Visions Academy. Though Mr. Davis complains about how expensive it is to feed an extra guest, Mrs. Morales reassures her son's best friend: "Ganke, wash your hands and sit down. You know you're always welcome here, even if it's for dinner number two. Tonight we're having chicharón de pollo" (5). Ganke looks to Miles's father, whom he calls Mr. Jeff, for an explanation of what his wife is about to serve, only to be reassured it's a Puerto Rican version of fried chicken. Ganke's presence requires a culinary translation. When Miles is by himself thinking about his favorite meal, "pasteles," the narrator does not let readers know that this dish is a Puerto Rican version of a tamal, with a masa made from plantains or yuca rather than corn, wrapped in banana leaves, and boiled (6).

Cooking and eating are only two of the ways in which the novelization highlights the Caribbean American dimensions of Miles's home life. Later in the novel, Miles arrives home from school bearing a pizza and a rose for his mother, only to find his parents dancing along to salsa music sung by Afro-Cuban singer extraordinaire, Celia Cruz. When he expresses mock disgust at the spectacle of his parents enjoying themselves, Rio, his mother, twirls Miles around and instructs him on how to move properly on the dancefloor: "Less culo, more waistline. Hip. Hip. Let your body do what it wants" (174). This bit of instruction contrasts with the solitary and painful trial-and-error process Miles has followed as he learns how to use his new Spider-powers. Finally, though there are no descriptions of Puerto Rican flags anywhere, the novel does feature more than a few instances where Rio Morales exclaims, "Wepa!" the all-purpose Puerto Rican catchphrase.[8] Miles never says this to himself, nor does he ever think in Spanish at all according to the narrator.

In contrast, the film version of Miles Morales's tale, *Spider-Man: Into the Spider-Verse,* shows the young man deftly navigating his family's bicultural heritage by responding in English or Spanglish to his mother's Spanish language harangues.[9] These brief domestic scenes take place early in the film,

---

8. The advanced trailer for the PS5 videogame, *Marvel's Spider-Man: Miles Morales,* more than makes up for the absence of Puerto Rican flags from previous iterations of this story. Rio and Miles have left Brooklyn and moved to Harlem, where Rio is running for office. As Miles and Ganke make their way through the crowded street-fair to go listen to her stump speech, they are surrounded by a surfeit of mini-Puerto Rican flags for sale from street vendors and various stalls.

9. Miles's American accent when saying a few words of Spanish recalls a young Rudy Huxtable's efforts to be a part of her mother Claire's phone conversations with her own Dominican relatives in *The Cosby Show.* In a listicle celebrating the show's thirtieth anniversary, Fisher, Ruffolo, and Meeser explain that Claire was supposed to be Dominican and Phylicia Rashad's ability to speak Spanish was what won her the role.

proving that while this is an aspect of the teenager's life, it is not how he publicly defines himself. Ultimately, the most important aspect of the multimodal representation of Miles Morales as a new kind of superhero comes down to representation. By showing a Blatino character who is smart, educated, hardworking, and dedicated to saving his neighbors from dangerous evil forces, this new iteration of the Spider-Man franchise lets readers see themselves in Miles and celebrate his achievements as not only possible but desirable. Miles Morales is the intersectional superhero version of the protagonists in the YA novels discussed in chapter 4: his biggest problem is figuring out who he wants to be and how his education can open doors for him while it has apparently warped so many other brilliant minds toward the petty pursuits of power and greed.

PART 3

SEEING OURSELVES REFLECTED BACK

CHAPTER 6

Visualizing Belonging

The most iconic moment of the Super Bowl LVI's halftime show may have been Jennifer Lopez's grand gesture of opening her Star-Spangled-Banner feather cape to reveal the Puerto Rican flag on the inside. This sartorial display of dual allegiance to the United States and Puerto Rico was matched sonically by the singer/dancer/actor calling out verses from her song "Let's Get Loud" as her preteen, Emme, sang the chorus from Bruce Springsteen's most misunderstood anthem, "Born in the USA."[1] The scene had an even more moving beginning, with Emme and dozens of other children sitting inside silvery cages singing in chorus to their mother's song. Mother and child were eventually reunited on stage surrounded by the now-freed child dancers, a stirring protest of the Trump administration's family separation policy that kept immigrant children in custody away from their parents and US-based relatives. Choreographers Tabitha and Napoleon D'umo, who have worked as J.Lo's creative directors for more than a decade, also collaborated with the singer/dancer/actor on this bold performance. David Mack from *Buzzfeed News* quotes Tabitha's explanation:

---

1. Bruce Springsteen spoke out against Ronald Reagan's efforts to appropriate the song for his reelection campaign (Chao). In the introduction, I discussed Jennifer Lopez's use of the refrain from "Let's Get Loud," during the medley she sang as a featured performer during Joe Biden's inauguration as president of the United States.

> I think it started, from a musical standpoint, having "Born in the USA" in there for a little moment and it just was a natural evolution. . . . We had a great partnership with Versace and Rob [Zangardi], her stylist, saying, "Let's just do this in a way that everyone feels that American pride."
>
> I don't think we were trying to be heavy-handed with anything. I think we were just celebrating all that is beautiful about this country—Puerto Rico being part of this country.

I include this excerpt here to illustrate two things about visual media and messaging: The first is that all such performances are the result of a creative team rather than representing only the featured artist's singular vision. The second reason is that Tabitha D'umo, the person publicly explaining how the choreography and wardrobe worked in sync to celebrate the Americanness of J.Lo's Caribbean American identity, is white. Thus, the creative team's shared vision of a multicultural America serves as the official version of how the J.Lo corporate persona defines her Caribbean Americanness within mainstream American cultural life.

Ms. Lopez shared both the stage and top billing with Colombian singer Shakira, whose performance kicked off the spectacle. Like J.Lo, she explicitly referenced her birthplace in her show, which highlighted two Afro-Colombian dances, the champeta and the mapalé (Cabo). Interestingly, the two singers took radically different approaches to explaining the meaning or intention behind their performances. While J.Lo delegated the task to D'umo, Shakira took to Instagram after the performance and personally thanked her native country and its culture for providing her the inspiration for the dances she performed. Though she has publicly acknowledged that the choreographers taught her dance styles she did not grow up performing, Shakira's post takes sole credit for the artistic vision of her half of the show and classifies it as distinctly Afro-Caribbean: "I want to thank Colombia for giving me the mapalé, the champeta, the salsa and the Afro-Caribbean rhythms that allowed me to create the Super Bowl Halftime Show that I dreamed of more than a decade ago."[2] The women were later joined onstage by Puerto Rican trap singer Bad Bunny (Benito Antonio Martínez Ocasio), who appeared with Shakira while Colombian reggaetón singer J Balvin (José Álvaro Osorio Balvin) sang with Jennifer Lopez.

---

2. Shakira's original post was in both Spanish and English. I have cited the English for the sake of convenience. However, the original Spanish caption reads as follows: "Quiero agradecer a mi Colombia por darme el mapalé, la champeta, la salsa y los ritmos afro caribeños que me han permitido realizar el Super Bowl que desde hace más de una década soñé."

David Bauder's review of the show for the *Associated Press* optimistically proclaimed, "it was a reminder to a television audience that approached 100 million that a different part of America was making a powerful statement in favor of inclusion," but left his key terms undefined. The *New York Times*' Jon Pareles interpreted this "different part of America" solely through the lens of ethnicity as a "no-nonsense affirmation of Latin pride and cultural diversity in a political climate where immigrants and American Latinos have been widely demonized." By emphasizing the halftime show's display of *latinidad*, these reviews lose the broader sense of complexity embedded within the concept of a Caribbean American identity, one defined by ties to or heritage from the various countries and islands of the archipelago, regardless of race, language, or religion. Also lost in this calculus is the importance of Miami as what the *Tampa Bay Times* has called "the capital of Caribbean exile" (Adams).

In this chapter, I offer a close reading of the Super Bowl halftime show and its performers that privileges the regional lens of a Caribbean American sense of belonging through the trope of family ties. This brief interlude will lead into a more extensive analysis of how Caribbean American visibility within two media that trade in the serialized circulation of images—televisual texts available for streaming and comic books—challenge assumptions about ethnic assimilation by remixing dominant culture texts and reshaping them to reflect the peculiarity of their own experiences of American society. The Super Bowl halftime show, televisual texts, and comic books share the episodic nature of their overall narrative arcs. Part of the pleasure their audiences take from engaging with televisual texts and comic books comes from the combination of the comfort of recognizing the familiar with the thrill of the surprise variation.

As reboots or offshoots of original shows that captured the cultural moment in which they first appeared, the three televisual texts I analyze here further emphasize the sense of the uncanny or of making the familiar seem new again: the Cuban American reworking of Norman Lear's feminist sitcom *One Day at a Time*, the Cuban American offshoot of Jada Pinkett Smith's *Red Table Talk* featuring Gloria Estefan's family, and the updated *Queer Eye*, featuring Jamaican Cuban social worker Karamo Brown in the culture expert role first played by Puerto Rican Jai Rodríguez in the Bravo original *Queer Eye for the Straight Guy*. The comic book franchises I discuss here engage in a parallel but distinct form of revision: they expand a known or established universe by inserting Caribbean American characters within it rather than undertaking a wholesale revision of original source material like the Miles Morales intertexts. The audience experiences the uncanny when they see a Puerto Rican grandmother identify Groot from the *Guardians of the Galaxy* as a ceiba tree from her island, or meet the newest generation of Puerto Rican White Tiger within the world inhabited by blind Irish American superhero *Daredevil*.[3] Haitian Doctor Voodoo (Jericho Drumm) replaces Doctor Strange as the new Sorcerer Supreme within the *New Avengers* series and novelist Gabby Rivera introduces a lesbian America Chavez alongside Captain Marvel and a female Hawkeye in her Marvel series.[4] Whether expanding or relaunching, the comic book and televisual texts under discussion here jointly communicate the notion that belonging within the United States takes place through membership within a family unit, whether it be biological or chosen, nuclear, extended, or provisional. These depictions of family life expand our collective notion of what the "all-American" family can look, sound, and act like.

PATRIOTISM AND THE SUPER BOWL HALFTIME SHOW

The Super Bowl halftime show itself is an annual popular culture spectacle that transcends individual team allegiances or, frankly, any interest in sports at all. From the high-priced advertisements featuring A-list talent, to the potential for wardrobe malfunctions, audiences of all kinds tune in to the show to know what their friends and their social media feeds will be talking about the next day. In anticipation of the 2020 Super Bowl, the *New York Times* culture critics published an edited transcript of their discussion on the topic, admitting in the title that the game is "problematic" but asking "why can't we look away?" Caryn Ganz further admits:

> Football is the quintessential problematic fave. And like Michael Jackson, it's too challenging to cancel, too big to fail, too embedded in the fabric of American leisure to rip out. (For now, at least.) The Super Bowl is drama, emotion, identity, catharsis, spectacle, skill, power: It's nearly impossible to find a viewer beyond its scope. It's no longer possible to keep up with everything happening in television, movies, music and digital media, but the Super Bowl is one of the last gasps of the monoculture. It's a given and a gimme: It has almost no barrier for entry—one network channel, one block of time when nobody is expected to be doing anything other than watching the Super Bowl.

---

3. The *Daredevil* comic series is also the site where the Afro-Cuban *Santerians* appear. For reference, consult Aldama (2017). I will not be discussing them here for the sake of the chapter's overall coherence.

4. America Chavez is a featured character in the newest Doctor Strange film, *Doctor Strange in the Multiverse of Madness* (2022).

I agree with Ganz's assessment of the lingering associations with monoculture agriculture, but I contend that the halftime show warrants this fascination more than the game itself, which often tends to be a lopsided, underwhelming victory. Wesley Morris admits to participating in the ritual less frequently of late due to the National Football League's controversial attempts to squelch players' free-speech in acts as varied as the celebrations in the end-zone to the silent kneeling protests during the playing of the national anthem. Thus, it is not surprising that he strikes a more nostalgic tone:

> A lot of us remember the alleged simpler times when it was easier to pretend that entertainment was all it was. On one Sunday, we can pause Everything Else and just enjoy a miraculous helmet catch or a commercial for a job-finding company. It's also a stable structure. We all know it. We know it will never change and therefore never challenge most people to confront more than their losing team. There's no M.C. to be urbane or smug or real. Setting aside the violence at its center, it's safe, a haven from so much. History in the making but also passionately ahistorical. Americana on the one hand, sure. But also just America.

This passage perfectly encapsulates the downside of nostalgia that has driven such deep divisions within American society since the election of Donald Trump in 2016: a fact-free glorification of a past-that-never-was fueling a virulently passionate patriotism that equates the idea of "America" exclusively with heterosexual white, Anglo-Saxon culture.

The Super Bowl LVI's halftime show challenges such sepia-toned depictions of the genre's appeal by holding a mirror up to both "Americana" and "just America" in one fell swoop through the musical number described in the opening paragraph. According to the *Associated Press*, Dominican American rapper Cardi B turned down the chance to headline the Super Bowl halftime show in 2019, citing her support for former NFL quarterback Colin Kaepernick, who knelt during the playing of the national anthem in protest over police brutality and racial profiling, an act that earned him the league's disfavor. Just a year earlier, US-based Barbadian singer and fashion mogul Rihanna also declined the NFL's invitation to perform the halftime show in solidarity with Kaepernick's activism and his cause. These Afro–Caribbean American artists' public statements of support for a Black athlete's silent protest of police brutality in the United States affirm their common cause with non-Caribbean Blacks who suffer from disproportionately large rates of racial profiling, incarceration, and the lack of infrastructure and disinvestment in their communities.

Against this context, I read J.Lo's and Shakira's decision to participate in the 2020 Super Bowl not as evidence of anti-Blackness or support for the NFL's crackdown on athletes' rights to free expression but, rather, as a savvy use of a large public platform on which to stage their protest against the inhumane immigration policies enacted by the Trump administration, the impact of which went beyond Latin American migrants. Not all critics agree with my assessment, however. Writing in the *Washington Post,* Petra Rivera-Rideau cites both Cardi B's and Rihanna's decisions not to perform in the halftime show prior to describing J.Lo and Shakira's performance as simultaneously an affirmation of *latinidad* and a missed opportunity to proclaim solidarity with Blacks and Afro-Latinos: "The message of unity promoted by J.Lo and Shakira neglected to address these racial politics that have shrouded the NFL. And while their performance at moments expressed Latino pride, Shakira and Lopez missed an important opportunity to ally themselves with black communities, including Afro-Latino ones." I agree with Rivera-Rideau's assessment of J.Lo and Shakira's show as emblematic of how white or white-passing Latinx performers use elements from Afro-Latinx culture without incorporating Black performers onstage. However, I consider the performance through the lens of Caribbean Americanness because it allows for a more complex understanding of the interrelationship of cultural capital and race, ethnicity, and belonging.

For example, though Cardi B supports Kaepernick, she also was physically present at the stadium during the Shakira/J.Lo performance, thereby making it difficult for scholars to read her boycott of the NFL as either absolute or all-encompassing. Cardi B went on *Instagram Live* after the show and explained that she felt flattered by Shakira's inclusion of one of her songs within her show. *Bustle* describes the rapper's reaction as "fangirling" and quotes from Cardi B's recorded comments: "I already knew that Shakira was going to perform 'I Like It.' For me to even know that she was going to perform 'I Like It,' I just be like, 'Yo, that sh*t is crazy.' . . . I really grew up listening to these people and just seeing them in person, performing. That sh*t is beyond, like, a blessing" (Schremph). I pause on this to illustrate that Afro–Caribbean American performers like Cardi B sometimes discuss feeling a sense of belonging to Black American, Afro-Latinx, and Caribbean American communities simultaneously without any of these identities being mutually exclusive. Likewise, Shakira's use of Cardi B's song allowed the Dominican rapper's creativity to be celebrated without asking her to compromise her ideals; this inclusion shows Shakira's commitment to staging an "Afro-Caribbean" show went beyond her Colombian roots and centered other Afro-Caribbean traditions.[5]

---

5. Shakira's claim about the "Afro-Caribbeanness" of her show is interesting because her own heritage is mixed: her mother is Colombian while her father is Lebanese.

The 2020 show was especially important for Caribbean American visibility because of its location in Miami, a city that is home to two Caribbean diasporic hubs: Little Haiti and Little Havana. More broadly, the state of Florida itself has become a site for increasing Puerto Rican migration centering around Orlando due to both the island's economic woes and the devastation wrought upon it by Hurricane Maria.[6] Caribbean Americans have been more prominently represented in the field of entertainment than in football proper. The online publication *Jamaicans.com* celebrated two Jamaican American football players who participated in the Super Bowl: Laken Tomlinson, an offensive guard for the San Francisco 49ers who hails from Savanna la Mar, Jamaica, and hometown hero, Rashad Fenton, a cornerback for the winning Kansas City Chiefs, who was born in Miami Gardens to a Jamaican father and a Bahamian mother. None of the mainstream national, regional, or sports publications mentioned any of their players' Caribbean American heritage. This erasure could be due to the player's own reticence to discuss their family background, but it could also be seen as an example of how Anglophone Afro–Caribbean Americans blend in to, or choose to ally with, Black society in the United States due to their shared experiences of anti-Black racism.

TELEVISING THE CHANGING AMERICAN FAMILY

By singing along with Emme, J.Lo tied her Super Bowl halftime show performance to a long series of televised depictions of Caribbean American people as members of family units rather than as individuals. Beginning 1969, American families agreed to let their young children spend an hour visiting their muppet friends on *Sesame Street*. Once there, they became part of a culturally diverse virtual neighborhood where adults and children paused to learn or review basic elements of literacy, numeracy, and emotional intelligence. Among the central figures from 1971 until her retirement in 2015 was the character of Maria Figueroa Ramirez. While I fondly think of her as "everybody's Puerto Rican mother," journalist Andrew S. Vargas's description of the character emphasizes how three-dimensional this fictional character is as a "small business owner, caring mother, and second-floor resident of 123 Sesame Street." As a bilingual, Latina, feminist character, however, Maria, did not emerge in a vacuum. When she was in college, the actress who played the role, Sonia Manzano, watched an episode of the children's show and was inspired by Loretta Long's portrayal of another resident, Susan Robinson. It

---

6. Puerto Rican migration patterns have changed especially after Hurricane Maria. Recent waves of migrants have preferred to settle in and around Orlando, Florida, rather than New York City (Alvarez).

suddenly dawned on Manzano that unlike other television shows, *Sesame Street* depicted people like the ones in her neighborhood when she was growing up. In her memoir, *Becoming Maria,* Manzano describes this epiphany as a realization of absence:

> And then a beautiful black couple appears. He is handsomeness personified with a mustache. She has a smile that goes on for miles.
>
> I am amazed when I realize that in all the years I watched television in the South Bronx I hardly ever saw any people of color. But I am watching them now—on a show called *Sesame Street.* (245)

Manzano is no less accomplished than her fictional counterpart. Vargas reminds us that "after becoming a permanent cast-member in 1974 Manzano also started writing for *Sesame Street,* for which she's earned a total of 15 Emmy Awards." Thus, Manzano became a trailblazer while also validating elements from her own Caribbean American life, like speaking Spanish on air.

Whereas *Sesame Street* became a cultural touchstone as a long-lasting and ever-evolving television franchise, contemporary depictions of Caribbean American family units take place through the prism of the television reboot. Because reboots present familiar narratives recast in a new light, these updated versions of beloved television shows help make Caribbean American characters more legible and thus less foreign to their compatriots. Two of the most high-profile instances of this phenomenon are the new *Queer Eye* featuring Jamaican American culture expert Karamo Brown and Norman Lear's Cuban American version of his 1970s feminist sitcom, *One Day at a Time*. Despite premiering in the age of show streaming and binge-watching, these reboots have been around for the past few years and have developed their own loyal viewing audiences.

While the 1975 *One Day at a Time* really emphasized how isolated the tight-knit single-mother household was from any other relatives, the twenty-first century update situates the single-mother household vertically, with the presence of the grandmother, and horizontally with repeated references to and appearances by extended family like cousins, aunts, and uncles each with their own style of being Cuban American. When Netflix cancelled the show after only three seasons, fans of *One Day at a Time,* with a little high-profile help from Lin-Manuel Miranda's Twitter feed, successfully petitioned to keep their beloved sitcom on air via Pop TV (Porter). Sadly, the coronavirus pandemic accomplished what Netflix tried to do in 2019: bring about the end of the Cuban American *One Day at a Time*. The show chalked up one more innovation on the way to cancellation: the showrunners released an animated episode focusing on politics and the upcoming election. Regular cast members voiced their avatars while Miranda and Gloria Estefan put in guest appearances as the conservative members of their extended family (Villareal).

Likewise, the new *Queer Eye* franchise has extended the reach of its televisual forbearer both culturally, by making over women, trans people, and queer men rather than the more defined original demographic of "the straight guy" and geographically, by filming a four-episode mini-season in Japan during 2019 and then spawning spin-offs in Germany and Brazil in 2022. The current show's definition of "queer" has also broadened to encompass grooming expert Jonathan Van Ness's nonbinary gender identity and HIV+ status as well as Canadian food and wine expert Antoni Porowski, who identifies as "queer" rather than "gay." Both American versions of the show problematize the idea of the "all-American family" in multiple ways. They depict the Fab Five group as an emotionally supportive "chosen family" twice over: first selected individually by producers, and subsequently chosen by one another as they perform affective ties during their interactions at the group's shared loft and throughout the course of various episodes. The Fab Five family includes immigrants like Antoni, who is Canadian, and Tan France, who is originally from Britain. The cast members also discuss their own families with the featured "heroes" whom they set out to help, another marked change from the original. Bobby and Tan regularly mention their husbands, while Karamo often speaks about his sons. Puerto Rican Jai Rodríguez, who was the culture expert in the original show, has told reporters that the new cast members' openness in discussing their family lives is one aspect of the new version of the show he wishes had been possible when he was on *Queer Eye for the Straight Guy* because his mother's lack of acceptance of his sexual orientation caused a lasting breach that still haunts him (Ragusa).

A relatively recent entry into this entertainment space is *Red Table Talk*, a web television talk show streaming on Facebook Watch. Jada Pinkett Smith launched the show in 2018; now there is also a podcast version available. The show features conversations between the three generations of Pinkett Smith's family, herself, her mother, and her daughter Willow, during which they share their respective views on hot-button issues and interact with famous friends. During late fall of 2020, the show branched out with the launch of the Cuban American version featuring Gloria Estefan, her daughter Emily, and niece and *Univisión* host Lili Estefan as the central female family members. This new iteration of a successful web venture into reality entertainment strikes its own tone while also staying true to the formula that earned the first one's success: the chance for viewers to eavesdrop on family conversations that make visible the younger members' struggles to speak their respective truths as queer individuals and demand both respect and understanding from their more old-fashioned or simply conventional elders. Both the original *Red Table Talk* and *Red Table Talk: The Estefans* center multi-generational family ties as the lens through which they present and discuss contemporary life in the United States, but the original depicts vertical kinship lines of grandmother, mother, and child while the Cuban version incorporates the horizontal ties of kinship that include a matriarch, niece, and daughter. The pattern of Caribbean American reboots continues in this case as well because the introduction of the Miami-based Estefan version of what they call "la mesa roja," though airing simultaneously with the original, revitalizes the Smith version and both benefit from their coexistence as mutually supporting but independent versions of nondominant American family life.

Whereas the original and reboot sitcom find humor in the perceived universality of the lower-middle-class /working families' experience, what makes the two talk shows so compelling is the chance to hear iconic entertainers discuss the mundane aspects of their lives with one another for the benefit of their audience. The resulting performances are heavily edited and follow along loosely prescribed genre conventions but maintain the illusion of being spontaneous. In this way, they occupy a hybrid space between scripted television shows and unscripted "reality" television shows like *The Real World* or formulaic lifestyle improvement programs like *Queer Eye*.[7]

Despite belonging to different genres, *One Day at Time* following in the tradition of the half-hour family comedy while *Red Table Talk: The Estefans* is a conversation-based talk show, these televisual texts share some didactic elements: they depict Cuban American families discussing important topics with one another and sharing their (sometimes radically) different opinions; celebrate the value of therapy as one tool for people to manage their mental health; model acceptance for and value of queer family members; and welcome intercultural communication and exchange.[8] Both shows feature the teenage daughter's coming out story as a lesbian. In its first season, *One Day at a Time* had a multiple episode story arch depicting Elena's (Isabella Gomez) awareness of her own same-sex desire, coming out to her shocked but supportive mother Penelope (Justina Machado) ("Sex Talk"), facing her conserva-

---

7. Interestingly, Karamo Brown starred in both reality shows. In his memoir, he discusses his time as a cast member of *The Real World: Philadelphia* (2004–5) and *Queer Eye*.

8. Although the Alvarez family at the heart of *One Day at a Time* is supposed to be Cuban, most of the actors who portray them are actually Puerto Rican: Rita Moreno, who plays the Cuban matriarch, Lydia; Justina Machado, who plays Penelope, the mother; and Marcel Ruiz, who plays Alex, Penelope's son. The notable exception to this pattern is Isabella Gomez, who plays Elena, Penelope's daughter; she is Colombian American.

tive grandmother's (Rita Moreno) acceptance via the Pope's example ("Pride and Prejudice"), and ultimately her father's (James Martinez) public rejection of his queer daughter during her quinceañera ("Quinces"). The second episode of *Red Table Talk: The Estefans* features a tearful Emily telling her mother Gloria that even though she is a gay icon, she was not a particularly supportive parent during her own coming out process. The family discusses how members saw the situation and how therapy helped them heal. Interspersed with the conversation are photos of Emily and her partner, which visually confirm that the family has come to a new appreciation for and acceptance of each other's autonomy.

Together, *Queer Eye*, *One Day at a Time*, and *The Red Table Talk: The Estefans* portray American families where Caribbean American members celebrate immigrants as fellow Americans, speak openly about their feelings, warmly welcome non-Caribbean people to their domestic spaces, make common cause with people who sometimes disagree with them, and generally enjoy spending time with one another. Whether or not biology has any part in their make-up, the Caribbean American families on display have different phenotypes and understand gender and sexuality as gradients on a spectrum. Trauma has marked the fictional family of *One Day at a Time* as well as the Estefans and the chosen family of the Fab Five, but all three use their public platforms to normalize people acknowledging their mental health struggles and getting professional help. Though I have enumerated their shared positive qualities, I do not wish to suggest that *Queer Eye*, *One Day at a Time*, or *The Red Table Talk: The Estefans* present utopian ideals. Fair critiques can be made against individual episodes of each televisual text. However, as a group these televisual shows serve as a counter narrative to the nepotism that dominated the Trump White House from 2016–20. And their emphasis on togetherness can be read, like J.Lo's Super Bowl halftime show performance, as an ardent critique of the family separation policy that determined how the United States treated migrants and refugees at its borders during this time.

COMIC BOOKS SERIALIZING DIVERSITY

Though both televisual and comic book texts operate on the premise of serial publication, people who want to see what happens next in the ongoing saga of the fight of good vs. evil have to either buy a copy of a particular comic book issue or borrow it from the library. Jason Dittmer analyzes the demands that fan culture and the profit motive both impose upon comic books as a medium and calls it the "tyranny of the serial" (252); he explains that fans are driven by a desire to preserve narrative continuity within a series while also demanding the inclusion of plot elements that resonate with their own lived experience. Dittmer argues that together these pressures result in limiting the medium's potential to promote radical social change within their pages thereby perpetuating a type of conservatism. However, Dittmer argues that comic books are political texts that do tend to reflect the times in which they are published:

> over time change in the society in which comic book producers are embedded is reflected in the texts that they produce. Therefore, there are two parallel processes: one which takes the events of the real world and build it into the events of the comic book serial . . . and another that prevents the narratives of the comic book serial from fundamentally altering their own representation of the real world. (253)

The closest parallel to this "tyranny of the serial" within the televisual archive described earlier was the organized fan campaign to find a new home for *One Day at a Time* after *Netflix* refused to renew it beyond a third season. Dittmer's analysis of comic books emphasizes their role as "tools to influence geopolitical imaginations" deployed by the US government, among other entities (248). He reads Captain America as the imagined embodiment of the United States and argues: "The seriality of the nationalistic comic book parallels the seriality of the nation itself. Indeed, it is useful not to think of the nation as a timeless essence, but instead as a continually shifting storyline in which the characters change, grow, and interact but certain plot elements remain the same" (258). In what remains of the chapter, I contend that the chief "continually shifting storyline" about Caribbean American comic book superheroes and televisual characters is their membership within a family unit figured as their primary claim to belonging within American society writ cosmically.

Several of the Caribbean American public figures discussed in this book have expressed their appreciation of comic books as a defining element of their youths. In *My Beloved World*, Sonia Sotomayor drew on her love of comic book superheroes for inspiration and a model of courage for handling her diabetes: she learned to regard her ability to inject herself with insulin as a young child as one of her superpowers since both her parents were too nervous to help with this task. Now her last name graces the intergalactic institution of higher learning at the heart of the *America Chavez* storyline: Sotomayor University (Rivera). When he was a kid, TV actor John Huertas from the series *This Is Us* felt such a strong identification with the Puerto Rican hero White Tiger that he raised enough money to fund an independent movie adaptation (or "fan film") of the comic book.[9] More recently, Colombian American comedian and actor John Leguizamo uses the preface to the comic book adaptation of *Freak*, the one-man Broadway show telling own immigrant family's story in New York, to give a shout out to one of the less celebrated Caribbean American pioneers of the comic book industry: "Back in the 1920s, Alex Schomburg, a Puerto Rican from Aguadilla, Puerto Rico first arrived to New York City with his two brothers to open their own art studio. This lead to Schomburg drawing Captain America for Timely Comics before it became Marvel Comics." Leguizamo's public acknowledgement serves two purposes: it leverages the comic/actor's considerable fame to share the spotlight with a forgotten figure and it also legitimates his own independent comics endeavor by aligning it with the innovation of a Caribbean American forbear. Within the narrow niche of comic book industry insiders, however, Schomburg's contributions did receive acclaim. His official estate website includes a statement from Stan Lee in which he praises Schomburg's comic book artwork: "I've always felt that Alex Schomburg was to comic books what Norman Rockwell was to The Saturday Evening Post. He was totally unique, with an amazing distinctive style. You could never mistake a Schomburg cover for any other artist's. When it came to illustrating covers, there was simply no one else in Alex's league" (lack of italics in original). Since this assessment comes from Stan Lee, I guess that makes it part of the Marvel "canon."

Caribbean Americans have continued thriving within the comic book world. The late George Pérez, the illustrator who created White Tiger's iconic look, attained the highest degree of public renown of any Latinx artist in the industry. In a Marvel book celebrating his distinctive artwork, Pérez explains how he drew from his own family background to give this new Puerto Rican superhero some recognizable cultural capital:

> Despite the fact I am Puerto Rican, Bill came up with the idea of White Tiger.... But I had the advantage that I could dig into my own upbringing to be able to provide a sense of verisimilitude to the character. The White Tiger facially, I based on my brother. His mother was obviously inspired by my own. It was the age of a lot of social consciousness, so Bill wanted to do

---

9. See Umberto Gonzalez, who quotes Huertas as follows:

> It would have been great to have a superhero that influenced me and made me feel like this guy understands my experience, and then finally I found the White Tiger.... He's a Puerto Rican from the Bronx—just like me—and he wanted to clean up his neighborhood. He inspired me to be a better person, a better man and always do the right thing.

some stories that were more than just kickass and which had some kind of social relevance. (Harrold 19)

Pérez celebrates the collaboration that made it possible for him to draw on his heritage to give the new Caribbean American superhero a recognizable look that amounted to authentic representation. Because comic books are collaborative products that depend on various artists' skills—writers, artists, colorists, letterers—I discuss a given character's Caribbean American identity based on its linguistic and visual performance, rather than on the race or ethnicity of the superhero's creators. This collaborative process recalls the dynamic messaging created by J.Lo's artistic team more than reflecting the single artist's vision, as was the case in Shakira's Super Bowl halftime show performance.

In the wake of the huge success of the *Miles Morales* reboot of the *Spider-Man* franchise, there has been talk about how the comic book industry's recent embrace of diversity is a good business practice to reach new(er) markets and reinvigorate their key franchises. The high-profile hires of Caribbean American writers to revamp existing or create new superhero franchises such as Marvel's hiring of Haitian American Roxane Gay, who collaborated with Black journalist Ta-Nehisi Coates and poet Yona Harvey on *Black Panther: World of Wakanda*. Novelist Gabby Rivera was the first Latina to write for Marvel and the character "America Chavez" was the first LGBTQ+ woman to have her own starring comic series, though it lasted less than a year (Pulliam-Moore). While America's Caribbean Americanness is not explained until the third volume of the series, fans have read her through her creators' subject position.

Though the premises were promising, both series were eventually cancelled in 2017 and fans' critique and outrage were swift. Writing for *Polygon*, a gaming site in partnership with Vox Media, Susana Polo explains that there was no corporate announcement from Marvel about the cancellations of the series *Generation X, Gwenpool, Luke Cage, Iceman, Hawkeye*, and *America Chavez* but that the creative teams took to social media to share the sad news themselves. In the wake of these cancellations, fans have questioned the veracity of Marvel's supposed commitment to diversity. Polo writes:

> Most of them had diverse creative teams. All of them featured lead female characters, lead characters of color or lead queer characters. Generation X followed the X-Man Jubilee, in her adventures with a group of students at Xavier's school. Iceman was the original X-Men character's first solo series since coming out as gay. Hawkeye followed the adventures of Hawkeye's partner, Kate Bishop (whose superhero name is also Hawkeye). America was the first solo series for America "Miss America" Chavez, a long-time

fan-favorite and queer Latina superhero. In fact, America and Iceman were the only queer characters with solo series at Marvel.

The audience for *America* (America Chavez) was not much different from *One Day at a Time*'s fan-base: queer and Latinx folks. Pop culture critic Charles Pulliam-Moore's own response to the cancellations aligns with the backlash from fans. In an article for *Gizmodo*, he points to *America*'s fate as emblematic of the lackluster effort that entertainment entities like Marvel put into the production of content that helps them say they are reaching out to broad audiences while not changing much about their regular business model:

> It isn't at all surprising that *America* could be ending; comics cancellations happen all the time, and the entire comics industry is in a rather tight spot right now. At the same time, though, the book seems to have suffered from the exact same issue that affects so many other comics with leads who aren't straight white men. The books came out, there was little to no promotion around them, sales slumped, and now they're most likely being axed.

These two comments acknowledge that comic book publishers perpetuate the "tyranny of the serial" that Dittmer discussed earlier by refusing to change their basic economic model. Thus, while they make periodic attempts to reflect the cultural mores that define an age, executives refuse to invest considerable funds behind their ideological commitments and to break the power comic bookstores have to order titles in advance. The comic book industry could use a disruption of their funding model along the lines of how Napster and its followers changed the music recording system and streaming services altered the movie rentals business model.[10]

The official Marvel response to the charges that its claim to diversity amounts to window-dressing gestures came in the form of a tweet. Joe Quesada, who is Cuban American and was the chief creative officer at Marvel at the time, tweeted the following in response to a fan calling the cancellations "tone deaf": "If a comic finds an audience it will stick around regardless of the

---

10. In an article for *Vox*, Alex Abad-Santos explains how a monopolistic bottleneck at the heart of comic book publishing's business model determines the fate of individual storylines and characters:

> Every major US comic book company—Marvel, DC, Image, etc.—relies on one company, Diamond Comic Distributors, to print and ship their books to independent retailers, a.k.a. the owners of comic book shops. Diamond sells comics to comic book shops as final sale, meaning owners aren't allowed to return or exchange books that didn't sell. This is in contrast to traditional book retailers, which can sell back the books they weren't able to sell.

lead character or creator's gender, ethnicity, sexual preference or identification. You can claim we're tone deaf but we PUBLISHED those books but you guys ultimately decide what survives." Quesada's tweet points to Marvel's long history of introducing diverse characters since the 1970s.

White Tiger is one of those early characters: his alter ego was Puerto Rican-born Hector Ayala. His impact was primarily to increase representation since no story line plot in the *Daredevil* universe hinged on the character's ethnicity. White Tiger has been revamped of late in a manner similar to the transformation that Thor has undergone; both roles are now played by women. Ayala's niece, Angela del Toro, assumes the mantle of her uncle's powers after his death, though again it is unclear what she does to or for Puerto Rico or Puerto Ricans (E. Garcia, 105). The *Daredevil* universe also saw the rise of the Afro-Caribbean group *The Santerians,* created by the same Joe Quesada who blamed cancellations on low sales (E. García 102). Perhaps the white title character's blindness makes this an appropriate context in which to highlight ethnic and racial difference because it echoes the often-repeated claim white people make about being colorblind or not seeing race. However, as Ibram X. Kendi reminds us, "the language of color blindness—like the language of 'not racist'—is a mask to hide racism" (9). Whether the choice of *Daredevil* as the appropriate storyline to host the various Caribbean American superheroes before they strike out on their own was strategic or coincidental, the symbolism is powerful.

Political science scholar Christian Davenport uses chronology to outline three periods during which Black superheroes gained prominence in comic books; the first was between 1973–78 and included: "Black Goliath, Black Lightning, the Black Panther, Brother Voodoo, the Falcon, Luke Cage, and Storm" (200). The subsequent periods in his system were from 1983–87, and then from 1991–94; he did not hold out much hope for "the future of future of black superheroes and diverse representations" (207) from his vantage point in the early decades of the twenty-first century. However, Davenport's pessimism may have been premature. There is still a glaring absence of Anglophone Caribbean American superheroes. One of the few is Bushmaster, a Jamaican superhero who appears in the *Luke Cage* comic books and plays a villain in the second season of the Netflix live action series. Actor Mustafa Shakir explains the reason why the character appealed to him:

> You've got Wakanda and you've got this African nation and you've got Oakland, and it expands to the Caribbean and Harlem and Brooklyn. I feel like there's more attention being paid to the diaspora, but to see it as not monolithic, because there's a lot of different voices in it, and so I feel like between

"Black Panther" and "Luke Cage," a lot of different people within the diaspora will feel heard and represented. ("Mustafa Shakir")

Though Shakir's reference is specifically to the African diaspora in this context, his assessment applies to the Caribbean diaspora as well. Both are multivocal and have many outposts across the United States. However, Bushmaster's storyline does not involve family in the same way that the comic books that constitute the archive of this chapter's second part do.

I analyze three comic book series—*America (America Chavez)*, the new Angela del Toro *White Tiger*, and Haitian American *Doctor Voodoo*—alongside a single special issue of the *Guardians of Infinity* featuring a Puerto Rican Groot, and compare the depictions of Caribbean American families in these texts to the patterns discussed earlier with respect to the televisual shows. Both types of serial visual representation of Caribbean American characters center the family unit as a defining characteristic of how one belongs or fits within American society.

Two of the comic books present Caribbean American families that welcome or take in supernatural or intergalactic strangers in an informal context closely related to adoption or a heterosexual take on the idea of "chosen family." The first is America Chavez, who explains how she came to claim a Caribbean American identity even though she was born in the planet Fuertona (Spanish slang word meaning strong woman) in a parallel universe. In the third volume of the series, she explains that after her two mothers are killed, she fled her dimension and ended up with "the Santana family BBQ, [in] Bronx NY." America has an epiphany about her ethnicity when they serve her a plate of food: "Once Abuela Santana offered me that first plate of arroz con gandules, I was one of hers, no questions asked. Didn't even know what a Puerto Rican was. I just knew these folks looked like me and let me in" (Rivera, 2017). The drawing depicts a preteen America receiving a plate of food from a kindly bespectacled and apron-clad *abuela*. Commensality becomes the mechanism through which new family ties are forged in this context and it is no coincidence that the dish in question, rice and pigeon peas, is one of the mainstays of a typical Puerto Rican diet both on the island and throughout the diaspora. The next panel down shows an older teenage version of America sitting atop a tree branch in "Cartagena, Colombia, los Manglares" with a new family, "the Mejias," who "soothed the ache for my moms with adventures in the manglares, fresh empanadas, and cumbias about falling in love." Both these interactions with Latinx families help America mourn for the loss of her mothers and begin to heal emotionally. In this way, these interactions affirm the female-centric discussions of *Red Table Talk: The Estefans* and the empathetic approach of *Queer Eye*. During her journey of self-discovery on Earth, America explores her *latinidad* by traveling from the urban New York City streets to the mangroves of Colombia in a pattern that resonates with the Colombia / Puerto Rico connections discussed in both Leguizamo's comic book *Freak* and the Shakira/J.Lo collaboration during the Super Bowl halftime show. Interestingly, the key cultural touchstones that affirm America's sense of self are food and music.

A New York–based Puerto Rican *abuela* is once again the catalyst for an intergalactic superhero's epiphanic self-recognition as a Caribbean American member of the family in the third volume of *Guardians of Infinity* featuring the arboreal character Groot from *Guardians of the Galaxy* and The Thing from *Fantastic Four*. The superheroes crash-land on New York's Lower East Side and team up to defeat the evil Plantman, who fights gentrification in NYC with an army of evil carnivorous plants. An Afro–Puerto Rican *abuela* recognizes Groot as a ceiba tree from her natal island and helps him regain control of himself after Plantman hypnotizes him into submission. Both the *America* series and the *Guardians* issue were written by Puerto Rican authors and the texts celebrate New York City as the capital of the Puerto Rican diaspora in the United States.[11] As a group these texts center the family unit or family ties as the primary means through which the Caribbean American characters show themselves and one another that they belong.

The Puerto Rican grandmother figure has become so emblematic a representation of the Caribbean American family that *The Atlantic* ran a story about this particular issue of *Guardians of Infinity*, where the pop culture critic describes the character with deep admiration: "The brown-skinned bilingual abuela, who is never named and thus feels like an archetypal, mythical being, recognizes Groot as a relative of the Ceiba, the gnarled, giant tree venerated in the Caribbean as a repository for ancestral spirits" (Carolina González). Though she does not explain that American readers would be more familiar with the ceiba tree's English name, the white silk-cotton tree, González reaffirms the conflation of ethnic representation with familial celebration by pointing out the connections between the story's characters and Miranda-Rodríguez's own Puerto Rican family members. The grandson "shares a name (Kian) with Miranda-Rodríguez's eldest son" and explains that Miranda-Rodríguez's depiction of grandmother honors his two godmothers: "Iris Morales, former Young Lord and documentary filmmaker, and Marta Moreno Vega, longtime cultural activist and director of the Caribbean Cultural Center in Harlem" (Carolina González). This description echoes with George Pérez's

---

11. Edgardo Miranda-Rodríguez co-wrote the Groot issue.

account of drawing inspiration from his family to create the look of the White Tiger character.

The other two comic book texts depict a considerably smaller family unit organized primarily along horizontal lines of kinship: uncle/niece and twin siblings. The *White Tiger* reboot is the work of two white writers: YA author Tamora Pierce and her husband, Timothy Liebe. This was another of the "diverse" storylines that were published during Quesada's time as Marvel's editor in chief. Frederick Aldama and Christopher González describe "Hector Ayala as *White Tiger* (and later his niece, Angela del Toro)" as two of "the most engaging [DC and Marvel] superheroes to date" (10). As this description makes clear, current discussions of White Tiger recover the earlier incarnation, Hector Ayala, primarily to recast him as the current superhero's ancestor; del Toro has no other family. This avuncular relationship is important within the context of comic books because it echoes Spider-Man's own family ties—to Uncle Ben, who is murdered, and Aunt May, who becomes Peter Parker's only parent figure. More broadly, we discussed earlier in the chapter that the female lineage of the Cuban American family in *The Red Table: The Estefans* includes Emilio Estefan's niece, Lili. Writing for NBC news online, Nicole Acevedo quotes Emily Estefan as saying that collaborating on their joint project altered how she regards both her mother and aunt: "through the process of this show, they've become superheroes for me, and I think they will for everybody else." Whereas Emilio Estefan is alive but largely absent from the feminine space that is *The Red Table,* Hector Ayala does not appear in the new *White Tiger* series because he has been shot dead some time before the comic opens. However, Angela often invokes her uncle especially with regards to the amulets she inherited from him and uses to claim her superpowers and fight crime.

In a Haitian twist on family ties, the comic book hero Doctor Voodoo's only family member is his twin brother, who is dead but joined to him in spirit. The corporate biography at the end of the comic book collection *Doctor Voodoo: Avenger of the Supernatural,* explains that Jericho Drumm (Doctor Voodoo) had left Haiti and studied psychology while his twin, Daniel Drumm, stayed behind and became a vodou priest. When Daniel falls prey to a false god, Jericho returns to Haiti and studies vodoun with his brother's religious guide, a process that conjoins the siblings to one another for eternity: "Papa Jambo then tutored Jericho in the ancient ways of their people, culminating in a ritual that summoned forth the Loa (or spirit) of his brother Daniel and bound it to Jericho." Doctor Strange can see and hear Daniel's spirit and Jericho in the flesh, perhaps due to his own sorcerer status. These interactions between Jericho and Daniel Drumm and Doctor Strange represent a momentary break with the *Doctor Strange* continuity during which he is demoted; however, Doctor Voodoo's ascendancy as Sorcerer Supreme is short lived. Like the Wakanda and America series, this one was also cancelled; however, Doctor Voodoo is back in a new Marvel series called *Strange Academy* where he now serves as the titular school's principal (Marnell).

While this twinning or doubling takes place at the level of the hero's origin story, as a cultural product the character itself ends up being its own double as the competing honorifics Brother/Doctor Voodoo convey. In the preface to the same collection, writer Roy Thomas provides his origin story as a commodity within the Marvel Universe. Thomas claims to have dreamed up the superhero first when he was a teenager, then he shared his idea with Stan Lee, who was looking for a way to bring back *Strange Tales* the series that gave rise to the mystical sorcerer Doctor Strange. Lee decided to change the character's name from "Doctor" to "Brother" to reflect the parlance of the times and gave Thomas the go ahead to write the origin story. Thomas recounts his devotion to the hero he created despite the lack of a proper context in which to let him shine:

> Despite all the talent involved, alas, Brother Voodoo didn't have a long solo life that first time around. Five issues of *Strange Tales* . . . a story or two in *Tales of the Zombie*. Still, we knew he was a hero with potential, so we—and those who've come after us—rung him in from time to time, teaming him up with Doc—or Spider-Man—or whoever.
> Jericho Drumm was waiting for his chance to prove himself.
> And to become, as he was always meant to be—Dr Voodoo!
> It's taken 35 years . . . but hey, that's just a few months in Marvel time!
> (ellipses in original)

This brief genealogy conveys Brother/Doctor Voodoo's hybrid nature as a Caribbean American icon: he is the creation of a white man but performs the identity of an Afro-Caribbean immigrant to the United States with a base of operations in another mainland Caribbean American metropolis: New Orleans. Not coincidentally, this new phase in Brother/Doctor Voodoo / Jericho Drumm's career at Marvel took place during Quesada's tenure as editor in chief. So, much in the same way that J.Lo's Super Bowl half-time show was a collaboratively constructed vision of Caribbean American belonging, so is Doctor Voodoo's promotion to Sorcerer Supreme.

The second element that these comic book texts perform slightly differently than the televisual texts discussed earlier is the linguistic dimension of belonging. Where *One Day at a Time* and *Red Table Talk: The Estefans* feature a range of different Spanish-accented versions of spoken English, the comic books that feature Puerto Rican characters depend more heavily on the use of code switching, or the inclusion of Spanish language words or phrases within the written text to indicate a Caribbean American character's distinct linguistic performance of otherness. After the intrepid abuela breaks the Plantman's mind-control over Groot, he utters his catchphrase "I am Groot" but in Spanish, "Yo soy Groot," thereby signaling that he has internalized his Puerto Rican incarnation as a ceiba tree. Tamora Pierce's version of Angela del Toro as White Tiger often finds herself on the receiving end of Spanish language exchanges rather than speaking it. When she first goes to have her superhero costume fitted, one of the seamstresses urges her to leave the dressing room and show off the costume by saying, "Do it Tigresa Blanca!" The image depicts this woman as Asian American, thereby rendering her use of Spanish even more unusual. In contrast, Gabby Rivera's *America Chavez* storylines have plenty of Spanish sprinkled throughout, such as the exclamation she utters when she first encounters Storm from the *X-Men*: "Whoa, hey, You're Storm—like, Storm-from-the X-Men-Storm! Santa Juanga in heaven!" There is no saint by that name, but by invoking a saint at all, America sounds like a Puerto Rican who was raised Catholic.

In contrast, the *Doctor Voodoo* comics rely more heavily on alternative spellings of standard words (like "dat" for "that") or missing grammatical structures ("he no aid you now" instead of "he will not help you now") to convey a character's Caribbeannness. Paul Humphrey reminds us that such linguistic affectations are relics of a different era but no less objectionable because of it: "it must be recognized that the original series suffered numerous shortcomings with regards to the representation of its protagonist and other Haitian characters with whom he interacts, such as the objectification of the black male body and the use of stereotypical modes of speech common in the blaxploitation cinema of the period" (122), the latter of which still remain in the volume *Doctor Voodoo: Avenger of the Supernatural.* On the plus side of such linguistic marking of the characters within this storyline, Paul Humphrey points out that the Haitian Creole references to spirit names and those describing elements of the vodou ritual render these less exotic even if the specific nuances of their meaning are not immediately apparent to readers:

> By not glossing most of these different elements as they appear ... the series situates characters who might ordinarily be considered on the periphery of New York City, New Orleans and the Caribbean as integral parts of the real-world and narrative metropolises in which they are depicted. By extension, readers who might identify with them both see themselves represented in the dominant narrative and able to more deeply understand the character's origins. (123)

Humphrey's analysis of how linguistic mainstreaming of terms associated with Afro-Caribbean religions in both *Doctor Voodoo* and *The Santerians* accords with my reading of how audiences agree to share the virtual neighborhood with the Caribbean American superheroes who inhabit the pages of the comic book they enjoy. For me, Rivera's cultural references to food and music and the use of *White Tiger*'s Spanish-language moniker by the Asian American seamstress constitute similar acts of linguistic remapping of the center and the periphery; they expose mainstream audiences to Caribbean American culture as one of the many flavors of what makes American society work.

The visual dimensions of comic book texts and televisual shows make it possible for audiences of all kinds to see themselves sharing space with Caribbean American interlocutors. These texts break down boundaries by making the intimate domestic realm of people's existence central to how characters present themselves. Their kinship ties further cement the idea that the audience's consumption of these cultural products constitutes its own kind of virtual hospitality, a dynamic process now further enhanced by audience's ability to "talk back" to these shows and books through social media posts and comments. Like the lyrics of the *Sesame Street* theme song, we may not know quite how to get to our ultimate Caribbean American destination, but once there we know what we expect to see:

> It's a magic carpet ride
> Every door will open wide
> To happy people like you
> Happy people like
> What a beautiful
> Sunny Day
> Sweepin' the clouds away (Raposo et al.)

The lyrics' charming optimism emphasize happiness and beauty. What I find significant here, however, is the reference to the very transparency that the children's show as well as the sitcoms, makeover shows, talk shows, and comic books discussed here provide through the mechanism of having "every door . . . open wide." By presenting their protagonists or featured performers not as individuals but as members of a family, these visual texts open their doors to audiences and invite them to the shared homeland of the United States of America.

CHAPTER 7

Staging Caribbean American Lives in the Shadow of *West Side Story*

On July 3, 2020, the filmed version of the smash Broadway hit *Hamilton* premiered on the streaming service Disney+, more than a year earlier and on a smaller screen than its announced release date of October 15, 2021. While this was undoubtedly a decision made in light of the closing of all live theater productions around the world due to the COVID-19 pandemic, *New York Times* theater reporter Michael Paulson reminds us that the timing of the premiere on the new streaming service was entirely calculated to align with the audience's patriotism: "The release date is not accidental: the musical depicts the American Revolution, and July 4 is Independence Day in the United States." The release date also coincides with the temporal setting of Lin-Manuel Miranda's earlier smash musical, *In the Heights,* over three days between July 3–5. Regardless of whether Miranda was involved in the discussions with Disney +, the actor/playwright/composer/rapper embraces the symbolism of Independence Day as the nation's myth of origin and his artwork across media makes the case that subsequent Americans' own stories of arrival or belonging enhance and feed into this larger narrative.

The *Hamilton* film's release took place amidst a racially charged summer in which people joined in solidarity with the Black Lives Matter movement and took to the streets to protest police brutality and the murder of George Floyd. Perhaps because of the musical's obvious appeal to civics, audience reaction to *Hamilton,* while overwhelmingly positive, still called the show's celebration of its protagonist's anti-slavery sentiments into question. In a tweet, Lin-Manuel Miranda acknowledged the audience feedback on this topic, saying "All the criticisms are valid. The sheer tonnage of complexities & failings of these people I couldn't get. Or wrestled with but cut. I took 6 years and fit as much as I could in a 2.5 hour musical. Did my best. It's all fair game." When asked, cast members Daveed Diggs and Okieriette Onaodowan also acknowledged that the musical sidesteps any real acknowledgement of the Founding Fathers' complicity in perpetuating the slave economy within the framework of the new nation they built (Viswanath).

However, some high-profile Black fans of the show, including Michelle Obama, attributed their new-found sense of identification with their nation's history directly to the musical's intentional casting of nonwhite actors in the main roles other than King George. An article in *The Atlantic* quotes the former First Lady voicing this very sentiment: "With a cast as diverse as America itself, including the outstandingly talented women, the show reminds us that this nation was built by more than just a few great men—and that it is an inheritance that belongs to all of us" (Kornhaber). Even something as stodgy as a scholarly edited collection, *Historians on Hamilton: How a Blockbuster Musical Is Restaging America's Past*, grudgingly attests to the show's success and influence in shaping the next generation's sense of self and belonging as Americans: "Children across the country have dressed up as characters from the show for Halloween; there are *Hamilton*-themed birthday parties and bat mitzvahs complete with colonial costumes" (Romano and Potter). Whether people had attended live performances, heard the music, or simply bought into the social media whirlwind that surrounded *Hamilton*, Americans of all ages were suddenly invested in the story of the nation's origins and developed a new appreciation for the Founding Fathers' radical hipness.

Six years after it made a splash on Broadway, the availability of what fans have nicknamed "the Hamfilm" through the new streaming platform marks the culmination of Lin-Manuel Miranda's efforts to share the Pulitzer-prize winning musical with audiences writ large, something he began during the show's original run by posting the official cast recording of the soundtrack free of charge on YouTube. His subsequent efforts to reach beyond the usual Broadway regulars include the #HamforHam preshow lottery for $10 tickets to the Broadway and touring shows (Boffone), #EduHam Project education campaign for New York high school students (Romano and Potter), the publication of an annotated version of the musical's libretto, *Hamilton: The Revolution* (which fans dubbed the "Hamiltome"), and the YouTube release of *The Hamilton Mixtape* featuring various artists' remixes of the show tunes. In May 2020, soon after the announcement that the film version would stream on Disney+,

Miranda hosted a master class of the AP US History exam preparation.[1] These efforts showcase not only Miranda's great talent for cross-platform promotion and marketing but also demonstrate his commitment to effect change in how Americans, young and old, relate to their country's history. By portraying one of the Founding Fathers as "the poor kid from the Caribbean who made the country rich and strong, an immigrant who came here to build a life for himself and ended up helping to build the nation," Miranda's *Hamilton* universe of interconnected texts promotes a sense of civic pride and belonging to the United States as a nation of immigrants (McCarter, 15). And Puerto Rico figured very prominently in Miranda's expansive definition of belonging to the United States.

Jeremy McCarter, Miranda's collaborator on *Hamilton: The Revolution*, argues that the musical tells the intertwined stories of two distinct yet overlapping regime changes:

> There's the American Revolution of the 18th century, which flares to life in Lin's libretto, the complete text of which is published here, with his annotations. There's also the revolution of the show itself: a musical that changed the way that Broadway sounds, that alters who gets to tell the story of our founding, that lets us glimpse the new, more diverse America rushing our way. (10).

McCarter qualifies the second of these claims with a reminder that despite the show's undeniable impact on how Broadway does business, the Great White Way was not the original venue or platform Miranda envisioned for his hip-hop rendition of Alexander Hamilton's life story. During a performance at the White House on May 11, 2009, Miranda sang the part of Aaron Burr and explained that the song was a demo of sorts for his planned concept album, *The Hamilton Mixtape*. A revised version of this rap became the musical's opening song and Miranda eventually recycled the album title as mentioned earlier. The central conviction that more Americans should become familiar with and care about their nation's founding and its history has been a throughline in the project all along.

After surprising the Obamas with his performance of new work rather than highlights from his award-winning musical *In the Heights*, Miranda went on to trade on *Hamilton*'s value as a hot commodity while he carried out his own civic-minded quests. He first used it to advocate on behalf of the contro-

---

1. To watch the class, go to the Advanced Placement YouTube channel and search for, "AP US History: Special Edition with Lin-Manuel Miranda." It was posted on May 1st, 2020.

versial and now much-critiqued PROMESA Act in a featured performance on *Last Week Tonight with John Oliver* that aired only four days before the May 1 deadline for the bill's passage.[2] In the show, Miranda first debuted a new rap song, "100 Miles," accompanied on piano by *Hamilton* music director Alex Lacamoire and then renewed his offer to perform the musical at Speaker of the House Paul Ryan's home if he agreed to bring the legislation to a vote, thereby preventing the island from defaulting on its debt since it is forbidden by law from declaring bankruptcy. Congress passed the bill and President Obama signed it into law. No word on whether Miranda had to make good on his offer.

The next time Miranda leveraged *Hamilton*'s cultural capital was in 2017, soon after Hurricane Maria made landfall in Puerto Rico, wiping out its energy grid and leaving the entire island and its archipelago without power or water.[3] Miranda and the show's producer, Jeffrey Seller, agreed to do two things: the first was to take the show to San Juan even though most touring versions of Broadway shows never make it there. The second thing was to use the show as a fundraiser to benefit the arts in Puerto Rico. Miranda also agreed to reprise the title role (Pollack-Pellzner). Though there was a mixed reaction to this decision based, in part, on island Puerto Ricans' disapproval of Miranda's advocacy for the PROMESA legislation given the draconian austerity measures it ushered into place, local audiences nonetheless showed up alongside US-based celebrities to support the show. During the publicity circuit in advance of the performance, Miranda explained that he has since changed his support of PROMESA and now advocates on behalf of debt forgiveness as the only feasible way for the island to overcome its crippling economic stalemate.

The third and most explicit way in which Miranda leveraged the public platform of the musical's cultural capital to advocate on behalf of specific legislation took place on November 18, 2016, when Vice President–elect Mike Pence attended the musical on Broadway. Miranda collaborated on a statement with the show's director, Thomas Kail, and producer, Jeffrey Seller to voice their concerns regarding the Trump administration's derogatory comments about immigrants during the campaign leading to their electoral vic-

---

2. For a scholarly assessment of the impact of the PROMESA Act on Puerto Rico's economy, see Edwin Meléndez, "The Politics of PROMESA."

3. Though most discussions of Puerto Rico on mainstream media imply that there is only one island involved, Puerto Rico is itself an archipelago made up of the main island, two other inhabited islands—Vieques and Culebra—as well as smaller islands Mona, Desecheo, and Caja de Muertos.

tory. Brandon Victor Dixon, the actor performing the role of Aaron Burr, spoke on behalf of the cast and the show's creators when he pleaded:

> Vice President-elect Pence, we welcome you and we truly thank you for joining us here at *Hamilton: An American Musical*, we really do. We, sir, we are the diverse America who are alarmed and anxious that your new administration will not protect us—our planet, our children, our parents—or defend us and uphold our inalienable rights, sir. But we truly hope that this show has inspired you to uphold our American values and to work on behalf of all of us. *All* of us. (Miranda et al.)

The repeated use of the adjective "American" in this statement, both within the musical's subtitle and then as a modifier of the "values" the cast beseeches the future Vice President to uphold, suggests that the Trump administration exists outside of the e pluribus unum at the heart of the show's vision of the United States. After all, the use of "sir" twice in direct address to Pence marks both him and "your administration" as distinct from the first-person plural included at the heart of the proclamation: "we are the diverse America who are alarmed and anxious that your new administration will not protect us— our planet, our children, our parents." The phrasing also recalls the show's second song, "Aaron Burr, Sir" which *Screen Rant*'s James Hut interprets as an overt condemnation of the man who would kill the titular character: "And, given the audience is supposed to connect with Alexander, the 'Sir' then puts Burr above the viewer's status too, better positioning him as the de facto villain of the story (such as one exists)." Intentional echoes notwithstanding, the cast statement is simultaneously an appeal to and a challenge for the Trump-Pence administration not to prove their fears well-founded.

While some found the cast's activism shocking, drama critic and professor Brian Eugenio Herrera explains that the *Hamilton* public address to Vice President Pence was firmly grounded within the well-known theatrical tradition of "the curtain speech on behalf of Broadway Cares / Equity Fights with AIDS (BC/EFA)" (240). This is a decades-long fundraising effort strategically situated at curtain-calls to ask for donations to nonprofit organizations working to promote women's health and care for those with HIV/AIDS. In Herrera's view, Mike Pence's public disregard for such health concerns during his term as governor of Indiana and the resulting spike in HIV/AIDS cases in the state made him an ideal target for this type of direct public intervention (Gonsalves and Crawford). However, Herrera acknowledges that this context was not apparent to those unfamiliar with Broadway customs:

> As an example of the disparity between how *Hamilton* plays within and beyond the theater, the brisk erasure of the actual theatrical context for Dixon's "Broadway Cares" speech does signal the easy elision of the varied theatrical traditions anchoring *Hamilton's* innovations and provocations, especially when news about them moves briskly within the Broadway bubble. As the *Hamilton* phenomenon continues to exceed the theatrical limits of its beginnings, the musical's theatrical histories may or may not remain central to broader considerations of the musical's significance. (Herrera, 241)

This excerpt clearly signals how *Hamilton* the musical performs its own sense of belonging to distinct and overlapping communities simultaneously. The words of the speech Dixon read are political and can be interpreted as a rhetorical slap in the face to the incoming Trump administration tantamount to issuing a challenge to an ideological duel. The very act of speaking during curtain call, however, signals the musical's cast and creators' belonging to the theater community's activist, feminist, and queer communities. And the subsequent media reporting on the exchange constitutes an act of translation between those in "the room where it happen[ed]" and those who were not in attendance, the left and the right, the theater nerds and the policy wonks.

The three Broadway musicals under discussion—*Hamilton*, *In the Heights*, and *On Your Feet!*—portray the Caribbean American experience as a central lens through which to understand problems or dynamics that impact the rest of the American nation. Whether it be the revolutionary impulse motivating Alexander Hamilton and his cronies to battle the British, the rising rent that prices people out of the New York City neighborhoods where they have spent their formative years, or the desire to create a decade-defining sound, the Nevisian, Dominican, and Cuban Caribbean American protagonists of these works of musical theater speak for all of us when they draw on their particular heritages for the inspiration and motivation to create a more open and welcoming American culture. Though they each engage in different scales of world-making—a new nation in *Hamilton*, a close-knit community in *In the Heights*, and an international music scene in *On Your Feet!*—all three musicals share an optimistic and celebratory tone about the possibilities open to immigrants and their descendants in the United States. Precisely because they set their stories against the backdrop of the foundational myths of the United States as both a nation of immigrants and a land of opportunity, these musicals' appeal extends beyond their featured ethnic groups. All three hold up a more diverse mirror up to nature, so to speak, to illustrate what American society can look like in the twenty-first century. These works grow out of a Caribbean American space first envisioned, if not realized, by an earlier Broadway musical that made a crossover splash as a film: *West Side Story*.

THE LEGACY OF *WEST SIDE STORY*

As an artist, Lin-Manuel Miranda finds himself at the center of a trio of Broadway musicals successfully turned into movies: besides *Hamilton*, the film adaptation of Miranda's first Broadway musical, *In the Heights*, directed by Jon M. Chu, debuted in June 2021 simultaneously in theaters and via the streaming service HBO Max. The third is the 1961 film adaptation of *West Side Story*, to which Miranda feels indebted for making him feel seen as a child due to its portrayal of Puerto Ricans (Bernstein Experience). The show is a staple of the American high school musical theater repertoire. Miranda famously directed the show while he was in high school (Todd). He incorporated a couple of lines from his favorite song in the musical, "Maria," as the English language refrain in the single he released to raise funds for hurricane recovery in Puerto Rico, "Almost Like Praying." And Miranda had previously translated some of the songs in the musical into Spanish for a Broadway revival of the show (Todd). To call Miranda a *West Side Story* super-fan is to put it mildly.

The lead characters' points of view in *In the Heights* and *Hamilton* represent the two ends of the spectrum of how Caribbean immigrants adapt to life in the United States, with either blind ambition or sappy nostalgia, a debate that is at the heart of *West Side Story*'s New York-based Puerto Rican community as depicted in the song "America." Usnavi, the male lead in *In the Heights*, demonstrates a Root identity because he idolizes the homeland his parents left when he was an infant; he dreams about saving money so he can move back to the Dominican Republic. His nostalgic view of the Caribbean nation echoes the positive memories the character Rosalía voices about her birthplace in the opening lyrics of the Broadway version of "America" from *West Side Story*: "Puerto Rico, / You lovely island . . . / Island of tropical breezes. / Always the pineapples growing, / Always the coffee blossoms blowing" (westsidestory.com). In contrast, the titular Founding Father in *Hamilton* could adopt the song's refrain "I want to live in America," as his personal motto after being left orphaned and destitute as a young man in St. Croix, a Caribbean island that is now part of the United States Virgin Islands.[4] While *In the Heights* and *Hamilton* depict the protagonists' Caribbean homeland in diametrically opposed ways, both musicals' respective story arcs show that each man makes a concerted decision to stay in the United States rather than returning to the Antilles. Miranda's Usnavi and Alexander Hamilton see themselves as intrinsically involved in the life of their respective communities, whether Washington Heights or the newly established United States, and each

---

4. Although Alexander Hamilton was born in Nevis, his family moved to St. Croix.

character eventually sacrifices his individual pursuit of happiness in favor of helping their new homes achieve a greater measure of stability.

In both the stage and screen versions of *West Side Story*, the song "America" encapsulates these tensions within the same migrant group: those Puerto Ricans who desire to improve their circumstances in the United States bicker or debate with their compatriots who feel nostalgic for the island and way of life they left behind when they migrated. The 1961 Hollywood adaptation of the film stridently promotes the Puerto Rican characters' celebration of the United States as a land of opportunity, but that optimism is tempered by a surprisingly explicit acknowledgement that systemic racism in the United States narrows the horizons of possibility for full integration. Two key exchanges during the song demonstrate that this discussion is distinctly gendered, with the chorus of women singing the praises of the United States while the men refute their idealized views with frank examples from their own working lives. The first takes place in the context of a couple's bickering; Anita declares her intention to settle down in the United States, "I'll get a terrace apartment," to which her lover Bernardo retorts, "Better get rid of your accent" (westsidestory.com). The second has the chorus of "All Girls" declare, "Life is all right in America," to which the chorus of "All Boys" replies, "If you're all-white in America." These lyrics contain stark reminders of how a person's brown or black skin tone and/or their Spanish accent limit their prospects for employment and make them subjects of redlining and other types of discrimination.

In the original lyrics for the Broadway show, in contrast, the tension between idealism and nostalgia is staged primarily as an argument between female characters, namely Rosalía and Anita; the men say nothing about the humiliations they have endured while looking for employment in the United States. In the show lyrics, the Puerto Rican characters resent the invisibility of their status as fellow Americans more than the hypervisibility of their skin tone or accent as markers of racial or ethnic Otherness in this stanza sung by all the cast: "Immigrant goes to America, / Many hellos in America; Nobody knows in America / Puerto Rico's in America!" Though this appears to be a shared sentiment, most of the rest of the song contains negative stereotypes of Puerto Rico as overpopulated, lacking in basic infrastructure, beset by tropical diseases, and overrun with violent men and overly fertile women.

My reading of how the competing views of migrant idealism and diasporic nostalgia vie for space within the show-stopping song "America" suggests that *West Side Story*'s Puerto Rican subject matter had a clear nation-building dimension in both media. Between the musical's Broadway premiere in September 1957 and the subsequent 1961 release of the Hollywood film adaptation, the United States grew from a nation with forty-eight states to fifty through the admission of the noncontiguous former territories of Alaska and Hawai'i as states in the Union. Following Camilla Fojas, who argues that "the Elvis-in-Hawai'i films are colonial narratives that tacitly reflect upon the role of the colonies in the U.S. empire" (194), I argue that the stage and screen versions of *West Side Story* are also colonial narratives. Whereas "the Elvis-in-Hawai'i films" Fojas studies invite the audience to adopt a touristic gaze and project themselves into the exotic island locale that is now a part of the United States, the stage and screen versions of *West Side Story* use the lens of the ethnic tensions and gang turf battles to render the American homeland uncanny because of the presence of Caribbean Americans within its most iconic city.

Though *West Side Story* plays up the ethnic gang turf battles in New York City to strengthen the echoes to *Romeo and Juliet* as its source material, this subject matter corresponded with historical tensions in the era. The musical's sympathetic portrayals of both female leads, Maria and Anita, echo the paternalistic language used by American government officials to discuss Puerto Rico's newly conceived role within the American political structure after the passage of the 1952 Commonwealth Act and the approval of its constitution. That same year, Vernon Northrop, acting US secretary of the interior, included the following explanation in a letter to the secretary of state:

> Puerto Rico has not become an independent nation; neither has it become a State of the Union. It remains a territory of the United States. The action of the Congress in authorizing and approving the constitution of the Commonwealth was taken under the constitutional power of the Congress to make needful rules and regulations respecting the territory of the United States. Puerto Rico's foreign relations, like those of the other territories and, it may be added, like those of the States, will continue to be conducted by the United States.

This statement sums up Puerto Rico's in-between status, which endures to this day. By the time the curtain falls in the musical, Maria and Anita face an uncertain future after their lovers' murders. Like Puerto Rico, the island from which both characters hail, Maria and Anita are neither independent (nations) nor are they wives (states), but rather occupy the in-between status of female migrants. Thus, they and their island depend on the United States and its oversight. Whether for good or bad, the musical *West Side Story* set a precedent for how the genre of musical theater imagines, portrays, and discusses the meaning of Caribbean Americanness.

Proof of this can be found in how Puerto Ricans themselves use *West Side Story* as a point of reference through which to better understand their own presence in the United States. Juliet Palante, the protagonist of the YA novel

Juliet Takes a Breath, reflects on the degree to which US-based Puerto Rican parents promote a love of the Hollywood adaptation of the musical in their children in the mistaken belief that its mostly symbolic representation was all they could lay claim to. After learning about Puerto Rican nationalist Lolita Lebrón's 1954 assault on Congress[5] to demand an end to American colonization of the island while doing research for her internship, Juliet fundamentally rethinks her family's identification with *West Side Story*:

> We watched *West Side Story* every Thanksgiving, rooted for the Sharks and cried for María's heartbreak and grieved with her. Our identity as Puerto Ricans was tied into a movie where both lead actors was [sic] white. My parents didn't tell me that either. I had to find out on AMC that Natalie Wood was white and I cried like a bitch that day. I felt robbed of something as if a lie had been woven into the narrative of my Nuyorican identity. Why was a musical more important to have on a loop in our home but not an act of bravery in the name of a free Puerto Rico? Maybe America just swallowed all of us, including our histories, and spat out whatever it wanted us to remember in the form of something flashy, cinematic, and full of catchy songs. (132)

This passage reflects a decolonial perspective that recognizes Puerto Ricans' long history pro-independence activism. It acknowledges how the previous generation of Nuyoricans made the pragmatic choice to celebrate the limited representation the musical gave the community regardless of how it reproduced stereotypes about Puerto Rican criminality and cast white actors in key roles. Juliet's newly awakened feminist Caribbean American consciousness makes her champion the controversial Lebrón rather than the more famous Rita Moreno, who earned an Oscar for her performance of Anita.[6]

While Rivera's feminist critique of the musical is effective, fellow Puerto Rican actor and comedian Suni Reyes takes a more meta-theatrical approach to critiquing the legacy of *West Side Story* by recording a parody of the signa-

---

5. Given the insurrection of January 6, 2021, we can now regard Lebrón's involvement as an eerie precursor of sorts. For a timeline detailing the 1954 attack on the Congress floor, consult the Office of the Historian's entry on the event: https://history.house.gov/Exhibitions-and-Publications/1954-Shooting/Essays/Timeline/.

6. In her memoir, Rita Moreno acknowledges that her success as Anita came at the expense of a fellow Puerto Rican actress, Chita Rivera, who had originated the role on Broadway: "My future role as Anita, the one that won me that golden Oscar, was played on the Broadway stage by Chita Rivera. It had to have been very difficult for Chita, who performed brilliantly in the play, not to appear in the movie. Compound that with the fact that her husband, Tony Mordente, played in both" (184).

ture song, "America." Recorded a year after Hurricane Maria, Reyes's parody calls out white Americans' fascination with the musical *West Side Story*, the eponymous song's dismissal of Puerto Rico's natural resources, the rolling blackouts that still plague the island, the traces of Spanish colonialism evident in the flamenco-inspired choreography of the film's dance sequence, and the film version's use of brown-face makeup on the actors who played Puerto Ricans, even including Rita Moreno. Finally, the song calls into question white Americans' ability to distinguish between Puerto Ricans, who have US citizenship, and Latinx peoples of different national origins given the Trump administration demonization of all Latinx peoples as undesirable law breakers. The conclusion that Suni Reyes's character comes to by the end of the song is that there is no real need to remake the musical.

Both Reyes's and Rivera's critique of *West Side Story* as a foreign and flawed reduction of Caribbean American life comes in the wake for their desire to have more and broader access to information about the histories of both Puerto Rican migration to the mainland United States as well as of the decolonial struggle for self-determination. For them, as millennials, *West Side Story* is a dated narrative that promotes negative stereotypes. Comedian and novelist / comic book writer are creating new chapters in the ongoing story of Caribbean American presence in the United States. In contrast, older Nuyoricans like Sonia Manzano and Sonia Sotomayor remember a time before there was any representation of Hispanophone migrants at all on the national scene. They fondly recall how the film adaptation of the Broadway show changed the calculus and acknowledged some of the ethnic and linguistic diversity that made New York City neighborhoods distinctive.

Sonia Manzano dedicates an entire chapter of her memoir, *Becoming Maria*, to the *West Side Story* film. She first saw it when one of her teachers took her and two classmates to a screening. Manzano recalls feeling overcome with emotion as she recognized the urban settings in which the various scenes took place: "I stare at the screen with some mental distance so I can reason and figure it out but there is no figuring to do, because when the actors sing and dance on a roof about being in America my heart takes over and begins to beat faster and faster until it makes a racket in my ears that roars" (Manzano, 125). As a memoirist, Manzano recreates on the page the thrill of recognition as well as the less glamorous aspects of seeing one's life represented on the screen: the tears, the nose blowing, and the embarrassment of having an emotional outburst in public. Manzano boils down this feeling of empowerment she felt as a child into three distinct affirmations that guide her through her studies in high school and college, and on to a career as a professional actress:

1. "This movie makes things possible." (126)
2. *"If people can make that movie, what can I do?"* (128)
3. "The movie made me strong. I can fight now." (129)

In showcasing these different perspectives about the impact of the 1961 film version of *West Side Story* on Nuyorican public figures' sense of self and how it shaped their notion of belonging to American society, the expanding canon of Caribbean American Broadway musical film adaptations has a democratizing effect, making the genre accessible to people who could not afford to have paid for the live theater experience. The same is true for the film adaptations of *In the Heights* and the new Steven Spielberg adaptation of *West Side Story*, which includes culturally appropriate casting and features Rita Moreno back in a new role.[7]

West Side Story's popularity in the repertoire of high school theater departments around the nation since its Broadway debut signals its canonical status within American culture. Generations of teenagers have played Tony or Maria or rumbled over turf as either a Jet or a Shark. The benefit of such broad acceptance and security within mainstream culture is that the musical continues to generate discussions about how best to cast for the roles, whether to alter the lyrics or modify the book, or what the benefits and limitations such restagings present to new generations of actors, singers, directors, choreographers, and contemporary audiences as the 2019 Broadway revival of the show made eminently clear.

However, there is a downside to such short-hand definitions of what it means to have Caribbean heritage in the United States. In *My Beloved World*, Sonia Sotomayor references the film version of the musical when trying to rationalize why her first Princeton roommate seemed afraid of her even though both young women identified as Latinas: "all Dolores knew of Puerto Ricans came from *West Side Story*, and I suspect that initially she was half-afraid I'd knife her in her sleep" (161). To be fair, in the next sentence the judge admits she had no points of reference against which to understand Dolores's Southwestern background. The impact of this long-ago interaction exemplifies the lasting damage that stereotypical depictions of a group of people can have beyond the context in which these first appear. Sotomayor recently participated in a Kennedy Center panel discussion about the 1961 film version and

---

7. The Spielberg *West Side Story* opened in theaters nationwide on December 10, 2021. Patricia Guadalupe of *NBC News* explains that Moreno's new role is as "Doc, the shopkeeper, who was a man in the original movie." Spielberg's interpretation of "culturally appropriate casting" has been to cast Latinx actors, rather than simply Puerto Ricans, to fill out the main roles. For example, Colombian American actress Rachel Zegler played the part of María.

Spielberg's remake. She spoke about the original film's political overtones and the importance of making the new adaptation speak to current potential viewers: "'I think in some ways it was ahead of its time. As I rewatch it now, I realize this is pretty upfront stuff and very complicated for 1960,' Sotomayor said. 'The question now is how to advance the issues for a new audience without losing the film's hold on audiences'" (Guadalupe). With the benefit of hindsight and sufficient distance from the profiling incident of her youth, Sotomayor hopes that the new version of this story can continue challenging her fellow Americans to be more accepting of their compatriots with Caribbean heritage.

NEW CARIBBEAN AMERICAN BROADWAY SHOWS

I will now turn to a discussion of *In the Heights* and *Hamilton* by Lin-Manuel Miranda and the jukebox musical *On Your Feet!*, featuring music and lyrics by Gloria and Emilio Estefan, with a book by Alexander Dinelaris. Both *On Your Feet!* and *In the Heights* center the Hispanophone Caribbean American experience and incorporate whiteness or the dominant society only at a distance, as an aspirational representation of what it means to have made it. In contrast, the arc of the founding father's life story on display in *Hamilton* thematizes the very privilege conferred upon an Anglophone Caribbean man of limited means but gifted intellect to summarily incorporate himself into the fabric of a new nation even as the lyrics from the song "Yorktown" remind everyone he's one of the immigrants who "get the job done." The irony is, of course, that a cast made up of BIPOC actors upholds the very values of whiteness that have marginalized people who look like the performers. The musical scores are another way in which these shows signal their belonging. *Hamilton* owes much more to hip hop and Broadway showstoppers than to reggaetón or salsa, despite being the product of the same Caribbean Americans musical team that staged *In the Heights*: Lin-Manuel Miranda and Cuban American Alex Lacamoire. In contrast, the infectious score of *West Side Story* arguably primed audiences to accept both the Latin Pop sounds of the Miami Sound Machine that make up the plot of *On Your Feet!* and the Latin beat at the heart of the score for *In the Heights*.

IN THE HEIGHTS

Lin-Manuel Miranda has often said that when he first came up with the idea for *In the Heights*, he was trying to do a Latino version of the Broadway rock musical *Rent*.[8] In an interview with *The Gothamist*, Miranda said that watching *Rent* as a teenager was very influential in his artistic development. He also talked about how gentrification made it impossible for him to afford to rent an apartment in Washington Heights after coming back from college and prompted his move to mid-town (Del Signore). The rock opera and the Latin hip hop musical share a concern with gentrification and displacement of low-wage earners, but there are some important differences in how each approaches this theme. *Rent* follows a diverse group of young artists struggling to afford living in a specific building in New York City while juggling relationships and the threat of HIV/AIDS. *In the Heights* also showcases young people's struggles to make their way in the world but also incorporates a multigenerational dimension to life and work in the city that better reflects the cultural reality of Hispanophone Caribbean and Latinx community. However, in its exuberant celebration of the idea of an actual place, *In the Heights* feels more reminiscent of a show like *Oklahoma*. While there are no competing groups like the cowboys and farmers, the hairstylists, drivers, and bodega owners of Washington Heights in their own way articulate a worldview that resonates with the title song of that musical: "We know we belong to the land / and the land we belong to is grand" (Hammerstein and Rodgers). Each community in these musicals feels anchored to a particular place within the larger imaginary of the United States—the physical landscape of the Oklahoma countryside on the one hand, or the urban Caribbean archipelago that is Washington Heights, on the other.

Gentrification becomes the main antagonist in *In the Heights*. This looming uncertainty about who can afford to keep on living or working in the neighborhood of Washington Heights lends the persistent salsa-flavored title song "In the Heights," a nostalgic air celebrating a tight-knit community that is no longer there. Like *West Side Story*, *In the Heights* praises immigrants' can-do spirit in the face of insurmountable odds, but whereas Maria and the other Puerto Ricans navigate racism, pressures to assimilate, and aural discrimination due to their accents on a daily basis as well as the prospect of gang turf warfare in 1950s New York, contemporary bodega owner Usnavi, retiree Abuela Claudia, and hair salon owner Daniela face the encroaching specter of gentrification, with its increasing rents that force them to cut back on necessities or even relocate their businesses elsewhere. The economic strain even impacts freshman Nina at Stanford, who has to work too many hours to pay the fees not covered by her scholarship: "I couldn't work two jobs and study for finals and finish my term papers" (Miranda/Hudes 1.5.36). While

---

8. Jonathan Larson drew inspiration from Puccini's opera *La Bohème* when writing *Rent*.

Nina's predicament recalls Cuban American college student Lizet Ramirez in *Make Your Home Among Strangers,* the biggest difference between the two first-generation students is that the Rosario family of Washington Heights comes together and encourages Nina to earn her degree whereas nobody in the Ramirez household approves of Lizet's academic ambitions. The musical's bittersweet resolution of this problem sees Mr. Rosario selling his taxi business to pay for the rest of Nina's education while she agrees to return to Stanford in the fall and focus on her studies.

Miranda began working on the idea for the play while he was still a student at Wesleyan University and eventually collaborated with playwright Quiara Alegría Hudes for the book. As mentioned earlier, the action of the play takes place between July 3 and 5, when everyone celebrates the community and the ties of affection that geography has facilitated. The stage directions explicitly mention the temporal setting, thereby emphasizing how important the Miranda/Hudes creative team consider this story of the Caribbean diaspora community in a corner of New York City to be emblematic of the larger American story. The opening minute of the season 37 episode of PBS's *Great Performances* documentary series featuring the Tony-award-winning musical *In the Heights* reinforces this point. In this excerpt, lyricist and composer Miranda calls the play "a classic American story" and says, "It's really about these three generations sort of trying to find home and what that means to them." In the documentary, though, Miranda reflects on how the writing process helped him think through what was involved in his own sense of belonging within the specific context of cultural and linguistic migration, an experience US-born Puerto Ricans like Supreme Court Justice Sonia Sotomayor explicitly ascribes to immigration.

During the show's initial run Miranda played Usnavi, a Dominican American character, who dreams of making enough money to return to his parents' ancestral land.[9] However, his statement can also be understood autobiographically: "There's a whole first-generation of immigrants. You grow up with your parents' traditions, you go to school with a completely different set of traditions, and you try to find yourself within the margins. Um, I certainly have. I've tried to write a show working that out for myself." Though both Miranda and Hudes are US-born Puerto Ricans, the characters who populate this fictionalized version of Washington Heights come from different parts of the Hispanophone Greater Antilles. Usnavi is Dominican American, Abuela Claudia is a Cuban exile, Nina's family is Puerto Rican. The musical showcases

---

9. In the film version, directed by John Chu, Miranda plays the role of the piragua guy. Usnavi is played by Anthony Ramos.

a new type of Caribbean American ethnicity through a secondary character, Carla, who celebrates her family's hybrid genealogy in the song "Carnaval del Barrio": "My mom is Dominican-Cuban, My Dad is from Chile and P.R., which means: / I'm Chile-Domini-Curican, but I always say I'm from Queens!" (Miranda/Hudes 2.5.118). The emphasis on these Caribbean populations' Hispanic roots highlights the linguistic and cultural commonalities that unite this ethnic enclave even as the musical acknowledges that the looming threat of gentrification threatens their continued presence in this part of New York City.

The *New York Times* did a story tracking the changing face of ethnic immigration in the city by pulling data from the previous census as well as the 2005–9 community survey. The highest density of the Caribbean population was mapped onto Washington Heights, Corona, and Brookville. In their analysis, reporters Ford Fessenden and Sam Roberts noticed trends that accord with how the musical portrays the rising economic dilemmas that the characters face: "Whites are supplanting Dominicans in northern Manhattan neighborhoods. In parts of southeast Queens, Jamaicans, Haitians and Guyanese are moving in as U.S.-born black populations decline. In Corona, Caribbean immigrant populations have declined as Latin Americans have moved in." These demographic trends suggest that the idyllic neighborhood envisioned in *In the Heights* was on its way out even as Usnavi used Abuela's lottery winnings to anchor his bodega more firmly in the community.[10] However, Usnavi has a last-minute epiphany when he sees the beautiful work his cousin Sonny has commissioned from Graffiti Pete. The finished mural prompts Usnavi to accept that since Abuela Claudia has died, it is up to him to claim the mantle as the neighborhood keeper of memories and he can do so precisely because, like her, his family roots are firmly planted in the Caribbean American neighborhood:

Abuela, I'm sorry,
but I ain't goin' back because I'm telling your story!
and I can say goodbye to you smilin', I found my island
I've been on it this whole time.
I'm home! (Miranda/Hudes 2.14.152)

---

10. The official Warner Brothers trailer for the film adaptation of *In the Heights* explicitly references the Trump-era threats to the Dreamer program established by President Obama to regularize the status of undocumented young people who were brought to the United States as children by their families. A young man with his arm around a girl (possibly Sonny) says, "They're talking about kicking out all the Dreamers" and the next shot features Usnavi and a small child holding a Dominican flag amidst a crowd of people dancing in the street.

This conclusion suggests that the Caribbean is a state of mind and just as present stateside as it is on the map. This is the moment when Usnavi relinquishes the Root identity he inherited from Abuela and embraces the Relation identity of his barrio, his Caribbean Americanness. However, the audience perceives this as an instance of situational irony, since Usnavi has been performing the role of barrio storyteller for the length of the performance.

Given Miranda's stated desire to avoid duplicating the social stereotypes *West Side Story* associates with the New York–Puerto Rican diaspora, it makes sense to consider the three external factors that heighten the precarity of the community the musical celebrates. The first is the acknowledgement that the increasing rents have forced Daniela to close her salon, as she tells Vanessa, Usnavi's love interest: "Can you believe the salon's moving to the Bronx?" (1.6.40). Vanessa's response illustrates how her own understanding of the city is filtered through racial and ethnic lenses: "Gettin' out of the barrio, and headin' to the hood" (1.6.40). Rather than depicting this shift as new, the musical acknowledges that it is cyclical when Kevin, Nina's father, sees a picture of the garage's previous owner, "Mr. O'Hanrahan. When half this block was Irish" (2.8.133). Through this reference to the changing ethnic profile of the same plot of land, *In the Heights* reinforces the idea that New York City, and the United States as a whole, have been shaped and transformed by various waves of immigration across time.

A blackout is both the second external threat the musical depicts and a common feature of summer life in New York City. The more idealistic members of the neighborhood join Usnavi in appreciating how the sudden darkness makes it possible to see the fireworks better against the darkness of the night sky. For the more cynical characters like Sonny and Graffiti Pete, the blackout is ominous in its potential to give rise to violence or cover up acts of vandalism as this exchange reveals.

> SONNY: "Naw, man, I can't leave. we gotta guard the store."
> GRAFFITI PETE: "They gonna bombard the store until you ain't got a store no more!"
> SONNY: I got a baseball bat on a rack in the back.
> GRAFFITI PETE: I got a couple roman candles, we can distract the vandals!
> (1.12.90)

The prospect of losing the store makes Sonny gain a new appreciation for what his cousin Usnavi's bodega means to the community and to their family. However, the young men's efforts are not sufficient to prevent the store from being burgled. The stage directions for act 2, scene 2, emphasize the physical evidence of the aftermath of the evening's events: "USNAVI outside the bodega. The awning is slashed, the window is broken. Neighbors stand by looking at the damage" (2.2.101). Regardless, Sonny shows a new maturity when he recognizes that protecting the bodega is his responsibility. This changes the cousins' relationship, making it into more of a partnership, which helps explain why Usnavi now relishes his role as Sonny's mentor thereby claiming his own new status as an elder.

The third external element that influences how events transpire in the play is the lottery as a deux ex machina. Playing the lottery is a cultural tradition common both to Caribbean islands across the archipelago and throughout the many states in the Union. Within the musical, the stakes for the community are made clear in the first act during the song, "96,000" when all the main characters share ideas about what they would do with the money if they won. This becomes a more pressing issue in the second act, when Abuela dies after having cashed in the winning lottery ticket. Though we first find out she won at the end of the song, "Paciencia y Fé / Patience and Faith," it is not until the beginning of the second act when the audience learns that nobody stole the money during the blackout. Abuela's plans for it are to distribute the winnings equally between herself, Usnavi, and Sonny as she reveals in the song, "Hundreds of Stories" in scene 3 (105). After Abuela's death, Usnavi reconsiders the plan and decides to be generous by addressing the languishing problem that has stymied Vanessa's independence: her mother's alcoholism. He works with Daniela to get Vanessa an apartment away from Washington Heights where she can use her salary to support herself rather than enabling her mother. Thus, even though Usnavi changes his mind about leaving for the Dominican Republic, *In the Heights* affirms that a community's affective ties are what keep it together even as its members become dispersed across the city. The musical enacts its own kind of Caribbean diaspora defined not by everyone's island of origin, as was the focus of the spontaneous "Carnaval del Barrio," but by the ties of friendship (Daniela-Vanessa, Sonny and Graffiti), family (Usnavi-Sonny, the Rosario family), and affection (Sonny and Nina, Usnavi and Vanessa) that mark their time in the Caribbean American enclave of Washington Heights.

ON YOUR FEET!

On Your Feet! explicitly situates itself as a work of the exilic experience and its focus is on the process of building community across difference or Relation identity in the United States rather than simply resisting the Castro authoritarian rule of the island the family left behind. In this emphasis, it echoes the grassroots vision of Marco Rubio's *American Dreams*. The first act often recalls the family's opposition to the Castro regime and their patriotism toward their new country via the father's army service during the Vietnam War. This memory work takes place through anecdotes spoken by Gloria Estefan's mother and grandmother; it signals the family's ideological belonging to Miami's Cuban American community. Otherwise, the musical uses Miami as a backdrop against which to understand the Estefan family's Cuban American success story. However, the action onstage quickly switches to reflect the itinerant nature of a band's touring schedule. This highlights how hard the musicians had to work to cross-over from Spanish-language radio and connect with audiences in the English-language media landscape. Place and locality are less important to the story arc here than it was in *In the Heights* precisely because the community the Estefans and their band members sought to create was one that transcended cultural specificity and focused on the universal appeal of the band's musical rhythms. Thus, this immigrant success story deploys the Horatio Alger trope of success through individual effort but gives it a Caribbean American twist: *On Your Feet!* celebrates a single family's rise from rags to riches and credits their success to persistence and hard work rather than to any community ties or help.

This autobiographical jukebox musical leverages the strength of Gloria Estefan (née Fajardo) and the Miami Sound Machine's discography to narrate the singer's rise to stardom. This is a triumphant tale that celebrates various accomplishments: the Fajardo family's escape from Cuba and new life in the United States, the central love story between Emilio and Gloria Estefan, their band's rise to the top of the American charts, and Gloria's miraculous recovery from a near-catastrophic back injury while on tour. It is light entertainment that counts on the audience's familiarity with the top forty hits to flesh out the protagonists' Cuban American background in more detail. *On Your Feet!*'s Broadway run lasted from November 2015–August 2017, followed by a national tour. Cuba's former president and the leader of its long-lasting revolutionary regime, Fidel Castro, died in November 2016. And, in one of his last official presidential actions, Barack Obama announced the end of the Clinton-era "wet foot / dry foot" policy that had allowed Cuban immigrants who reached the United States mainland to request an immigration parole and apply for permanent residence status, while those who were apprehended at sea were returned to Cuba or a third country (DHS) in January of 2017.

With the end of the special status, Cuban immigrants seeking entry into the United States became subject to the same restrictions and the possibility of deportation as any other immigrants. Adrian Florido a contributor to NPR's podcast on race, *Code Switch*, asked Cuban American sociologist Guillermo Grenier about the likely implications of this on the Cuban American community. Florido reports that, "Grenier said he expects the end of wet-foot, dry-foot to gradually change notions of Cuban-American identity as newer migrants become subject to the construct of 'illegality' that drives so much of the policy and rhetoric around immigration in the United States." Up until 2017, Cubans who arrived in the United States were considered political exiles rather than economic migrants. After the repeal, Cuban nationals became subject to the Trump administration's draconian immigration policies. Emilio Estefan's introduction to the *On Your Feet!* cast performance during the Tony Awards show in December of 2016, signals his growing awareness of immigrant groups' new precarity in the wake of the election. Proclaiming that "Broadway is about diversity" and thanking audiences and the Broadway establishment for the warm welcome the show has received, Estefan mentions his wife will make a guest appearance before joking that the show's organizers "told me for sure that I have to announce this. All the cast of *On Your Feet!*, we all have papers. And they all, believe it or not, they all [sic] legal." While the joke was in questionable taste, the line earned big laughs from the assembled audience, perhaps due to the shared recognition that immigration and the threat of deportation would take a central role in the political life of the nation for the next four years.

On Your Feet! briefly recounts that earlier Cuban immigrant story of fleeing repression and adds it to the pantheon of other immigrant tales that gave rise to the idea of the United States as a nation of immigrants. Three main overlapping story lines coalesce around the idea of the band's success. The first is its lead singer's coming of age: Gloria Fajardo is a bright, talented young Cuban American woman struggling to break free from her conservative Cuban mother, who cannot adapt to the informal social mores of their family's new country. Gloria falls in love with fellow Cuban expatriate Emilio Estefan after joining his band. Through the trope of Gloria's estrangement from her mother, the musical suggests that only those Caribbean Americans who embrace elements from both sides of their heritage—their island culture and the opportunities available in the United States—can successfully connect with their compatriots across the differences of their respective experiences in Relation identity. By forging something new, a hybrid combination of dynamic Cuban rhythms and English language lyrics understandable by all, the Estefans found the key to their crossover success in the 1980s.

Emilio Estefan's struggle to convince record companies of his band's crossover potential from Spanish-language radio to the English-language top 40 is a secondary and complementary story of achievement. This through line leans heavily into the idea that music's universal appeal makes it an ideal means to foment an appreciation for diversity. The conga-line conceit that communicates this is somewhat heavy-handed but ultimately succeeds because it resonates with so many of the audiences' personal experiences with this music: the Estefans perform their set at a bar mitzvah, an Italian wedding, and a Shriner's convention before a music executive finally agrees to record their English-language songs. The image of a multicultural conga line serves as a visual pun that comically conveys the notion of the musical "melting pot" at work. The third motif is the overcoming of adversity discussed earlier.

In a generally positive review of the *On Your Feet!*, Charles Isherwood remarks upon the show's explicit celebration of diversity as a defining aspect of Americanness by pausing on a pivotal moment: "'You should look very closely at my face,' a heated Emilio says, 'because whether you know it or not . . . this is what an American looks like.' (This applause-baiting line hits its mark)" (ellipsis in original). I agree that this is the show's most anticipated moment and one that is clearly telegraphed ahead of time. It is an explicit declaration of Caribbean American belonging to the social and cultural life of the United States that illustrates the dynamic nature of immigration: it changes the nation that welcomes the immigrants as much as it inspires the new arrivals to become something different than who they were in the place they left behind. Though he admits the musical's book relies a bit heavily on cliched dialogue and that some of the musical numbers stand in the way of the plot development, Isherwood celebrates the musical's insistence on broadening the definition of who is American and contrasts it to Miranda's blockbuster show.

The review's last line first invites and then refutes such comparisons: "Does 'Hamilton' have a cute little Jewish boy leading a conga number? I think not." Though this might seem like a spurious comparison, Isherwood points to the different Americas each show invokes. Despite its multiracial/ethnic cast, *Hamilton* is set in colonial America. The much-celebrated drafting of the Constitution ensures not only a stable form of government that endures until today, but the show necessarily glosses over the white supremacist three-fifths compromise of article 1, section 2, which defines an enslaved person as only having a fraction of the value of a free person. *On Your Feet!* flows in the opposite direction of *Hamilton* and travels beyond the urban insularity of *In the Heights*. Emilio and Gloria Estefan move from the heart of the Cuban American enclave in Miami to international success and the musical's focus ends up being back on the biological family rather than celebrating community. And it is in the family-centric context of bar mitzvahs and weddings that anyone is likely to encounter the Estefan's music now, as we conga together to mark rites of passage.

The show's final overlapping story of achievement concludes the entertainment; it depicts the lead singer's miraculous recovery from the injuries sustained in the tour bus crash and the birth of the couple's second child, Emily, who now co-stars with her mother in *Red Table Talk: The Estefans*. Coincidentally, this last phase in the Estefans' success story entails the end of the Miami Sound Machine as an entity. Whereas the band name tied the couple geographically to the city where they got their start (and still live), Gloria Estefan's emergence as a solo performer frees the couple from these constraints. However, the musical version of their courtship and professional lives triangulates by using the imperative verb form implicit in its title, (Get) *On Your Feet!* to invite the audiences to participate in their performance and thus, become part of the act itself. This act of belonging is communal and explicitly cross-cultural. It contrasts with *West Side Story*'s tragic ending.

HAMILTON

By way of conclusion, I return to *Hamilton* to consider how the story arc depends for its success on two fundamental breaks with the Caribbean. The first is geographical and the second is with the typical Caribbean celebration of extended family. The founding father's backstory makes up the content of the show's first song, "Alexander Hamilton" and his friends, foes, and loved ones convey the details in what Miranda calls, "a debt to the prologue of *Sweeney Todd*" (Miranda 2016, 16). Aaron Burr's evocation of the Caribbean island where Hamilton was born, a "forgotten / Spot in the Caribbean . . . impoverished, in squalor" echoes some of the scorn that the pro-US chorus members of *West Side Story* had toward Puerto Rico in the song "America" (16). Hamilton's wife, the wronged Eliza, recounts her husband's unhappy childhood:

> When he was ten his father split, full of it,
>   debt-ridden,
> Two years later, see Alex and his
>   mother bed-ridden,
> Half-dead sittin' in their own sick,
> The scent thick. (16)

The final element contributing to his degradation was a devastating hurricane that hit the area. Together these three touchstones constitute the bulk of what we can describe as Hamilton's Caribbean upbringing. It is no wonder this immigrant was ready to buy into the show's version of the American dream, which promises, "In New York you can / be a new man" (17). The promise of a fresh start is what motivates all immigration, yet the undeniable fact of Hamilton's comparative privilege as a white, English-speaking, autodidact man of very limited means, rather than the brown-skinned, unskilled laborers with a Spanish accent like the Estefan and Fajardo families in *On Your Feet!*, Usnavi's parents in *In the Heights,* and the migrants from Puerto Rico in *West Side Story,* meant he had more leeway in "not throwing away [his] shot" whereas the others never quite got theirs.

The second way in which Hamilton fails to live up to the type of Caribbean identity imagined in *On Your Feet!, In the Heights,* and *West Side Story* is the break with the extended family. As an orphan, Alexander Hamilton had to make his own way in the world even though the musical acknowledges he only arrived on the US mainland due to the generosity of his community, who paid for his passage. Once in New York, he is alone; his ambition drives him to fulfill the promise of his talent. The show's depiction of its titular hero portrays his need to express himself by writing as simultaneously his greatest strength and his most tragic flaw since his constant need to narrativize his actions is what prompts him to recount every sordid detail of his extra-marital affair in a bid to escape being blackmailed. This act of hubris alienates him from his wife, their children, and his trusted confidante/sister-in-law, to say nothing of his former colleagues in the United States government. Hamilton's fall from grace is the inverse of Usnavi's epiphany to claim his voice and role as community storyteller. While the loss of their son in a duel reconciles him with Eliza, Hamilton is a diminished figure who never quite recovers from the shock.

The musical ends with Eliza's apotheosis as the person who carries out her husband's vision. In refusing to share the details of her own biography and instead founding an orphanage and rehabilitating her husband's legacy, Eliza Hamilton emerges as the cultural translator figure that Broadway and Disney+ also play. All three versions of the story—written text, Broadway musical, and filmed performance—disseminate information about this minor character in the nation's history and, in so doing, open up the door for Dreamers and current citizens, born or naturalized, to imagine themselves as the rightful heirs to the tradition of making the United States a "more perfect union" every day.

CONCLUSION

Aspirational Whiteness and the Limits of Belonging

Whereas the previous chapters have explored conflicting aspects of the Caribbean American experience and sense of belonging from the perspective of civil servants, celebrities, and fictional characters inhabiting the page, screen, and/or stage who all reside within the continental United States, Tiffanie Drayton's recent memoir, *Black American Refugee: Escaping the Narcissism of the American Dream* (2022) discusses her complex emotional relationship to the United States from the geographic vantage point of the homeland she left behind as a young child: Trinidad and Tobago. As the subtitle suggests, it is only by returning to her birthplace that Drayton can "escape" the disappointment and frustration with the nation's inability to let her belong fully as an American citizen while living in the United States. Drayton's self-designation as a "Black American" and the positionality she claims in the prologue's first line as someone writing "from exile" clearly indicate she does not entirely foreclose the possibility of returning to the United States at some future time (1).

Neither the Caribbean region nor its people mark Drayton's tale in any substantive way; the islands fade into the narrative's background until Drayton vaguely recalls her occasional youthful sojourns there to attend Carnival as paradisiacal respites from her humdrum American existence. In these passages, Drayton narrates from the vantage point of a tourist rather than claiming insider status as an island-born person. According to cultural critic Marita Sturken, American tourists "are outsiders to the daily practices of life in tourist destinations, and they are largely unaware of the effects of how tourist economies have structured the daily lives of the people who live and work in tourist locales" (9–10). Beyond situating herself spatially as a resident of Trinidad and Tobago, Drayton never includes any other specific detail of her contemporary Caribbean reality, such as which of the islands she lives in with her own American-born children, any interactions she may have with other Trinidadians, or her experience of the rich cultural and ethnic traditions and fierce political rivalries that characterize public life at the tail end of the Antillean archipelago. Despite her physical distance from the United States, Drayton's convenient silence on Trinidad and Tobago's own fraught race relations between the descendants of people from Africa, India, China, and Europe as well as the mixed-race population, and the lack of any acknowledgement of the islands' imperial past with its legacies of enslavement and indentured servitude mark her text as a fundamentally American work of life writing. So, belonging works in this text in two simultaneous ways: first, through Drayton's choice not to identify herself as Trinidadian (the closest she comes is by describing the islands as "the home my mother left behind when I was a child") and second, through her repeated complaints about being denied full citizenship status as an American within the United States (Drayton 1).

I read *Black American Refugee* and its performative rejection of the United States as the final example of belonging in this study. Though it stridently critiques the interpersonal and systemic racism Drayton experienced while growing up in the United States, the memoir also occasionally falls into its own form of anti-Blackness when Drayton objects to how her Caribbean Americanness is unintelligible or even invisible to her compatriots in statements such as, "In America, I am a Black woman," a race-based designation that does not capture the fullness of Drayton's lived experience (1).[1] A few pages later she contrasts how she experiences her race differently in the majority-white society of the United States and in Trinidad and Tobago, where the two largest racial/ethnic groups are people descended from Africans and Indians:

> In America, my Black life was narrowly defined in a way that colored it gray, dark, and dingy—rife with grit, hardship, and constant disappointment. Upon my return to Trinidad, my Black life became one enveloped

---

1. Drayton later describes her own life choices and situations, such as being pregnant out of wedlock and receiving government-backed health insurance, through a joking reference to living up to damaging stereotypes about Black women being considered "welfare queen[s]" (248). I find Drayton's pattern of voicing and using demeaning caricatures about Black women problematic precisely because Drayton often speaks about not fully identifying with the Black American community.

in the greens and blues of the ocean; mocha, caramel, and mahogany faces; and the rainbow of pinks, oranges, teals, and yellows of glittering Carnival costumes. (3)

The false contrast set up in this passage is especially problematic because it uses maximalist generalizations of both experiences. The passive voice with which Drayton describes her experience of Blackness in this passage as being "narrowly defined" suggests that neither she nor any African American has agency over their own lives whereas Trinidadian people of color are mere caricatures who live in sync with the elements, party nonstop, and apparently have no responsibilities. Drayton's tendency to exaggerate her critique of the home she left behind and oversimplify the joy and respite she finds in life in the Caribbean constitutes a clear example of how Sturken contends American tourists position themselves with regards to history and world events: "The mode of the tourist, with its innocent pose and distanced position, evokes the American citizen who participates uncritically in a culture in which notions of good and evil are used to define complex conflicts and tensions" (Sturken 10). Drayton's calculus about the limits of her Black life in the United States plays into such uncritical categories. The memoir further displays the tourist mode by contrasting Drayton's mobility, signaled through her own and her family's repeated trips to Trinidad, with those (presumably Black) Americans who could not afford to leave the US and are thus, "trapped in the turmoil" (Drayton 5). Drayton participates in the very political economy of ignorance that she wishes to escape from when she sets up faux contrasts within her narrative like these two examples. In so doing, however, she gives short shrift to the rich complexity of people's lives across various points in the African diaspora, especially through the stereotypical and reductive Carnival trope she repeatedly uses as a shorthand to communicate her feeling of comfort within Trinidad and Tobago.

As a critique of how the United States fails to deliver in its promise of full citizenship and inclusion of BIPOC into the body politic, *Black American Refugee* fares better when it explains the depths of Drayton's disillusionment through the prism of her own dysfunctional romantic life, suggesting that her family's adopted country has treated her as badly as have her abusive ex-lovers. This is evident in the text's chapter titles, which correspond to the spectrum of coercive behaviors typical of a manipulative romantic partner: 1. Love-Bombing, 2. Devalued, 3. Discarded, 4. Calm, 5. Moving the Goalposts and Gaslighting, 6. Healing, 7. Hoovered, 8. Lethal Abuse, 9. The Breakup, Epilogue: Reconciliation. On the one hand, this catchy conceit renders the memoir immediately "relatable" to a segment of the reading public whose own relationship history is far from smooth and performs what Jeffrey Bennet, in the context of discussing panels from the AIDS quilt, has called "the emotive aspects of citizenship typically shunned in democratic practice" (134). The language of sexual or emotional trauma represents a broader set of experiences than the frustration from the disconnect between the ideal of full citizenship and one's own more limited access to the rights, privileges, and responsibilities therein. Thus, Drayton claims the moral high ground for herself and, by extension, for other survivors of such toxic entanglements by using the affirming vocabulary of breaking the cycle of violence that had kept one bound to an abuser and applying it to describe her relationship to the United States.

The biggest problem with the memoir's explicit conflation of the United States with the two problematic lovers about whom Drayton writes is that the latter are also Caribbean American. The first of these, Justin, comes from a privileged background in Ohio and has a grandmother who immigrated from Barbados (Drayton 208). He is indecisive and a bit of a freeloader; he would neither find a job nor commit to the relationship. In contrast, Gabriel is Haitian American man who lived with his parents but worked full time while also pursuing a master's degree (237). He fathered both of Drayton's children but was controlling and physically abusive toward her. After reflecting on her experience in the United States from her Caribbean dwelling, Drayton uses passive voice once more to frame her dramatic epiphany: "Finally, America, the abuser, was unmasked" (5). This infelicitous turn of phrase at once conveys Drayton's false modesty by not taking credit for performing the action of unmasking, and it also is emblematic of how the memoirist understands the individual's relationship to systemic racism as something so powerful and abstract that it defies all attempts at self-efficacy. By hiding behind the grammatical construction, Drayton effaces her own agency in calling out what she finds intolerable in the social and cultural life of the United States even as she eagerly embraces the subject position of the victimized or abused party.

Black American Refugee, thus, enacts what Caribbean literature scholar Donette Francis calls "sexual citizenship," a concept she adapted and broadened from David Evans, who coined it. For Francis, "sexual citizenship disrupts the boundaries between the public and the private while also unsettling the borders between nation and the diaspora. Connecting female sexual citizenship both inside and outside the region challenges the dichotomy that posits diaspora as an empowering 'elsewhere' of sexual liberation versus home as space for sexual oppression" (4). As a diasporic writer, Drayton flips this logic around: she equates the home she grew up in (the US) with oppression, while celebrating her birthplace as the site for sexual liberation even though neither Justin nor Gabriel stay in Trinidad long-term.

Black American Refugee suggests that the United States seduced Drayton into valuing aspirational whiteness at the expense of her Blackness. The memoir depicts the American public school system as the main purveyor and reinforcer of such self-defeating internalized racism:

> As I walked past the hallways filled with Black and Hispanic kids, I felt a deep sense of superiority and pride in the fact that I would be joining the white kids in the higher-level courses. I was one of the "smart" kids whom my teachers adored. Though I stood out as the only Black girl in my AP classes and battled some self-consciousness, I much preferred the absence of full acceptance over the outright fear of violence and ostracism. (Drayton 98)

Although the adult Drayton regrets the arrogance of her youth, this passage powerfully conveys how systemic racism reinforces an association between intellectual achievement and rewards while suggesting that the price one pays for mediocrity or lackluster performance is one's safety. Even when she moves from Texas to Florida, and then to New Jersey, Drayton finds other examples of young Black women disillusioned by their failure to realize the benefits associated with "proximal" whiteness. One such friend from her youth was Ashley; her parents had moved to the suburbs and Drayton suggests that the cultural isolation she experienced there was detrimental to her mental health, leaving her deracinated. Drayton recounts that Ashley routinely used a blond, blue-eyed avatar when playing *The Sims*, thereby further distancing her sense of self from her Black body. But rather than inspiring pity, Drayton's description of the spectacle of Ashley's performative whiteness once again reinforces her own arrogance: "The peculiarity of it all—the whiteness she described and subscribed to and the figment of Blackness that she created in her head—made us grateful for our 'underprivileged' lives among people of color" (120). While on its surface, this seems like a contradictory set of standards, this passage points to an interesting dichotomy in how whiteness signifies.

In the first example, whiteness functions as a sociocultural category associated with intellectual acuity and arbitered by the teachers in an academic setting. Kids in advanced classes, such as Drayton, become culturally white and, thus, belong within that intellectual space. The second instance depicts whiteness as a superficial attribute of appearance—Ashley is alone and nobody in the virtual space of the game can see through her digital whiteface. Drayton and her companions occupy the arbiter position and deem Ashley's understanding of Blackness to be less real than the European-looking avatar she claims as her own, calling the former a "figment." Drayton regards Ashley's performance of belonging within either Black or white communities as equally unsuccessful.

Within Drayton's account, these two valences of whiteness echo similar phenomena that social commentators have begun to see in white supremacist grassroots organizations like the Trump supporters who stormed the Capitol on January 6, 2021, or the multiracial membership of organizations like the Proud Boys. In a recent opinion piece published in the *Washington Post*, Cristina Beltrán explains the emergence of a complex racial category:

> Rooted in America's ugly history of white supremacy, indigenous dispossession and anti-blackness, multiracial whiteness is an ideology invested in the unequal distribution of land, wealth, power and privilege—a form of hierarchy in which the standing of one section of the population is premised on the debasement of others. Multiracial whiteness reflects an understanding of whiteness as a political color and not simply a racial identity—a discriminatory worldview in which feelings of freedom and belonging are produced through the persecution and dehumanization of others.

Beltrán argues that "multiracial whiteness" is a weaponized conflation of whiteness with European culture and therefore with belonging to dominant society in the United States.[2] In her discussions of aspirational or proximal whiteness in *Black American Refugee*, Drayton exemplifies just how frustrating the pursuit of such an ideal can be, especially for people who also experience casual racism due to their skin color and so forth. In contrast, white people's failure to understand whiteness as a racial category makes them assume "race" is something that applies only to Brown or Black people. As Ibram Kendi reminds us, "race is fundamentally a power construct of blended difference that lives socially. Race creates new forms of power: the power to categorize and judge, elevate and downgrade, include and exclude" (38). By aspiring to the power and privileges of American whiteness, Drayton and the white multiracial Proud Boys uphold the racist system that denies access to those who are neither phenotypically nor culturally white.

Kimberly Guilfoyle and Enrique Tarrio are two high profile public figures with Caribbean heritage and ties to the Trump administration: Guilfoyle's mother was Puerto Rican and her father was an Irish immigrant, whereas Enrique Tarrio identifies as Afro-Cuban. Besides dating the president's oldest son and namesake, Guilfoyle served as the National Chair of Trump Victory Finance Committee and led the "Women for Trump" aspect of his reelection campaign. Guilfoyle put her powers of persuasion on display during the

---

2. I want to clarify that Beltrán's concept of "multiracial whiteness" is not related to Kevin Brown's use of the term "Black Multiracials." Brown's neologism refers to multiracial people who have at least one Black parent. Her concept conveys the diversity of people who identify with aspirational whiteness as a cultural concept regardless of their parentage.

high-profile speech she delivered on the first night of the Republican National Convention in 2020. This marked yet another occasion in which Guilfoyle demonstrated how instrumental the memory of her mother is to her. While I do not assume that Guilfoyle has sole authorship over the speech she delivered, however, the facts of her biography correspond both to her political persona and to her personal background and family history and thus I will analyze them as such. Guilfoyle introduces herself to the audience by saying, "I speak to you tonight as a mother, a former prosecutor, a Latina, and a proud American" (PBS). A few moments later she qualifies that last identity to describe herself as "a first generation American" whose support for President Trump grows out of her fear of socialism and support for law enforcement. Guilfoyle then invokes a curated version of her genealogy to simultaneously celebrate the ideal of the immigrant American dream even as she then juxtaposes it to the failure of collectivist regimes in two iconic parts of the circum-Caribbean: Cuba and Venezuela.

> My mother, Mercedes, was a special education teacher from Aguadilla, Puerto Rico. My father, also an immigrant, came to this nation in pursuit of the American Dream. Now, I consider it my duty to fight to protect that dream. Rioters must not be allowed to destroy our cities. Human sex drug traffickers should not be allowed to cross our border. The same Socialist policies which destroyed places like Cuba and Venezuela must not take root in our cities and our schools.[3]

Mercedes Guilfoyle's occupation as a special education teacher has very little to do with any other part of this passage of Guilfoyle's speech. Kimberly's reference to it constitutes virtue signaling. The geographical markers that follow are all to Spanish speaking places—Aguadilla, Puerto Rico, Cuba, and Venezuela—while the rest of her family story consciously elides her father's Irish nationality and his white race.[4] This triangulation suggests that Caribbean countries that govern themselves independently of the United States are full of human traffickers, socialists, and rioters eager to cross the border and take over American cities and, specifically, their schools.

---

    3. I have cited the transcript version of the speech available through Rev.com. The capitalization of the word "Socialist" was present in this web version available at: https://www.rev.com/blog/transcripts/kimberly-guilfoyle-2020-rnc-speech-transcript.

    4. Also absent from this catalogue of places is California, the state where she was born and raised and where her first ex-husband (Gavin Newsom) now serves as governor, though she mentions it in the next segment of her speech as an illustrative example of how "the Democrats" have also "destroyed places" domestically, presumably due to their "Socialist policies."

Within this map of potential threats to the American way of life, Puerto Rico's status as a signifier is a bit unclear: as a territory of the United States, but a predominantly Spanish speaking island, it is a political Bermuda Triangle that could either serve as the first stop in these bad actors' attacks against America or as a source of reinforcements from where to recruit US citizens willing to protect the American Dream, most likely through the labor of their military service. While this last part is not overtly stated, the martial rhetoric of Guilfoyle's evocation of Cuba and Venezuela as "destroyed" societies reinforces Puerto Rico's importance as the last remaining US military stronghold in the Caribbean.[5]

Guilfoyle's language in this passage recalls the tone of President Trump's description of undocumented Mexicans as "bad hombres" (F. Garcia) during the third presidential debate against Hilary Clinton in the 2016 campaign (F. Garcia). However, Guilfoyle avoids two pitfalls of that earlier Trump insult: the use of mock Spanish and the focus on people from the region in question as embodying the undesirable qualities she decries. Guilfoyle's improvement or remix of this original dog whistle carefully avoids offending members of two key Republican voting blocs in Florida—Venezuelans and Cubans—by focusing the bulk of her critique on an abstract straw man, "Socialist policies." This is a savvy political move on her part since, as NBC News reports, these two groups of voters came out in huge numbers in support of the Trump ticket during 2020 (Sesin). Carmen Sesin reports that the Trump organization messaging strategy aimed at Latinx was well coordinated and disseminated across English and Spanish language media outlets: "Trump and Republicans misleadingly casting Biden as a socialist and even a 'Castro-Chavista,' referring to Fidel Castro of Cuba and Hugo Chavez of Venezuela." Thus, the text of Guilfoyle's speech is proof of her discipline and dedication to staying on-message for Donald Trump. Since she dates the president's oldest son, this ends up being personally beneficial to Guilfoyle whereas Tarrio has been charged with conspiracy due to his involvement with the Capitol insurrection (Tillman).

Enrique Tarrio leads both the far-right terrorist organization, the Proud Boys, as well as a grassroots campaign called "Latinos for Trump" that is unaffiliated with the official Trump political organization. Unlike former president Trump, Tarrio has made a show of publicly denouncing white supremacy (D. Sullivan), and he also proclaims that the Proud Boys is an organization he leads that has very few barriers to entry: "We accept people from all walks

---

5. Puerto Rico houses Fort Buchanan, an Army military base that bills itself as the "'Sentinel of the Caribbean' and the only federal military installation in Puerto Rico and the Caribbean" on its official military website. Full disclosure: I spent part of my youth living on base in Fort Buchanan.

of life. . . . We don't ask what your religion, cult background [sic] is when you join the Proud Boys. All it takes to become a Proud Boy is that you love America, and you're born with a penis. And if you're not born with a penis, we have a Proud Boys women's group" (D. Sullivan).[6] Despite these public statements, the FBI considers the Proud Boys to be "an extremist group with ties to white nationalism" since 2018 (Solomon).[7] In their leadership within gendered political activism groups, both Guilfoyle and Tarrio represent the dark side of Caribbean American activism through their public endorsement of exclusionary and divisive rhetoric that leverages the banner of "American-ness" and patriotism as shorthand for only those of their compatriots who share their Republican party affiliation and white supremacist views. Ironically, in so doing, Tarrio and Guilfoyle both invoke their Caribbean heritage as the source of their white supremacist American patriotism.

Unlike Guilfoyle, who has leveraged her life story into a career arc that may be described as that of a political entrepreneur, Tarrio's claim to fame is his leadership status within the Proud Boys organization. He made an unsuccessful run for elective office (D. Sullivan). Generally, Tarrio does not go out of his way to give controversial speeches for public audiences nor has he published any manifesto or biographical account though he occasionally speaks to mainstream news outlets. One such instance took place in August 2019 when he agreed to be interviewed by CNN's Sara Sidner at the site of the Portland Proud Boy's rally. During this exchange, he made reference to his own Afro-Cubanness and the family members he lost when they opposed the Castro government to refute charges that the organization he leads is racist. Responding to Snider's statement that Portland residents of color feel terrorized by some of the language used by groups like Proud Boys and Patriot Prayer, another white supremacist organization, Tarrio rejected this characterization by pivoting to his personal background:

---

6. Tarrio's vague reference to an affiliated women's group is more fraught than would appear at face value. Alexander Reid Ross, writing for *The Daily Beast*, explains that the national Proud Boys organization are at odds with the most recent version of a women's group, the "Proud Girls" started and led by Tara LaRosa, a former MMA fighter and the self-appointed "Den Mother." According to Ross, LaRosa started a "Proud Girls" channel on Telegram and featured a photo of herself alongside Enrique Tarrio. While some state chapters have recognized the group, others refuse to and have turned against those who support LaRosa. Ross also mentions that a previous incarnation of an affiliated women's group, the "Proud Boys' Girls" had a Facebook group page from 2016–18.

7. An article in *The Hill* published few months later reported that Renn Cannon, an FBI special agent in charge, claimed that the agency had not intended to designate the Proud Boys organization as an extremist group during a presentation to the Clark's County Sheriff's Office in Vancouver, Washington (Gstalter). Cannon suggested there was a miscommunication between the federal agency and the Sheriff's office, explaining that "the FBI tries to characterize potential threats from members of the Proud Boys but does not designate groups" (Gstalter).

ET: Just a second ago you mentioned people of color, right? And, you said—I'm a person of color, right? I'm Cuban, right? My family, two members of my family got killed in Castro's regime, so it's a difference of opinion whether people of color, white people, it's always about race. Our message isn't, today, our message wasn't about race, our message has never been about race.

SS: What is your message?

ET: When you join our ranks, when you join our ranks, we don't ask you what race you are, what religion you are, we just accept you for who you are. We have liberals, we have a lot of liberals, there's actually a high profile liberal here who's part of our ranks.

Although Tarrio spun his narrative about the Proud Boy's open recruitment policy during this interview, he has not sought the national spotlight like Guilfoyle has done, preferring instead to address his followers directly via the conservative social media platform Parler. Ironically, Tarrio's discipline about messaging primarily via across alt-right media platforms briefly forced major news outlets to legitimate Parler by quoting extensively from his posts on that platform whenever they want to refer to the group within the stories they file. After the January 6 invasion of the Capitol, Amazon, Google, and Apple all banned the Parler app (Nicas and Alba).

In their public statements, both Guilfoyle and Tarrio have demonstrated their adherence to white nationalist ideals as encapsulated by the Trump administration. They want to enlist others to their narrow view of patriotism defined by unqualified love of country, unquestioning adherence to the idea of American exceptionalism, and suspicion of foreigners and ethnic Americans who complain about not being treated fairly. Guilfoyle's and Tarrio's Caribbean American heritage is only useful inasmuch as it demonstrates their support for the United States as a policing power that keeps other nations, and internal dissenters in line. The relationship Guilfoyle and Tarrio imagine between themselves and their compatriots is the inverse of that espoused by all the Caribbean American candidates for the nation's highest office examined in the first chapter. However, in this divided nation, it is small wonder that Ted Cruz and Marco Rubio have publicly aligned themselves with aspects of the Trump version of white nationalism (Perano and Treene). As white Caribbean Americans Cruz, Rubio, and Guilfoyle enhance their already-privileged status by actively subverting their political opponents' efforts to build coalitions and enact a national plan to handle the rampant spread of the COVID-19 pandemic. Enrique Tarrio's deliberate acts of anti-Black violence and vandalism are engineered to draw attention away from his own Blackness, thereby ensuring that his most American story of leading a white supremacist organization keeps others from further integrating institutions and organizations in the United States unless they are willing to surrender their overlapping subject positions (racial, gendered, class) in the bargain.

Sociologist Richard Alba studies patterns of ethnic self-identification as "white" in the US Census and has concluded: "In a society where racial and ethnic origins historically have confined Americans to different social strata, the mainstream has been long associated with the social spaces and cultural practices of white Americans." Though Alba remarks that whiteness as an identity category, "has never been fixed; it is a malleable concept, and it is on its way to changing again, as it has before," he does not suggest that it can encompass or be available to all ethno-racial identities. Alba's analysis of people's self-identification with it suggests that this status comes at the expense of one's ethnic identity; the type of assimilation he describes effaces traces of difference in favor of emphasizing the commonality of skin tone. Even Alba's critics agree that "in the U.S. ethnoracial order, entrenched privileges and opportunities are afforded to some and not to others" (Mora and Rodríguez-Muñiz). In a response to his essay, G. Cristina Mora and Michael Rodríguez-Muñiz seize on Alba's use of Latinxs as an exemplary case study for the expansion of whiteness as a racial category in the United States due to this group's increasing tendency to identify as "white" in Census data given their rates of inter-marriage with whites and their socioeconomic entry into "mainstream" class. Mora and Rodríguez-Muñiz point out that there are more complex reasons behind Latinxs' increasing tendency to self-identify as white: "To be sure, some Latinos understand themselves as racially white. This identification may be interpreted as aspirational—a kind of racial passing—but it does not necessarily provide blanket evidence for the inevitable social inclusion of Latinos in the white-dominant mainstream." Mora and Rodríguez-Muñiz cite Julie Dowling's work on Mexican Americans and Mara Loveman's research on Puerto Ricans to suggest that the choice to identify as "white" on the Census reflects Latinxs' insecurities about their own status as a minority population more than it affirms their sense of belonging to a dominant society: "These examples suggest that white self-identification—the very evidence some scholars have used to make claims about the whitening or assimilation of Latinos—may in fact register conditions of ethnoracial exclusion. In other words, choosing whiteness is also related to the perils of living as a minority for many" (Mora and Rodríguez-Muñiz). Whereas Mora and Rodríguez-Muñiz theorized that some of the affinity people of color felt with whiteness as an idealized racial marker to describe themselves on the Census was motivated by their fear of "ethnoracial exclusion," Beltrán suggests in contrast that the driver is not fear but rather aspiration; they want to be judged within a system that values "colorblind individualism" rather than putting any stock on a given person's racial or ethnic identity.

Tiffanie Drayton recognizes a lot of the themes and dog whistles Tarrio and Guilfoyle use because that rhetoric was part of the false promises the beloved United States presented to her family of immigrants. Drayton extends a virtual invitation for readers who share her conflicted attraction to a nation that does not love them back to form community with her by reading her work. She clearly continues identifying as an American, albeit one in exile. But her most vivid depictions of belonging take place within her nuclear family rather than through interactions with either other Americans or any individuals in Trinidad and Tobago. Thus, hers is a narrative of belonging from afar.

This study about Caribbean American public figures' narratives of belonging ends with an acknowledgement that not all visions put forward by these writers are equally inclusive. By considering the reductive and vindictively narrow visions of who belongs to the United States, I hope to leave readers with a sense of urgency and a better appreciation for all the heavy lifting that the more creative, open, and inviting visions of a collaborative approach to nation and culture building have outlined for our consideration. The Tarrios and Guilfoyles of the Caribbean American community keep it from becoming anodyne and vapid. The Draytons call us to account. By challenging first principles, these figures force everyone else to articulate what values they hold dear and how they are going to work to share them with all their compatriots.

WORKS CITED

Abad-Santos, Alex. "Marvel Canceled Roxane Gay and Ta-Nehisi Coates' Black Panther Comics. The Problem Goes Beyond Marvel." *Vox*, 16 June 2017, https://www.vox.com/culture/2017/6/16/15804600/marvel-cancel-roxane-gay-ta-nehisi-coates-comic.

"Abolition of Slavery in Puerto Rico." *The World of 1898: The Spanish-American War*. Hispanic Division, Library of Congress, 11 June 2011, https://www.loc.gov/rr/hispanic/1898/slaves.html.

A Nation at Risk: The Imperative for Educational Reform: A Report to the Nation and the Secretary of Education, United States Department of Education. Washington, DC: National Commission on Excellence in Education, 1983.

Acevedo, Elizabeth. *With the Fire on High*. HarperTeen, 2019.

———. Book Review of *Juliet Takes a Breath*. Powell's.com, https://www.powells.com/book/juliet-takes-a-breath-9780593108178#SR.

Acevedo, Nicole. "Gloria, Lili, and Emily Estefan Get Real, Talk Candidly in New 'Red Table Talk.'" *NBC News*, 5 October 2020, https://www.nbcnews.com/news/latino/gloria-lily-emily-estefan-get-real-talk-candidly-new-red-n1242084.

Act, Jones–Shafroth. "Puerto Rican Federal Relations Act of 1917, Pub." (1917): 64–368. https://uscode.house.gov/view.xhtml?path=/prelim@title48/chapter4&edition=prelim.

Adams, David. "Miami: The Capital of Caribbean Exile." *Tampa Bay Times*, 8 October 2005, https://www.tampabay.com/archive/1994/12/08/miami-the-capital-of-caribbean-exile/.

Alba, Richard. "The Likely Persistence of a White Majority." *American Prospect*, 11 January 2016, https://prospect.org/civil-rights/likely-persistence-white-majority/.

Alcindor, Yamiche (@Yamiche). "What a moment for our country and for women of color in particular. The first Latina Supreme Court Justice, Sonia Sotomayor, administers the oath of office to the Vice President Kamala Harris, the first black, South Asian, and woman to hold this office." *Twitter*, 20 January 2021, 11:45 a.m., https://twitter.com/Yamiche/status/1351933767531827208.

WORKS CITED

Aldama, Frederick Luis. *Latinx Superheroes in Mainstream Comics.* University of Arizona Press, 2017.

———. *Your Brain on Latino Comics: From Gus Arriola to Los Bros Hernandez.* University of Texas Press, 2009.

Aldama, Frederick Luis, and Christopher González. "Latino Comic Books Past, Present, and Future—A Primer." *Graphic Borders: Latino Comic Books Past, Present, and Future,* edited by Frederick Luis Aldama and Christopher González, University of Texas Press, 2016, pp. 10–21.

Alonso, Axel. "Axel Alonso: Reinventing Today's Heroes." Interview with *LatinRapper.com,* 8 August 2011, https://www.webcitation.org/61oOqAiUw?url=http://www.latinrapper.com/axel-alonso-interview.html.

Alvarez, Lizette. "A Great Migration from Puerto Rico Is Set to Transform Orlando." *New York Times,* 17 November 2017, https://www.nytimes.com/2017/11/17/us/puerto-ricans-orlando.html.

American Library Association. "The Coretta Scott King Book Awards." *EMIERT: A Roundtable of the American Library Association,* http://www.ala.org/rt/emiert/cskbookawards.

Anderson, Greta. "Georgia Southern Defends Book Burning as Students' Right." *Inside Higher Ed,* 14 October 2019, https://www.insidehighered.com/news/2019/10/14/georgia-southern-students-burn-novels-after-author-visit.

"Announcement Trailer: Marvel's Spider-Man: Miles Morales." YouTube, uploaded by PlayStation, 11 June 2020, https://www.youtube.com/watch?v=gHzuHo8oU2M.

"AP US History: Special Edition with Lin-Manuel Miranda." YouTube, uploaded by Advanced Placement, 1 May 2020, https://youtu.be/1fSQkPJpBqM.

Asen, Robert. "A Discourse Theory of Citizenship." *Quarterly Journal of Speech,* vol. 90, no. 2, 2004, pp. 189–211.

Ariens, Chris. "Kimberly Guilfoyle in 'Total Disbelief' About Gretchen Carlson's Sexual Harassment Suit." *Adweek Network,* 10 July 2016, https://www.adweek.com/tvnewser/kimberly-guilfoyle-in-total-disbelief-about-gretchen-carlsons-sexual-harassment-suit/298398/.

Associated Press. "Cardi B Declined Super Bowl Halftime Show with 'Mixed Feelings.'" *Billboard,* 2 February 2019, https://www.billboard.com/articles/news/super-bowl/8496179/cardi-b-declined-super-bowl-halftime-show-kaepernick.

Avery, Fiona. *Araña: In the Beginning.* Marvel, 2005.

———. *Araña: Night of the Hunter.* Marvel, 2006.

———. *Araña: The Heart of the Spider.* Marvel, 2005.

Baker, Peter, and Jeff Zeleny. "Obama Hails Judge as 'Inspiring.'" *New York Times,* 26 May 2009, https://www.nyti.ms/2jONX7h.

Barlow, Aaron. *The Cult of Individualism: A History of an Enduring American Myth.* Praeger, 2013.

Bauder, David. "Lopez, Shakira in Joyful, Exuberant Halftime Show." *Associated Press,* 2 February 2020, https://www.washingtonpost.com/sports/lopez-shakira-in-joyful-exuberant-halftime-show/2020/02/02/d29d82ce-462f-11ea-91ab-ce439aa5c7c1_story.html.

Beltrán, Cristina. "To Understand Trump's Support, We Must Think in Terms of Multiracial Whiteness." *Washington Post,* 15 January 2021, https://www.washingtonpost.com/opinions/2021/01/15/understand-trumps-support-we-must-think-terms-multiracial-whiteness/.

Bendis, Michael. *Ultimate Fallout #4.* "Spider-Man No More," Marvel, 2011.

Benner, Katie. "The Leader of the Far-Right Proud Boys Was Arrested in Washington." *New York Times*, 4 January 2021, https://www.nytimes.com/live/2021/01/04/us/joe-biden-trump#the-leader-of-the-far-right-proud-boys-was-arrested-in-washington.

Bennet, Jeffrey. "A Stitch in Time: Public Emotionality and the Repertoire of Citizenship." *Remembering the AIDS Quilt*, edited by Charles E. Morris III, Michigan State University Press, 2010, pp. 133–58.

Beston, Paul. "When High Schools Shaped America's Destiny: An Early-Twentieth-Century Grassroots Movement for Mass Secondary Education Positioned the Nation for World Leadership." *City Journal*, 26 September 2018, https://www.city-journal.org/html/when-high-schools-shaped-americas-destiny-15254.html.

Betancourt, David. "Miles Morales Is a Spider-Man Who's Biracial Like Me. So, Why Wasn't I More Excited for His Movie? I was Skeptical of the Animated 'Spider-Man: Into the Spider-Verse' Until I Saw It." *Washington Post*, 13 December 2018, https://www.washingtonpost.com/arts-entertainment/2018/12/13/miles-morales-is-spider-man-whos-biracial-like-me-so-why-wasnt-i-more-excited-his-movie/.

———. "Mustafa Shakir Relishes the Chance to be a Marvel villain in Season 2 of 'Luke Cage.'" *Washington Post*, 22 June 2018, https://www.washingtonpost.com/news/comic-riffs/wp/2018/06/22/mustafa-shakir-relishes-the-chance-to-be-a-marvel-villain-in-season-2-of-netflixs-luke-cage/.

Bishop, Matthew, and Michael Green. *Philanthrocapitalism: How Giving Can Save the World*. Kindle edition, Bloomsbury Press, 2010.

Bliss, Jessica. "Latinx Author Whose Book Was Burned by Students Appears at Nashville's Southern Festival of Books." *The Tennessean*, 13 October 2019, https://www.tennessean.com/story/news/2019/10/13/latinx-book-burning-georgia-southern-university-nashville/3959225002/.

Bodnar, John. *Remaking America: Public Memory, Commemoration, and Patriotism in the Twentieth Century*. Princeton University Press, 1992.

Boffone, Trevor. "Ham 4 Ham: Taking *Hamilton* to the Streets." *HowlRound Theatre Commons*, 16 March 2016, https://howlround.com/ham4ham#sthash.qTcrpyUw.dpuf.

"Books for the First-Year Experience from Macmillan." macmillanfyebooks.wordpress.com, https://macmillanfyebooks.wordpress.com/tag/first-year-experience/.

Boot, Max. "Marco Rubio's Humiliating Transformation into a Trump Fan-Boy Is Complete." *Washington Post*, 20 June 2019, https://www.washingtonpost.com/opinions/2019/06/20/marco-rubios-humiliating-transformation-into-trump-fan-boy-is-complete/.

Bosman, Julie. "Time to Throw their Books into the Ring." *New York Times*, 22 February 2007, https://nyti.ms/2hyb61Z.

Botelho, Maria José, and Masha Kabakow Rudman. *Critical Multicultural Analysis of Children's Literature: Mirrors, Windows, and Doors*. Routledge, 2009.

Brantley, Ben. "'Capeman' Outdoors, Starring the City." *New York Times*, 17 August 2010, https://www.nytimes.com/2010/08/18/theater/18capeman.html.

Brown, Abram. "The App that the Proud Boys Used to Celebrate Donald Trump's Debate Performance." *Forbes*, 30 September 2020, https://www.forbes.com/sites/abrambrown/2020/09/30/the-app-that-the-proud-boys-used-to-celebrate-donald-trumps-debate-performance/?sh=1a98627764fe.

Brown, Karamo, and Jancee Dunn. *Karamo: My Story of Embracing Purpose, Healing, and Hope*. Kindle edition, Gallery Books, 2019.

Brown, Kevin. *Because of Our Success: The Changing Racial & Ethnic Ancestry of Blacks on Affirmative Action*. Carolina Academic Press, 2014.

WORKS CITED

Cabo, Leila. "Shakira Brought These Two Colombian Dances to the Super Bowl Stage 2020." *Billboard*, 2 February 2020, https://www.billboard.com/articles/news/super-bowl/8549928/shakira-champeta-mapale-dances-super-bowl-halftime.

Cardelago, Christopher. "Kamala Harris Shamed by Jamaican Father Over Pot-Smoking Joke." *Politico*, 20 February 2019, https://www.politico.com/story/2019/02/20/kamala-harris-father-pot-1176805.

Cart, Michael. "How 'Young Adult' Fiction Blossomed with Teenage Culture in America." *Smithsonian.com*, 7 May 2018, https://www.smithsonianmag.com/arts-culture/how-young-adult-fiction-blossomed-with-teenage-culture-in-america-180968967/.

Cavna, Michael. "Miles Morales & Me: Why the New Biracial Spider-Man Matters." *Washington Post*, 4 August 2011, https://www.washingtonpost.com/blogs/comic-riffs/post/miles-morales-and-me-why-the-new-biracial-spider-man-matters/2011/08/04/gIQABzlGuI_blog.html.

CBS This Morning. "Miya Ponsetto Speaks Out About Viral Confrontation with Black Teen." YouTube, 8 January 2021, https://youtu.be/j3AYRvAvO58.

Chandrasekhar, Charu A. "Can New Americans Achieve the American Dream-Promoting Homeownership in Immigrant Communities." *Harvard Civil Rights-Civil Liberties Law Review*, vol. 39, 2004, 169–216.

Chao, Eveline. "Stop Using My Song: 35 Artists Who Fought Politicians Over Their Music." *Rolling Stone*, 8 July 2015, https://www.rollingstone.com/politics/politics-lists/stop-using-my-song-35-artists-who-fought-politicians-over-their-music-75611/bruce-springsteen-vs-ronald-reagan-bob-dole-and-pat-buchanan-28730/.

Clifford, James. *The Predicament of Culture: Twentieth-Century Ethnography, Literature, and Art*. Harvard University Press, 1988.

"CNN Reporter Presses Proud Boys Chairman at Dueling Protests in Portland, Oregon—CNN Video." *CNN*, 17 August 2019, https://www.cnn.com/videos/us/2019/08/17/portland-protest-proud-boys-antifa-oregon-sidner-sot-vpx.cnn.

Conde, Marco. "In Marvel's 'Spider-Verse,' Spider-Man's Mom Is Alive and Puerto Rican." *NBC News*, 13 December 2018, https://www.nbcnews.com/news/latino/marvel-s-spider-verse-spider-man-s-mom-alive-puerto-n947036.

Couch, Aaron. "'Spider-Man: Into the Spiderverse' Shows Off Eye-Popping Footage at Comic-Con." *The Hollywood Reporter*, 20 July 2018, https://www.hollywoodreporter.com/heat-vision/spider-man-spider-verse-casts-web-comic-con-1128280.

Cravalho, Auli'i. "Auli'I Cravalho." *American Like Me: Reflections on Life Between Cultures*, edited by America Ferrera and E. Cayce Dumont, Gallery Books, 2018, 149–53.

Crucet, Jennine Capó. *Make Your Home Among Strangers*. Picador St. Martin's Press, 2015.

Cruz, Ted. *A Time for Truth: Reigniting the Promise of America*. Broadside Books, 2015.

D'Alessandro, Anthony. "Viola Davis Attached to Star in 'The Fighting Shirley Chisholm,' for Amazon Studios." *Deadline*, 29 November 2018, https://deadline.com/2018/11/viola-davis-the-fighting-shirley-chisholm-amazon-studios-movie-1202510762/.

Danticat, Edwidge. *Mama's Nightingale: A Story of Immigration and Separation*. Dial Books for Young Readers, 2015.

———. "We Must Not Forget Detained Migrant Children." *New Yorker*, 26 June 2018, https://www.newyorker.com/news/news-desk/we-must-not-forget-detained-migrant-children.

Davenport, Christian. "Black Is the Color of My Comic Book Character: An Examination of Ethnic Stereotypes." *Drawing the Line: Comic Studies and Inks 1994–97*, edited by Lucy Shelton Caswell and Jared Gardner. The Ohio State University Press, 2017.

Dawsey, Josh. "Trump Derides Protections for Immigrants from 'Shithole' Countries." *Washington Post*, 12 January 2018, https://www.washingtonpost.com/politics/trump-attacks-protections-for-immigrants-from-shithole-countries-in-oval-office-meeting/2018/01/11/bfc0725c-f711-11e7-91af-31ac729add94_story.html.

Deaderick, Lisa. "Professor Admits to Lying About Being Black; Scholars Discuss How Racism Helped Enable Her Deception." *San Diego Union-Tribune*, 13 September 2020, https://www.sandiegouniontribune.com/columnists/story/2020-09-13/professor-admits-to-lying-about-being-a-black-woman-scholars-discuss-how-racism-helped-enable-her-deception.

Del Signore, John. "Lin-Manuel Miranda, *In the Heights*." *The Gothamist*, 7 March 2008, https://gothamist.com/arts-entertainment/lin-manuel-miranda-emin-the-heightsem.

Department of Homeland Security. "DHS Fact Sheet: Changes to Parole and Expedited Removal Policies Affecting Cuban Nationals." 12 January 2017, https://www.dhs.gov/sites/default/files/publications/DHS%20Fact%20Sheet%20FINAL.pdf.

Díaz, Junot. *Islandborn*. Dial Books for Young Readers, 2018.

———. "The Silence: The Legacy of Childhood Trauma." *New Yorker*, 9 April 2018, https://www.newyorker.com/magazine/2018/04/16/the-silence-the-legacy-of-childhood-trauma.

Dittmer, Jason. "The Tyranny of the Serial: Popular Geopolitics, the Nation, and Comic Book Discourse." *Antipode*, vol. 39, iss. 2, 2007, pp. 247–68, DOI: 10.1111/j.1467-8330.2007.00520.x.

Drayton, Tiffanie. *Black American Refugee: Escaping the Narcissism of the American Dream*. Kindle edition, Viking, 2022.

Duggan, Paul. "Novelist H. G. Carrillo, Who Explored Themes of Cultural Alienation, Dies After Developing COVID-19." *Washington Post*, 23 May 2020, https://www.washingtonpost.com/local/cuban-american-author-hg-carrillo-who-explored-themes-of-cultural-alienation-died-after-contracting-covid-19/2020/05/21/35478894-97d8-11ea-91d7-cf4423d47683_story.html.

"Emily's Coming Out Story." *Red Table Talk: The Estefans*, 14 October 2020, https://www.facebook.com/redtabletalkestefans/videos/807185940045400/.

@elainaaan. "so after our FYE book's author came to my school to talk about it . . . these people decide to burn her book because 'it's bad and that race is bad to talk about.' white people need to realize that they are the problem and that their privilege is toxic. author is a woman of color." *Twitter*, 9 October 2019, 11:33 p.m., https://twitter.com/elainaaan/status/1182136933754929152.

Estefan, Emilio. "Gloria Estefan & The Cast of On Your Feet—Megamix (The 70th Annual Tony Awards)." YouTube, uploaded by Gloria Estefan Official Fan TV, 13 December 2016, https://youtu.be/hq9HryqmHZs.

Feeney, Nolan. "The 8 Habits of Highly Successful Young-Adult Fiction Authors." *The Atlantic*, 22 October 2013, https://www.theatlantic.com/entertainment/archive/2013/10/the-8-habits-of-highly-successful-young-adult-fiction-authors/280722/.

Ferrera, America, and E. Cayce Dumont, editors. *American Like Me: Reflections on Life Between Cultures*. Gallery Books, 2018.

Fessenden, Ford, and Sam Roberts. "Then as Now—New York's Shifting Ethnic Mosaic." *New York Times*, 22 January 2011, http://archive.nytimes.com/www.nytimes.com/interactive/2011/01/23/nyregion/20110123-nyc-ethnic-neighborhoods-map.html?hp.

Figueroa, Yomaira (@Dr.YoFiggy). "The only reason Jessica Krug finally admitted to this lie is bec on Aug 26th one very brave very BLACK Latina junior scholar approached two senior Black Latina scholars & trusted them enough to do the research & back her up. Those two scholars made phone calls & reached out to . . ." *Twitter*, 3 September 2020, 3:28 pm., https://twitter.com/DrYoFiggy/status/1301602923026284551.

Fish, Amy. "'Leave Us Good News': Collective Narrations of Migration in Mama's Nightingale." *Research On Diversity on Youth Literature*, vol. 2, iss. 2, https://sophia.stkate.edu/cgi/viewcontent.cgi?article=1085&context=rdyl.

Fisher, Luchina, et al. "*The Cosby Show* Turns 30: 30 Things You May Not Have Known About the Show." *ABC News*, 20 September 2014, https://abcnews.go.com/Entertainment/cosby-show-turns-30-30-things-show/story?id=25605293.

Florido, Adrian. "End of 'Wet Foot, Dry Foot' Means Cubans Can Join the Ranks of 'Undocumented.'" *Code Switch*, 15 January 2017, https://www.npr.org/sections/codeswitch/2017/01/15/509895837/end-of-wet-foot-dry-foot-means-cubans-can-join-ranks-of-the-undocumented.

Fojas, Camilla. "Paradise, Hawaiian Style: Tourist Films and the Mixed-Race Utopias of U.S. Empire." *Global Asian American Pop-Cultures*, edited by Shilpa Dave, LeiLani Nishime, and Tasha Oren, NYU Press, 2016, pp. 183–96.

Francis, Donette. *Fictions of Feminine Citizenship: Sexuality and the Nation in Contemporary Caribbean Literature*. Palgrave Macmillan, 2010.

Gajanan, Mahita. "'I Couldn't Be an Enabler.' Rihanna Discusses Why She Turned Down the 2019 Super Bowl Halftime Show." *TIME*, 9 October 2019, https://www.time.com/5696356/rihanna-super-bowl/.

Gandhi, Lakshmi. "A History of Indentured Labor Gives 'Coolie' Its Sting." *Code Switch*, 25 November 2013, https://www.npr.org/sections/codeswitch/2013/11/25/247166284/a-history-of-indentured-labor-gives-coolie-its-sting.

Garcia, Enrique. "The Industry and Aesthetics of Latina/o Comic Books." *The Routledge Companion to Latina/o Popular Culture*, edited by Frederick Aldama, Routledge, 2016, pp. 101–9.

Garcia, Feliks. "Donald Trump Labels Mexican Criminals 'Bad Hombres' to Much Derision During Final Presidential Debate." *The Independent*, 20 October 2016, https://www.independent.co.uk/news/world/americas/us-politics/bad-hombres-donald-trump-mexican-immigration-third-presidential-debate-a7370756.html.

Gay, Roxane. *Bad Feminist: Essays*. Harper Perennial, 2014.

———. *Hunger: A Memoir of (My) Body*. Harper, 2017.

———. "Louis C. K. and the Men Who Think Justice Takes as Long as They Want It To." *New York Times*, 29 August 2018, https://www.nytimes.com/2018/08/29/opinion/louis-ck-comeback-justice.html.

———, editor. *Not That Bad: Dispatches from Rape Culture*. Harper Perennial, 2018.

———. "Roxane Gay." *American Like Me: Reflections on Life Between Cultures*, edited by America Ferrera and E. Cayce Dumont, Gallery Books, 2018, 58–62.

———. "Roxane's Reviews: Juliet Takes a Breath." *GoodReads.com*, 1 February 2016, https://www.goodreads.com/review/show/1534210055.

Gilchrist, Tracy E. "Roxane Gay Explains why Junot Díaz's Explanations Don't Excuse Him." *The Advocate*, 4 May 2018, https://www.advocate.com/books/2018/5/04/roxane-gay-explains-why-junot-diazs-explanations-dont-excuse-him.

Glissant, Édouard. *Poetics of Relation*. Translated by Betsy Wing, University of Michigan Press, 1997.

Goldin, Claudia, and Lawrence F. Katz. "Human Capital and Social Capital: The Rise of Secondary Schooling in America, 1910–1940." *Journal of Interdisciplinary History*, vol. 29, iss. 4, 1999, 683–723.

Gonsalves, Greg, and Forrest Crawford. "How Mike Pence Made Indiana's HIV Outbreak Worse." *Politico*, 2 March 2020, https://www.politico.com/news/magazine/2020/03/02/how-mike-pence-made-indianas-hiv-outbreak-worse-118648.

González, Carolina. "Cosmic Latina Grandma Takes Over Latest Guardians of the Galaxy Comic." *The Atlantic*, 29 January 2016, https://www.theatlantic.com/politics/archive/2016/01/cosmic-latina-grandma-takes-over-latest-guardians-of-the-galaxy-comic/458904/.

Gonzalez, Umberto. "John Huertas Explains Why He Made 'White Tiger.'" *The Wrap*, 29 December 2016, https://www.thewrap.com/jon-huertas-white-tiger-making/.

Grunenwald, Joe. "Gabby Rivera's JULIET TAKES A BREATH to be Adapted as a Graphic Novel from BOOM! Studios." *The Beat: The Blog of Comics Culture*, 18 March 2020, https://www.comicsbeat.com/gabby-riveras-juliet-takes-a-breath-to-be-adapted-as-a-graphic-novel-from-boom-studios/.

Gstalter, Monica. "FBI Does Not Consider 'Proud Boys' an Extremist Group, Agent Says." *The Hill*, 8 December 2018, https://thehill.com/blogs/blog-briefing-room/news/420392-fbi-does-not-consider-proud-boys-an-extremist-group-agent-says.

Guadalupe, Patricia. "Many Latinos loved 'West Side Story' but not the stereotypes. Can new film version get it right?" *NBC News*, 17 April 2019, https://www.nbcnews.com/news/latino/many-latinos-loved-west-side-story-not-stereotypes-can-new-n990496.

Gubar, Susan. *Racechanges: White Skin, Black Face in American Culture*. Oxford University Press, 1997.

Guerrero, Jean. "How the Insurrection's Ideology Came Straight Out of 1990's California Politics." *LA Times*, 5 January 2022, https://www.latimes.com/opinion/story/2022-01-05/jan-6-anniversary-immigration-great-replacement-theory.

Guilfoyle, Kimberly. *Making the Case: How to Be Your Own Best Advocate*. HarperCollins, 2015.

———. "Kimberly Guilfoyle's Full Speech at the Republican National Convention." YouTube, uploaded by PBS Newshour, 24 August 2020, https://youtu.be/ErSd_YiRCAs.

Gunning, Monica. *A Shelter in Our Car*. Children's Book Press, 2004.

Gupta, Arun. "Why Young Men of Color Are Joining White-Supremacist Groups." *Daily Beast*, 6 September 2018, https://www.thedailybeast.com/why-young-men-of-color-are-joining-white-supremacist-groups.

Halloran, Vivian. "Circumscribed Citizenship: Caribbean American Visibility." *Caribbean Migrations: The Legacies of Colonialism*, edited by Anke Birkenmaier, Rutgers University Press, 2020, pp. 78–86.

Hammerstein II, Oscar, and Richard Rodgers. Lyrics to "Oklahoma!" *Genius*, 2016, https://genius.com/Shirley-jones-and-gordon-macrae-oklahoma-lyrics.

Harris, Kamala. "America's Promise." YouTube, 26 January 2019, https://youtu.be/stkkh8RyGno.

———. *The Truths We Hold: An American Journey*. 2019. New York: Penguin Press, 2019.

Harris, Kamala (@KamalaHarris). "Shirley Chisholm created a path for me and for so many others. Today, I'm thinking about her inspirational words: 'I am, and always will be, a catalyst for change.'" *Twitter*, 16 January 2021, 4:09 p.m., https://twitter.com/vp/status/1350550885265530882.

———. "Today I introduced a comprehensive marijuana reform bill that is the first step towards legalization. My bill will: ✓Decriminalize marijuana at the federal level ✓Expunge prior marijuana convictions ✓Use tax revenue from marijuana sales to help those w/prior convictions." *Twitter*, 23 July 2019, 9:50 a.m., https://twitter.com/KamalaHarris/status/1153708999734378503.

Harrold, Jess. *The Marvel Art of George Pérez*, Marvel, 2021.

Hayden, Joe. "Book Review: *Hoax: Donald Trump, Fox News, and the Dangerous Distortion of Truth* by Brian Stelter." *Journalism & Mass Communication Quarterly*, 16 October 2020, doi:10.1177/1077699020963639.

Heddon, Deirdre. *Autobiography and Performance*. Palgrave Macmillan, 2008.

Hermann, Peter. "Proud Boys Leader Says He Burned Black Lives Matter Banner Stolen from Church During Demonstrations in D.C." *Washington Post*, 18 December 2020, https://www.washingtonpost.com/local/public-safety/enrique-tarrio-proud-boys-black-lives-matter-sign/2020/12/18/c056c05e-415a-11eb-8db8-395dedaaa036_story.html.

Hermann, Peter, and Martin Well. "Proud Boys Leader Arrested in the Burning of Black Lives Matter Banner, D.C. Police Say." *Washington Post*, 4 January 2021, https://www.washingtonpost.com/local/public-safety/proud-boys-enrique-tarrio-arrest/2021/01/04/8642a76a-4edf-11eb-b96e-0e54447b23a1_story.html.

Hernandez, Laurie. "Laurie Hernandez." *American Like Me: Reflections on Life Between Cultures*, edited by America Ferrera and E. Cayce Dumont, Gallery Books, 2018, 224–33.

Hernández, Tanya Katerí. *Racial Innocence: Unmasking Latino Anti-Black Bias and the Struggle for Equality*. Beacon Press, 2022.

Hetrick, Adam. "Bilingual Adaptation of Oscar Hammerstein II and Georges Bizet's *Carmen Jones* Workshopped in NYC." *Playbill*, 26 March 2015, https://www.playbill.com/article/bilingual-adaptation-of-hammerstein-and-bizets-carmen-jones-workshopped-in-nyc-com-345194.

Heynen, Robert and Emily van der Meulen. "Anti-Trafficking Saviors: Celebrity, Slavery, and Branded Activism." *Crime, Media, Culture*, 2021, https://journals.sagepub.com/doi/pdf/10.1177/17416590211007896.

Hirsch, E. D., Jr. *The Making of Americans: Democracy and Our Schools*. Yale University Press, 2009.

Humphrey, Paul. "'Yo Soy Groot': Afro-Caribbean Religions and Transnational Identity in the Comic Metropolis." *Studies in Comics*, vol. 10, no. 1, 2019, pp. 115–24, DOI: 10.1386/stic.10.1.115_1.

Hunt, James. "Hamilton: Why Aaron Burr Is Always Called 'Sir' in the Musical." *ScreenRant*, 9 August 2020, https://screenrant.com/hamilton-musical-aaron-burr-sir-name-reason-explained/.

"In the Heights: Official Trailer." YouTube, uploaded by Warner Brothers, 12 December 2019, https://youtu.be/UoCL-ZSuCrQ.

Isaac, Allan Punzalan. *American Tropics: Articulating Filipino America*. University of Minnesota Press, 2006.

Isherwood, Charles. "Review: 'On Your Feet!' Rides the Rhythm of the Estefans." *New York Times*, 5 November 2015, https://www.nytimes.com/2015/11/06/theater/review-on-your-feet-rides-the-rhythm-of-the-estefans.html.

Jacobson, Louis. "Yes, Kamala Harris Is Eligible to Run for President." *Politifact*, 22 January 2019, https://www.politifact.com/truth-o-meter/statements/2019/jan/22/jacob-wohl/yes-kamala-harris-eligible-run-president/.

Jacoby, Richard. *Conversations with the Capeman: The Untold Story of Salvador Agron*, University of Wisconsin Press, 2004.

Jean-Pierre, Karine. *Moving Forward: A Story of Hope, Hard Work, and the Promise of America*. Hanover Square Press, 2019.

Kakutani, Michiko. "The Bronx, the Bench, and the Life In Between." Review of *My Beloved World: A Memoir*, by Sonia Sotomayor. *New York Times*, 21 January 2013, https://nyti.ms/VlcaAy.

Kaufman, Scott Eric. "Fox News's Kimberly Guilfoyle Slams 'Black Lives Matter': You Don't Hear the Irish Shouting 'Irish Lives Matter' Because They 'Got Over' Racism." *Salon*, 18 March 2016, https://www.salon.com/2016/03/18/fox_news_kimberly_guilfoyle_you_dont_hear_irish_people_shouting_irish_lives_matter_because_they_got_over_racism/.

Kendi, Ibrahim X. *How to Be an Antiracist*. Kindle edition, One World, 2019.

Kennedy, John F. *A Nation of Immigrants*. Kindle edition, Pickle Partners Publishing, 2016.

———. *Profiles in Courage*. Pickle Partners Publishing, 2015.

Kirschen, Bryan. "Multilingual Manipulation and Humor in 'I Love Lucy.'" *Hispania*, 2013, 735–47.

Korecki, Natasha, et al. "Inside Donald Trump's 2020 Undoing." *Politico*, 7 November 2020, https://www.politico.com/news/2020/11/07/this-f-ing-virus-inside-donald-trumps-2020-undoing-434716.

Kornhaber, Spencer. "*Hamilton*: Casting After Colorblindness." *The Atlantic*, 31 March 2016, https://www.theatlantic.com/entertainment/archive/2016/03/hamilton-casting/476247/.

Kraidy, Ute Sartorius. "Sunny Days on *Sesame Street*? Multiculturalism and Resistance Postmodernism." *Journal of Communication Inquiry*, vol 26, no.1, 2002, pp. 9–25.

Krug, Jessica. "The Truth, and the Anti-Black Violence of My Lies." *Medium*, 3 September 2020, https://medium.com/@jessakrug/the-truth-and-the-anti-black-violence-of-my-lies-9a9621401f85.

Lamme, Linda Leonard, et al. "Immigrants as Portrayed in Children's Picture Books." *The Social Studies*, vol. 95, no. 3, 2004, pp. 123–30, https://doi.org/10.3200/TSSS.95.3.123-30.

Lash, Cristina L. "Making Americans: Schooling, Diversity, and Assimilation in the Twenty-First Century." *RSF: The Russell Sage Foundation Journal of the Social Sciences*, vol. 4, iss. 5, 2018, 99–117.

Lee, Ashley. "Coronavirus Closes 'Once on this Island,' the First Broadway Tour to End Early." *Los Angeles Times*, 25 March 2020, https://www.latimes.com/entertainment-arts/story/2020-03-23/coronavirus-closes-once-on-this-island-broadway-national-tour.

Lee, Stan. *Amazing Spider-Man Epic Collection: Great Responsibility, Vol. 1*. Marvel Entertainment, 2016.

———. "Full Text Written by Stan Lee (Creator of 'Spiderman' and 'Hulk' about Alex Schomburg." *The Official Estate of Alex Schomburg Site*, 2003, https://www.alexschomburg.com/press_stan_lee.htm.

Leguizamo, John, writer. *Freak*, vol.1, Freak Comix LLC, October 2017.

Lepore, Jill. "Bound for Glory: Writing Campaign Lives." *New Yorker*, 13 October 2008, https://www.newyorker.com/magazine/2008/10/20/bound-for-glory.

Levy, Rachel. "Who Are the Proud Boys? The Group Trump Told to 'Stand Back and Stand By.'" *Wall Street Journal*, 6 November 2020, https://www.wsj.com/articles/who-are-proud-boys-11601485755.

Lewis, Tania. "'He Needs to Face His Fears with these Five Queers!': *Queer Eye for the Straight Guy*, Makeover TV, and the Lifestyle Expert." *Television and New Media*, vol. 8, no. 4, 2007, pp. 285–311.

Li, Stephanie and Gordon Hutner. "Introduction: Writing the Presidency." *American Literary History*, vol. 24, iss. 3, 2012, 419–23, https://www.jstor.org/stable/23249742.

Lopez, Jennifer. "Watch Jennifer Lopez Sing 'This Land Is Your Land' for Biden Inauguration." YouTube, uploaded by PBS News Hour, 20 January 2021, https://youtu.be/PEAtsgMsWmo.

Lozada, Carlos. "God, Family, and Donors: Inside the Book Acknowledgements of the 2016 GOP Field." *Washington Post*, 27 August 2015.

Lund, Jeb. "Ted Cruz Isn't Crazy—He's Much Worse." *Rolling Stone*, 4 December 2015.

Mack, David. "JLo's Super Bowl Creative Directors Explained the Meaning of the Kids in Cages and the Puerto Rican Flag." *Buzzfeed News*, 3 February 2020, https://www.buzzfeednews.com/article/davidmack/jennifer-lopez-super-bowl-halftime-meaning-cages-flag.

Malcolm, Zaria T., and Ruth McKoy Lowery. "Reflections of the Caribbean in Children's Picture Books: A Critical Multicultural Analysis." *Multicultural Education*, vol. 19, no.1, 2011, pp. 46–50.

Manzano, Sonia. *Becoming Maria: Love and Chaos in the South Bronx*. Scholastic Press, 2015.

Marnell, Blair. "Meet the Faculty of Strange Academy." *Marvel*, 4 March 2020, https://www.marvel.com/articles/comics/meet-the-faculty-of-strange-academy.

Martin, Ricky. *Me*. Celebra, 2010.

Marvel's Spider-Man. Playstation 4 version, Insomniac Games, 2018.

Marvel's Spider-Man: Miles Morales. Playstation 5 version, Insomniac Games, 2020.

Mayer, Jane. "The Making of the Fox News White House." *New Yorker*, 4 March 2019, https://www.newyorker.com/magazine/2019/03/11/the-making-of-the-fox-news-white-house.

———. "The Secret History of Kimberly Guilfoyle's Departure from *Fox*." *New Yorker*, 1 October 2020, https://www.newyorker.com/news/news-desk/the-secret-history-of-kimberly-guilfoyles-departure-from-fox.

McClary, Susan. *Georges Bizet: Carmen*. Cambridge University Press, 1992.

McDaniels, Darryl, and Edgardo Miranda-Rodríguez. "Guardians of the Lower East Side." *Guardians of Infinity: Millenium: Part Three*, vol. 3, Marvel, 2016.

Meléndez, Edwin. "The Economics of PROMESA." *Centro Journal*, vol. 30, no. 3, Fall 2018, pp. 72–103.

Miranda, Lin-Manuel. "100 Miles Across. Lyrics by Lin-Manuel Miranda, Music by Alex Lacamoire." *Tumblr*, 26 April 2016, https://linmanuel.tumblr.com/post/143385694570/here-are-my-lyrics-to-last-nights-john-oliver.

———. "Almost Like Praying (feat. Artists for Puerto Rico)." YouTube, uploaded by Atlantic Records, 6 October 2017, https://youtu.be/D1IBXE2G6zw.

———. "Lin-Manuel Miranda." *American Like Me: Reflections on Life Between Cultures*, edited by America Ferrera and E. Cayce Dumont, Gallery Books, 2018, 194–97.

Miranda, Lin-Manuel (@Lin_Manuel). "Appreciate you so much, @brokeymcpoverty. All the criticisms are valid. The sheer tonnage of complexities & failings of these people I couldn't get. Or wrestled with but cut. I took 6 years and fit as much as I could in a 2.5 hour musical. Did my best. It's all fair game." *Twitter*, 8 July 2020, 8:44 a.m., https://twitter.com/Lin_Manuel/status/1280120414279290881.

Miranda, Lin-Manuel, et al. "Statement on Behalf of the Show." Quoted in Brinlee, Morgan. "Read the 'Hamilton' Cast's Mike Pence Statement." *Bustle*, 19 November 2016, https://www.bustle.com/articles/196017-transcript-of-hamilton-casts-statement-to-mike-pence-doesnt-read-like-very-rude-harassment.

Miranda, Lin-Manuel, and Jeremy McCarter. *Hamilton the Revolution*. Grand Central Publishing, 2016.

Miranda, Lin-Manuel, and Quiara Alegría Hudes. *In the Heights: The Complete Book and Lyrics of the Broadway Musical*. Applause Theatre and Cinema Books, 2013.

Molina, Jacely. "Dear Miya Ponsetto, You Can Be Latinx and Still Be a Karen." *Refinery29*, 8 January 2021, https://www.refinery29.com/en-us/2021/01/10254014/soho-karen-miya-ponsetto-latina-arrested.

Mora, G. Cristina. *Making Hispanics: How Activists, Bureaucrats, and Media Constructed a New American*. University of Chicago Press, 2014.

Mora, G. Cristina, and Michael Rodríguez-Muñiz. "Latinos, Race, and the American Future: A Response to Richard Alba's 'The Likely Persistence of a White Majority.'" *New Labor Forum*, vol. 26, no. 2, 2017, SAGE Publications, https://newlaborforum.cuny.edu/2017/04/28/a-response-to-richard-albas-the-likely-persistence-of-a-white-majority/.

Moreno, Rita. *Rita Moreno: A Memoir.* Celebra, 2013.

Morin, Rebecca. "Kamala Harris Once Opposed Legalizing Marijuana. Now She Wants to Decriminalize it." *USA Today,* 23 July 2019, https://www.usatoday.com/story/news/politics/elections/2019/07/23/harris-introduces-federal-legislation-legalize-marijuana/1801194001/.

Morris, Wesley, et al. "The Super Bowl Is Problematic. Why Can't We Look Away?" *New York Times,* 30 January 2020, https://www.nytimes.com/2020/01/30/arts/television/super-bowl-why-watch.html.

Naidoo, Jamie Campbell. "Forgotten Faces: Examining the Representations of Latino Subcultures in Américas and Pura Belpré Picturebooks." *New Review of Children's Literature and Librarianship,* vol. 13, no. 2, 2007, pp. 117–38, https://doi.org/10.1080/13614540701760478.

Nama, Adilfu, and Maya Haddad. "Mapping the Blatino Badlands and Borderlands of American Pop Culture." *Graphic Borders: Latino Comic Books Past, Present, & Future,* edited by Frederick Luis Aldama and Christopher González, University of Texas Press, 2016, pp. 252–68.

Nededog, Jethro. "'Queer Eye's' Jai Rodriguez Confesses, 'I Was Not the Puerto Rican Emily Post.'" *The Wrap,* 18 October 2013, https://www.thewrap.com/queer-eyes-jai-rodriguez-confesses-puerto-rican-emily-post/.

Nguyen, Viet Thanh. "The Beautiful, Flawed Fiction of 'Asian American.'" *New York Times,* 31 May 2021, https://www.nytimes.com/2021/05/31/opinion/asian-american-AAPI-decolonization.html.

Nicas, Jack, and Davey Alba. "Amazon, Apple, and Google Cut Off Parler, an App That Drew Trump Supporters." *New York Times,* 13 January 2021, https://www.nytimes.com/2021/01/09/technology/apple-google-parler.html.

Noble, Safiya Umoja. *Algorithms of Oppression: How Search Engines Reinforce Racism.* New York University Press, 2018.

Northrop, Vernon D. "The Acting Secretary of the Interior (Northrop) to the Secretary of State." 9 October 1952, The Office of the Historian: Department of State, United States of America, https://history.state.gov/historicaldocuments/frus1952-54v03/d902.

"Nuyorican." *Merriam-Webster Dictionary,* accessed 29 July 2019, http://www.merriam-webster.com/dictionary/Nuyorican.

Office of the Historian. "Timeline of the 1954 Shooting Events." History, Art, and Archives: House of Representatives, https://history.house.gov/Exhibitions-and-Publications/1954-Shooting/Essays/Timeline/.

Oppenheimer, Jess, and Gregg Oppenheimer. *Laughs, Luck . . . and Lucy: How I Came to Create the Most Popular Sitcom of All Time.* Syracuse University Press, 1996.

Pareles, Jon. "Jennifer Lopez and Shakira Restore Sparkle to Super Bowl Halftime." *New York Times,* 2 February 2020, https://www.nytimes.com/2020/02/02/arts/music/super-bowl-halftime-review.html?auth=login-email&login=email.

Parker, Ryan. "Brian Michael Bendis Addresses Ganke/Ned Lees Similarities in 'Spider-Man: Homecoming.'" *MCU Exchange,* 7 April 2017, https://mcuexchange.com/brian-michael-bendis-addresses-ganke-ned-leeds-similarities-spider-man-homecoming/.

Paulson, Michael. "'Hamilton' Movie Will Stream on Disney Plus on July 3." *New York Times,* 12 May 2020, https://www.nytimes.com/2020/05/12/movies/hamilton-movie-disney-plus.html?smid=em-share.

Perano, Ursula, and Alayna Treene. "Cruz to Object to Certification of Arizona's Electoral College Votes." *Axios,* 5 January 2020, https://www.axios.com/ted-cruz-electoral-college-arizona-49c57cad-3a94-4ff9-a018-740c4d5eaab7.html.

Pierce, Tamora, and Timothy Liebe. *White Tiger: A Hero's Compulsion.* Nos. 1–6, Marvel Comics, 2007.

Platoff, Anne M. "Drapo Vodou: Sacred Standards of Haitian Vodou." *Flag Research Quarterly*, vol. 2, nos. 3–4, 2015, nava.org/digital-library/frq/FRQ_007_2015.pdf.

Pleck, Elizabeth. "The Making of the Domestic Occasion: The History of Thanksgiving in the United States." *Journal of Social History*, vol. 32, no. 4, 1999, pp. 773–89, DOI: 10.2307/3789891.

Pollack-Pelzner, Daniel. "The Mixed Reception of the *Hamilton* Premiere in Puerto Rico." *The Atlantic*, 18 January 2019, https://www.theatlantic.com/entertainment/archive/2019/01/hamilton-premiere-puerto-rico-stirs-controversy/580657/.

Polo, Susana. "Marvel Exec Insists Wave of Cancellations Not Motivated by Books' Diversity." *Polygon*, 22 December 2017, https://www.polygon.com/comics/2017/12/22/16810138/marvel-exec-insists-wave-of-cancellations-not-motivated-by-books-diversity.

Porter, Rick. "'One Day at a Time' Cast, Creators, Fans Rejoice at Pop TV Revival." *Hollywood Reporter*, 27 June 2019, https://www.hollywoodreporter.com/live-feed/one-day-at-a-time-cast-creators-fans-rejoice-at-pop-tv-revival-1221572.

Public Broadcasting System. "*In the Heights*: Chasing Broadway Dreams." *Great Performances*, Season 45, episode 5, 17 November 2017, https://www.pbs.org/video/in-the-heights-chasing-broadway-dreams-zbnlsx/.

"Puerto Rico: Last Week Tonight with John Oliver (HBO)." YouTube, uploaded by Last Week Tonight, 25 April 2016, https://youtu.be/Tt-mpuR_QHQ.

Pulliam-Moore, Charles. "It Sure Looks Like Marvel's Canceling Both Its Comics Starring Queer Characters." *Gizmodo*, 19 December 2017, https://gizmodo.com/it-sure-looks-like-marvels-canceling-both-of-its-comics-1821437768.

Quesada, Joe (@JoeQuesada). "If a comic finds an audience it will stick around regardless of the lead character or creator's gender, ethnicity, sexual preference or identification. You can claim we're tone deaf but we PUBLISHED those books but you guys ultimately decide what survives." *Twitter*, 21 December 2017, 2:03 p.m., https://twitter.com/JoeQuesada/status/943919768167440384.

Quintero, Sofia. *Efraín's Secret*. Ember, 2011.

Ragusa, Gina. "Jai Rodriguez of 'Queer Eye' Reveals His Private Pain While Filming the Groundbreaking Series." *Showbiz CheatSheet*, 17 March 2021, https://www.cheatsheet.com/entertainment/queer-eye-jai-rodriguez-reveals-private-pain-filming-groundbreaking-series.html/.

Raleigh, Elizabeth, and Grace Kao. "Do Immigrant Minority Parents Have More Consistent College Aspirations for their Children?" *Social Science Quarterly*, vol. 91, no. 4, 2010, pp. 1082–102.

Raposo, Joe, et al. "Sesame Street Theme." *Genius*, https://genius.com/Sesame-street-sesame-street-theme-lyrics.

Redding, LaTisha. *Calling the Water Drum*. Lee & Low Books, 2016.

Resto-Montero, Daniela. "Don Jr.'s Now-Deleted Birther-Style Retweet about Kamala Harris, Explained." *Vox*, 20 June 2019, https://www.vox.com/policy-and-politics/2019/6/30/20566571/kamala-harris-donald-trump-jr-tweet-2020-democratic-candidates.

Reyes, Suni. "'America': A Musical Parody." YouTube, uploaded 1 July 2018, https://youtu.be/_62C6rqppvM.

Reynolds, Jason. *Miles Morales: Spider-Man*. Marvel Press, 2017.

Richards, Sandra L. *Rice & Rocks*. Wise Ink Creative Publishing, 2016.

Rivera, Gabby. *America: The Life and Times of America Chavez*. Nos. 1–6, Marvel Comics, 2017.

———. *Juliet Takes a Breath*. Riverdale Books, 2016.

Rivera-Rideau, Petra. "What J-Lo and Shakira Missed in their Super Bowl Halftime Show." *Washington Post,* 4 February 2020, https://www.washingtonpost.com/outlook/2020/02/04/what-j-lo-shakira-missed-their-super-bowl-half-time-show/.

Roig-Franzia, Manuel. "Marco Rubio's Compelling Family Story Embellishes Facts, Documents Show." *Washington Post,* 20 October 2011.

Rojek, Chris. "'Big Citizen' Celanthropy and its Discontents." *International Journal of Cultural Studies,* vol. 17, no. 2, 2014, pp. 127–41.

Romano, Renee C., and Claire Bond Potter. *Historians on Hamilton: How a Blockbuster Musical Is Restaging America's Past.* Rutgers University Press, 2018.

Romo, Vanessa. "MIT Clears Junot Díaz of Sexual Misconduct Allegations." *NPR,* 20 June 2018, https://www.npr.org/2018/06/20/622094905/mit-clears-junot-diaz-of-sexual-misconduct-allegations.

Ross, Alexander Reid. "Proud Boys Are at War with Their Female Extremist Wing." *Daily Beast,* 31 December 2020, https://www.thedailybeast.com/proud-boys-are-at-war-with-their-proud-girls-female-extremist-wing.

Rubio, Marco. *American Dreams: Restoring Economic Opportunity for Everyone.* Sentinel, 2015.

———. *An American Son: A Memoir.* Sentinel, 2013.

Scott, Carole. "Dual Audience in Picturebooks." *Transcending Boundaries: Writing for a Dual Audience of Children and Adults,* edited by Sandra L. Beckett, Garland Publishers, 1999, pp. 99–110.

Schaefer, Sandy. "Donald Glover's Spider-Man: Into the Spiderverse Cameo Explained." *Screenrant,* 16 December 2018, https://screenrant.com/donald-glover-spiderman-spiderverse-cameo/#:~:text=Donald%20Glover%20makes%20a%20cameo,Sara%20Pichelli%20back%20in%202011.

Schremph, Kelly. "Cardi B. Totally Fangirled After Shakira Sang Her Song at the Super Bowl." *Bustle,* 3 February 2020, https://www.bustle.com/p/cardi-b-reacts-to-shakira-singing-i-like-it-at-the-super-bowl-halftime-show-21769383.

Sesin, Carmen. "Trump Cultivated the Latino Vote in Florida, and It Paid Off." *NBC News,* 4 November 2020, https://www.nbcnews.com/news/latino/trump-cultivated-latino-vote-florida-it-paid-n1246226.

Shakira. "Quiero agradecer a mi Colombia . . ." *Instagram,* 3 February 2020, https://www.instagram.com/p/B8HhF1nJIIz/.

"Shakira & J. Lo's FULL Pepsi Super Bowl LIV Halftime Show." YouTube, uploaded by NFL, 2 February 2020, https://www.youtu.be/pILCn6VO_RU.

Sheeler, Jason. "Ricky Martin Doesn't Want to Hide Who He Is Anymore: I Am a Man with No Secrets." *People,* 2 June 2021, https://people.com/music/ricky-martin-wont-hide-anymore-man-with-no-secrets-pride-cover/.

Shih, David. "Another Thing the Book Burning at Georgia Southern Reveals." *Inside Higher Ed,* 25 November 2019, https://www.insidehighered.com/views/2019/11/25/further-exploration-book-burning-georgia-southern-opinion.

Smith, David. "Trump Has a New Favourite News Network—And It's More Rightwing Than Fox." *The Guardian,* 15 June 2019, https://www.theguardian.com/tv-and-radio/2019/jun/15/oan-oann-fox-news-donald-trump.

Solomon, Maggie. "FBI Categorizes Proud Boys as Extremist Group with Ties to White Nationalism." *NPR,* 20 November 2020, https://www.npr.org/2018/11/20/669761157/fbi-categorizes-proud-boys-as-extremist-group-with-ties-to-white-nationalism.

Sondheim, Stephen. "America." *West Side Story.com*, The Leonard Bernstein Office, 2020, https://www.westsidestory.com/america.

Sotomayor, Sonia. *My Beloved World*. New York: Vintage, 2013.

———. *Turning Pages: My Life Story*. Philomel Books, 2018.

Spider-Man: Far from Home. Directed by Jon Watts, Marvel Studios, Columbia Pictures, Sony Pictures, 2019.

Spider-Man: Homecoming. Directed by Jon Watts, Marvel Studios, Columbia Pictures, Sony Pictures, 2017.

Spider-Man: Into the Spider-Verse. Directed by Bob Persichetti and Peter Ramsey, Columbia Pictures, Marvel Entertainment, and Sony Pictures Animation, 2018.

Staff Writer. "This NFL Player of Jamaican Descent Played for the Winning Super Bowl LIV Team, The Kansas City Chiefs." *Jamaicans.com*, 10 February 2020, https://www.jamaicans.com/this-nfl-player-of-jamaican-descent-played-for-the-winning-super-bowl-liv-team-the-kansas-city-chief/.

Stein, Sam. "Proud Boy Leader Says He Was Invited to White House. White House Says It Was Actually a Public Xmas Tour." *Daily Beast*, 12 December 2020, https://www.thedailybeast.com/proud-boy-leader-said-he-was-invited-to-white-house-white-house-says-it-was-actually-a-public-xmas-tour?ref=home.

Steinhauer, Jennifer. "2019 Belongs to Shirley Chisholm." *New York Times*, 6 July 2019, https://www.nytimes.com/2019/07/06/sunday-review/shirley-chisholm-monument-film.html.

Stelter, Brian. *Hoax: Donald Trump, Fox News, and the Dangerous Distortion of Truth*. Atria, 2020.

Sturken, Marita. *Tourists of History: Memory, Kitsch, and Consumerism from Oklahoma City to Ground Zero*. Duke University Press, 2007.

Sullivan, Dan. "Extremist Group Sits at the Fringes in Florida." *Tampa Bay Times*, 7 October 2020, https://www.tampabay.com/news/florida-politics/elections/2020/10/07/extremist-groups-sit-at-the-fringes-of-florida-politics/.

Sullivan, Kevin. "'I Am Who I Am': Kamala Harris, Daughter of Indian and Jamaican Immigrants, Defines Herself Simply as 'American.'" *Washington Post*, 2 February 2019, https://www.washingtonpost.com/politics/i-am-who-i-am-kamala-harris-daughter-of-indian-and-jamaican-immigrants-defines-herself-simply-as-american/2019/02/02/0b278536-24b7-11e9-ad53-824486280311_story.html?utm_term=.fe0643737ebc.

Swain, Carol M. *The New White Nationalism in America: Its Challenge to Integration*. Cambridge University Press, 2002.

Terrill, Robert. *Double-Consciousness and the Rhetoric of Barack Obama: The Price and Promise of Citizenship*. University of South Carolina Press, 2015.

Thomas, Roy. "Do, do that Voodoo That You Do to Me: The Origins of Brother Voodoo, 1973." *Doctor Voodoo: Avenger of the Supernatural*, Marvel, 2016.

Tillman, Zoe. "Proud Boys Leader Enrique Tarrio Has Been Charged with Conspiracy in the Jan. 6 Insurrection." *Buzzfeed News*, 8 March 2022, https://www.buzzfeednews.com/article/zoetillman/proud-boys-enrique-tarrio-conspiracy-charge.

Tobin, Paul. *Spider-Girl: Family Values*, #1. Marvel, 2011.

Todd, Kendall. "'Holy Sh*t! 'West Side Story' Is About Puerto Ricans?'—Lin-Manuel Miranda and the Enduring Legacy of 'West Side Story.'" *The Bernstein Experience*, 18 December 2017, https://bernstein.classical.org/features/lin-manuel-miranda-and-west-side-story/.

Tosh, Peter. "African." *Genius*, https://genius.com/Peter-tosh-african-lyrics.

Toure, Madina. "Shirley Chisholm Could Become 2nd Black Woman to Have Statue in US Capitol." *Observer*, 6 March 2018, https://observer.com/2018/03/shirley-chisholm-statue-us-capitol/.

Trombetta, Sadie. "Junot Diaz Has Been Accused of Sexual Harassment by Writer Zinzi Clemmons & Others." *Bustle*, 4 May 2018, https://www.bustle.com/p/junot-diaz-has-been-accused-of-sexual-harassment-by-writer-zinzi-clemmons-others-8988173.

Truitt, Brian. "A TV Comedy Assured New Spidey's Creator." *USA Today*, 2 August 2011, https://usatoday30.usatoday.com/life/comics/2011-08-02-new-spider-man-inside_n.htm.

Twitter. "Permanent Suspension of @RealDonaldTrump." 8 January 2021, https://blog.twitter.com/en_us/topics/company/2020/suspension.html.

US Army. *Fort Buchanan Puerto Rico*, https://home.army.mil/buchanan/index.php.

US Supreme Court. Downes v. Bidwell, 182 US 244 (1901). Downes v. Bidwell. No. 507. Argued January 8–11, 1901. Decided May 27, 1901*. 182 US 244.

Vargas, Andrew S. "A Look Back at the Latinos of 'Sesame Street.'" *Remezcla*, 9 July 2015, https://remezcla.com/lists/film/look-back-latino-sesame-street/.

Villareal, Yvonne. "'One Day at a Time' Gets Animated About Politics and Family in New Election Episode." *Los Angeles Times*, 16 June 2020, https://www.latimes.com/entertainment-arts/tv/story/2020-06-16/one-day-at-a-time-politics-family-animated-episode.

Viswanath, Jake. "*Hamilton* Stars Daveed Diggs & Okieriette Onaodowan Address the Show's Slavery Issue." *Bustle*, 8 July 2020, www.bustle.com/entertainment/hamilton-cast-members-respond-slavery-criticism.

Weiner, Tim. "Theodore C. Sorensen, 82, Kennedy Counselor, Dies." *New York Times*, 2010.

Weiser, M. Elizabeth. *Museum Rhetoric: Building Civic Identity in National Spaces*. The Pennsylvania State University Press, 2017.

Welna, David. "Rubio Tries to Clarify How His Family Left Cuba." *All Things Considered*, 24 October 2011, https://www.npr.org/2011/10/24/141663197/rubio-tries-to-clarify-how-his-family-left-cuba.

Wemple, Erik. "Yamiche Alcindor Wants an Answer, Thank You Very Much." *Washington Post*, 30 March 2020, https://www.washingtonpost.com/opinions/2020/03/30/yamiche-alcindor-wants-an-answer-thank-you-very-much/.

White House. "A Proclamation on National Caribbean-American Heritage Month, 2021." *White House.org*, 1 June 2021, https://www.whitehouse.gov/briefing-room/presidential-actions/2021/06/01/a-proclamation-on-national-caribbean-american-heritage-month-2021/.

Yoon, Nicola. *The Sun Is Also a Star*. Delacorte Press, 2016.

Young, Cynthia A. "Black Ops: Black Masculinity and the War on Terror." *American Quarterly*, vol. 66, iss. 1, 2014, pp. 35–67.

Zhao, Christina. "Trump Shares Clip Promoting January 6, D.C. Protests that Proud Boys Will Attend Incognito." *Newsweek*, 2 January 2021, https://www.newsweek.com/trump-shares-clip-promoting-january-6-dc-protests-that-proud-boys-will-attend-incognito-1558543.

Zoboi, Ibi. *American Street*. Kindle edition, Balzer + Bray, 2017.

INDEX

Acevedo, Elizabeth, 7, 17, 86, 87, 95
Ailes, Roger, 51, 61, 62n3, 63
Aldama, Frederick, 106, 107n2, 108–10, 113, 141
America Chavez (Rivera), 126, 126n4, 134, 136, 137, 139, 143
American Dreams (Rubio), 22, 23, 27, 28, 32, 33, 44–45, 48, 163
American Like Me (Ferrera), 1–2
American Son, An (Rubio), 32, 33, 40
American Street (Zoboi), 86, 87, 88, 89, 90, 92, 99, 101, 102–3, 105, 116
aspirational Caribbeanness, 15
aspirational whiteness, 15, 18, 168, 172, 173n2
autotopography, 28–29, 30, 33, 34, 37–39, 45

Bad Feminist (Gay), 48, 50, 53, 54, 59, 60
Because of Our Success (Brown), 15
Becoming Maria (Manzano), 130, 155
Beloved World of Sonia Sotomayor, The (Sotomayor), 72
Beltrán, Cristina, 173, 178
Biden, Joe, 8, 11, 47, 123n1

Big Citizens, 48–50, 55, 57, 58, 59, 64
Black American Refugee (Drayton), 18, 168–73
Blatino, 17, 108, 112, 119
Bodnar, John, 8
"Born in the USA" (Springsteen), 9, 123–24
Botelho, Maria José, 70, 71
Brief and Wondrous Life of Oscar Wao, The (Díaz), 67, 72
Brown, Karamo, 16, 48, 52, 54–55, 125, 130, 132n7
Brown, Kevin, 15, 16, 173n2
Byrne, Monica, 60

Calling the Water Drum (Redding), 68, 69, 71–72, 77–78, 80
Caribbean American Heritage Month, 11, 11n3, 12
Carillo, H. G., 15
celanthropy, 49, 49n1, 57
Chisholm, Shirley, 11n3, 22
Clemmons, Zinzi, 60
college aspirations, 88
Community, 108, 109n4

Cravalho, Auli'i, 3
Crucet, Jennine Capó, 17, 82, 82n1, 83, 85
Cruz, Ted, 16, 21–22, 31, 34n3, 45n6, 177
Cuba, 32–33, 35, 41, 47, 163, 174, 175

Danticat, Edwidge, 7, 17, 68, 75
Daredevil, 126, 126n3, 138
deterritorialization, 67, 103
Díaz, Junot, 17, 51, 60, 61, 64, 67
Doctor Strange, 126n4, 141, 142
Doctor Voodoo, 139, 141, 143–44
Drayton, Tiffanie, 18, 179
Drown (Díaz), 72

Efraín's Secret (Quintero), 86–87, 89, 93, 97, 102–4, 116
Estefan, Emilio, 7, 141, 157, 163, 164–65
Estefan, Gloria, 7, 125, 131, 163, 165–66

Ferrera, America, 1–2
Figueroa, Yomaira, 14
first-generation, 25, 42, 43, 82, 83, 159
Fish, Amy, 72, 76
Francis, Donette, 171

Gay, Roxane, 2, 6–7, 16, 48, 51, 53, 59–60, 64, 87, 136
gentrification, 140, 158, 160
Glissant, Édouard, 5
Glover, Donald, 108–9, 116
Gorman, Amanda, 9, 10
Great Replacement theory, 22, 83
Guardians of Infinity, 139–40
Guardians of the Galaxy, 125, 140
Guilfoyle, Kimberly, 18, 51, 61, 173–74, 174n4, 175–77, 179
Gunning, Monica, 68, 71, 80

Haddad, Maya, 112
Haiti, 36–39, 67, 68, 72–73, 77, 78, 86, 92, 102, 129, 141
Hamilton (Miranda), 9, 12, 17, 145–51, 157, 165
Hamilton Mixtape, The, 146, 147
Hamilton: The Revolution (Miranda), 145–47

Harris, Kamala, 10–12, 16, 21–22, 30–31, 39, 44, 94
HBCU, 39, 52, 94
Heaney, Seamus, 10
Heddon, Deirdre, 28–29, 32
Hernandez, Laurie, 3
Hudes, Quiara Alegría, 159
Hunger (Gay), 48, 50, 53–54, 60
Hurricane Katrina, 77
Hurricane Maria, 129, 129n6, 148, 155
Hutner, Gordon, 24

In the Heights (Chu), 151, 160n10
In the Heights (Hudes and Miranda), 17, 145, 147, 150–51, 156–60, 161–63, 165, 170
inauguration, 8–9, 11, 123n1
Islandborn (Díaz), 67–69, 71–73, 77, 78, 80

January 6 insurrection, 21, 154, 173, 177
Jean-Pierre, Karine, 16, 25, 35, 37, 45n6
J.Lo. *See* Lopez, Jennifer
Juliet Takes a Breath (Rivera), 86–87, 89, 90, 95, 97, 100, 102–4, 154

Kao, Grace, 88–89
Karamo (Brown), 48, 50, 64
Kendi, Ibram X., 138, 173
Krug, Jessica, 14–15

Lamme, Linda Leonard, 71
latinidad, 13, 47, 96, 109, 112, 114, 125, 128, 140
Leguizamo, John, 135, 140
Lepore, Jill, 23
"Let's Get Loud" (Lopez), 9, 123, 123n1
LGBTQ+, 25, 46, 48, 50, 56–58, 95–96, 136
Li, Stephanie, 24
Lopez, Jennifer (J.Lo), 7, 9, 17, 123, 123n1, 124, 128–29, 133, 136, 140, 142
Lowery, Ruth McKoy, 71

Machado, Carmen María, 60
Make Your Home Among Strangers (Crucet), 82–85, 87, 89, 90–91, 95, 99–101, 159
Making the Case (Guilfoyle), 61

INDEX

Malcolm, Zaria T., 71

Mama's Nightingale (Danticat), 68, 69, 71–73, 75–78, 80

Manzano, Sonia, 129–30, 155

Martin, Ricky, 16, 36, 48–51, 53–55, 57–59, 91

Marvel's Spider-Man, 107, 114

Marvel's Spider-Man: Miles Morales, 107, 118

Me (Martin), 48, 50, 64

#MeToo movement, 50, 51, 57, 59, 60–61

Miles Morales (Reynolds), 107, 113–15, 117

Miranda, Lin-Manuel, 2, 7, 9–10, 130, 145–47, 147n1, 151, 157

Molina, Jasely, 13

Moreno, Rita, 132n8, 133, 154, 154n6, 155–56

Moving Forward (Jean-Pierre), 25–28, 35, 37–38, 46

multiracial whiteness, 18, 173, 173n2

My Beloved World (Sotomayor), 25–28, 35–36, 42–43, 74, 134, 156

Naidoo, Jamie Campbell, 70

Nama, Adilfu, 112

Nguyen, Viet Thanh, 12–13, 15

Not That Bad (Gay), 48, 50, 53–55, 59–60, 64

Obama, Barack, 28, 30, 31, 163

Obama, Michelle, 42, 146

Oklahoma (Hammerstein and Rodgers), 158

On Your Feet! (Estefan and Dinelaris), 7, 17, 150, 157, 162–67

One Day at a Time, 7, 17, 113, 130, 132, 132n8, 133–34, 137, 142; Norman Lear's, 125, 130

Pence, Mike, 21, 148–49

Pérez, George, 135, 140

performative whiteness, 172

Poetics of Relation (Glissant), 5; Relation-identity, 5–6, 8–9, 11, 13, 23, 40, 44, 71, 74, 78–80, 115, 161, 162, 164; Root-identity, 5–6, 13, 23, 38, 44, 80, 89, 151, 161

Ponsetto, Miya, 13

PROMESA Act, 148, 148n2

Proud Boys, the, 18, 173, 175–76, 176n6

proximal whiteness, 172–73

Puerto Rico: and Alex Schomburg, 135; as archipelago, 148n3; and baseball, 111; in comic books, 138, 140; and Jennifer Lopez, 123, 124; and Kimberly Guilfoyle, 174; and Lin-Manuel Miranda, 147–48, 148n2, 151; and military bases, 175n5; and Ricky Martin, 57n2, 59; in picture books, 78, 79; and slavery, 101; and Sonia Sotomayor, 36–38, 42–43, 46, 72, 74; University of, 86; as US territory, 4, 36, 153, 175; and *West Side Story*, 151–55, 166–67; in YA fiction, 93, 94, 103, 105

Queer Eye, 50, 52, 55, 57, 125, 130–31, 132, 132n7, 133, 140

Queer Eye for the Straight Guy, 125, 131

Quintero, Sofia, 86, 87, 94

Raleigh, Elizabeth, 88–89

rape culture, 16, 48, 50, 54–55, 59–61

Red Table Talk, 125, 131, 132

Red Table Talk: The Estefans, 17, 132–33, 139, 142, 166

Redding, LaTisha, 68, 71, 77–78, 80

Rent (Larson), 158

Reynolds, Jason, 107, 117

Rice & Rocks (Richards), 68–69, 71–72, 78

Richards, Sandra L., 68, 71, 80

Rivera, Gabby, 86–87, 95, 97, 126, 136, 143–44, 154, 155

Rodriguez, Jai, 125, 131

Rojek, Chris, 49, 49n1

Rubio, Marco, 16, 22, 31–32, 35, 40, 163, 177

Rudman, Masha Kabakow, 70–71

Santerians, The, 113, 138, 144

Scott, Carole, 69

Sesame Street, 129–30, 144

sexual citizenship, 171

Shakira, 7, 17, 124, 124n2, 128, 128n5, 136, 140

Shelter in Our Car, A (Gunning), 68–69, 71–72, 79–80

"Silence, The" (Díaz), 68

Smith, Jada Pinkett, 125, 131

Sotomayor, Sonia, 7, 10, 16, 25, 35–36, 42, 53, 68, 72, 74, 75, 134, 155–56, 159

Spider-Man: Far from Home, 115
Spider-Man: Homecoming, 115, 116
Springsteen, Bruce, 9, 123, 123n1
Staub, Leslie, 75, 76n1
Sun Is Also a Star, The (Yoon), 86–87, 89–93, 97, 102–5, 116
Super Bowl Halftime Show, 142

Tarrio, Enrique, 18, 173, 175, 176n6, 177
Time for Truth, A (Cruz), 22–23, 27–28, 32, 34, 34n3, 41, 45, 47
tourists, 168, 170
toxic masculinity, 16, 55–56, 62
Trujillo, Rafael, 73
Trump, Donald, 21, 23, 31, 61, 127, 175
Truths We Hold, The (Harris), 22–23, 27–28, 30, 39, 44, 47
Turning Pages (Sotomayor), 68–69, 71–72, 74–75, 78, 80

Ultimate Spider-Man, 108, 109, 117

Walters, Barbara, 58
Weiser, M. Elisabeth, 7
Wemple, Erik, 11
West Side Story (Spielberg), 156n7
West Side Story (Wise and Robins), 92, 150–58, 166–67
wet foot / dry foot, 163, 164
white privilege, 13
white savior, 50, 55, 59
White Tiger (character), 126, 134, 135, 138, 141, 143
White Tiger reboot, 141, 144
With the Fire on High (Acevedo), 86–90, 94, 95, 100–104, 112, 116

Yoon, Nicola, 17, 86

Zoboi, Ibi, 17, 86, 91